Organizing and Reorganizing

Also by Lorna McKee and Ewan Ferlie

SHAPING STRATEGIC CHANGE (*with Andrew Pettigrew*)

Also by Lorna McKee

CHILDREN AND THE CHANGING FAMILY (*with Ann-Magritt Jenson*)

Also by Ewan Ferlie

THE NEW PUBLIC MANAGEMENT IN ACTION (*with Lynn Ashburner and Louise FitzGerald*)

THE OXFORD HANDBOOK OF PUBLIC MANAGEMENT (*with Laurence Lynn Jr and Christopher Pollitt*)

Related titles

Lyn Ashburner (ed.)
ORGANIZATIONAL BEHAVIOUR AND ORGANIZATIONAL STUDIES IN
HEALTH CARE

Ann L. Casebeer, Alexandra Harrison and Annabelle L. Mark (Eds.)
INNOVATIONS IN HEALTH CARE: A Reality Check

Sue Dopson and Annabelle L. Mark (eds)
LEADING HEALTH CARE ORGANIZATIONS

Annabelle L. Mark and Sue Dopson (eds)
ORGANIZATIONAL BEHAVIOUR IN HEALTH CARE

Organizing and Reorganizing

Power and Change in Health Care Organizations

Edited by

Lorna McKee
University of Aberdeen, UK

Ewan Ferlie
Royal Holloway University of London, UK

Paula Hyde
University of Manchester, UK

palgrave
macmillan

First published 2008 by
PALGRAVE MACMILLAN
Houndmills, Basingstoke, Hampshire RG21 6XS and
175 Fifth Avenue, New York, N.Y. 10010
Companies and representatives throughout the world

PALGRAVE MACMILLAN is the global academic imprint of the Palgrave
Macmillan division of St. Martin's Press, LLC and of Palgrave Macmillan Ltd.
Macmillan® is a registered trademark in the United States, United Kingdom
and other countries. Palgrave is a registered trademark in the European
Union and other countries.

ISBN-13: 978–0–230–54294–5 hardback
ISBN-10: 0–230–54294–8 hardback

This book is printed on paper suitable for recycling and made from fully
managed and sustained forest sources. Logging, pulping and manufacturing
processes are expected to conform to the environmental regulations of the
country of origin.

A catalogue record for this book is available from the British Library.

A catalog record for this book is available from the Library of Congress.

10   9   8   7   6   5   4   3   2   1
17   16   15   14   13   12   11   10   09   08

Printed and bound in Great Britain by
CPI Antony Rowe, Chippenham and Eastbourne

Contents

List of Figures, Tables and Boxes

Figures

Tables

Boxes

Preface

Health systems throughout the world, regardless of GDP per capita and its proportional spend on health, face serious challenges in terms of rising costs, sustaining quality and standards, motivating those who are professionally qualified and engaging those who provide care and advice either informally or from other sectors of civil society. How are these challenges to be faced? Science, technology and medical innovations will make a critical contribution; demography and epidemiology will map the scope of the challenge; politics and the market will interact in creating patterns of provision and consumption; but the creation of sustainable health systems will get nowhere without effective management and appropriate organisation. It is in contributing to this crucial space that we can judge the importance of the series of books, conferences and professional activity which are gathered under the rubric of Studies in Organisational Behaviour in Health Care.

This volume, brought together under the theme of *'Speaking Truth to Power'* continues a fine tradition of critical comment and original research designed for impact in academic circles, and in the many locations where everyday committed people struggle to find answers to fundamental issues of resource allocation, devolved decision-making and professional morale and motivation. It weaves together the fruits of fine scholarship, empirically based insights, and a comparative perspective from international engagement and cross-disciplinary conversations.

The creation of the Society of the Study of Organising in Health Care (SSHOC) as a learned society marks the coming of age of a movement begun some 15 years ago in which editors of the current volume were among the prime movers. They can look on this volume with pleasure as a mark of the speed and direction of change in creating a scholarly space in an area of the utmost importance to every political economy and civil society.

Sandra Dawson
Cambridge, 29 July 2007

Notes on Contributors

Perri 6 is Professor of Social Policy at the Graduate School of the College of Business, Law and Social Sciences at Nottingham Trent University, and a leading researcher in the policy sciences, health policy, and public management. His recent books include *Public Emotion* (2007, with Radstone, Squire, and Treacher), *Beyond Delivery* (2006, with Peck), *Managing Networks of Twenty First Century Organizations* (2006 with Goodwin, Peck, and Freeman), and a series of articles on managing tensions between inter-agency working and client confidentiality.

Julia Abelson is an Associate Professor in the Department of Clinical Epidemiology and Biostatistics, an Associate Member of the Department of Political Science and Director of the Centre for Health Economics and Policy Analysis at McMaster University. Her research interests include public values and health policy, health system governance and accountability, and health policy analysis. She teaches undergraduate and graduate courses in health policy. Through her research, education, and service activities, she has worked closely with provincial, regional, and local decision makers across Canada and is a member of several health research boards and committees.

Jane Banaszak-Holl is Associate Professor of Health Management and Policy and Associate Research Professor at the Institute of Gerontology, School of Medicine at the University of Michigan. She received her masters of art and PhD in sociology from Cornell University. Her work focuses on inter-organizational relationships, the strategy and prosperity of health care organizations, particularly long-term care providers, and the development of effective management practices. For 2006–2007, she is Division Chair of the Health Care Management Division in the Academy of Management and is a member of the National Institute of Mental Health's health services review committee.

Allan Best, PhD is Senior Scientist, Centre for Clinical Epidemiology and Evaluation, Vancouver Coastal Health Research Institute, and Clinical Professor, Health Care and Epidemiology, University of British Columbia. For the past several years, Dr Best has focused his research and training programme on community partnerships for health research. Current initiatives focus on prevention and management strategies for chronic disease, evidence-based decision-making by local health authorities, and systems approaches to promoting knowledge integration in the research to policy and practice cycle.

Jeffrey Braithwaite is Professor and Director, Centre for Clinical Governance Research, University of New South Wales, Australia. His research inquires into the changing nature of health systems, particularly the structure and culture of organizations, attracting funding of more than £6 million. He has published multiple times in the *British Medical Journal, The Lancet, Social Science & Medicine,* and many other prestigious journals. Jeffrey has received numerous national and international awards including a Vice-Chancellor's award for teaching from UNSW and a paper he led on organizational restructuring, published in Health Services Management Research, was one of the top 50 management articles in 2006.

Judith G. Calhoun is an Associate Professor in the Department of Health Management and Policy. She has a masters degree in educational psychology from the University of Iowa, and a doctorate in cognitive and organizational psychology from the University of Michigan. In addition, she has a masters degree in business administration from the University of Michigan, with specialization in marketing, market research, and information systems management. Currently, she is developing a model of leadership competencies for the National Centre for Healthcare Leadership and the Association of Schools of Public Health.

Ann Casebeer is an Associate Professor in the Department of Community Health Sciences and Associate Director of the Centre for Health and Policy Studies, both at the University of Calgary. She is also Faculty Director for SEARCH (a research literacy learning network), Canada. She combines an applied practice background with an academic grounding in organizational learning and change. Her understanding of innovation and broad social policy mechanisms for change within complex environments is grounded by 10 years in the UK National Health Service and in over a decade with SEARCH. Research expertise includes the use of qualitative and mixed methods in action-oriented contexts and for knowledge exchange and use, and for health care innovation and health gain.

Sue Dopson is the Rhodes Reader in Organizational Behavior at the Said Business School, University of Oxford and Fellow and Vice President of Templeton College. She has published widely in the area of health care management, change and innovation in public services. Her current research interests include the role of networks in innovation, the challenges of getting genetics research into practice, and the role of support workers in secondary health care settings.

Bernard Dowling is a Research Fellow in the National Primary Care Research and Development Centre at the University of Manchester. His research interests include relationships between public sector organizations, governance structures in primary care, and the use of quasi-markets in public health systems – particularly the commissioning of secondary care services by primary care agencies.

Mark Exworthy is Reader in Public management and Policy in the School of Management at Royal Holloway, University of London. His research interests focus on professional-managerial relations, decentralization, and policy aspects of health inequalities. This work lies primarily in the field of UK health policy and management but his work also has an international, comparative dimension.

Ewan Ferlie is Professor of Public Services Management and Head of the School of Management at Royal Holloway, University of London. He is also Director of the Centre for Public Services Organizations there. He previously worked at the University of Kent, Warwick Business School, and Imperial College London. He has published widely on organizational change, development, and restructuring in health care.

Louise Fitzgerald is Professor of Organization Development. Her research interests focus on the management of organizational change in complex organizations, and much of her recent work has been carried out in the health care sector. The themes of this work have been the development of network forms of organization; the roles of change managers, especially clinical hybrids; and the diffusion of innovation. Louise has held prior academic posts at Warwick, Salford, and City Universities.

Pierre-Gerlier Forest is the President of the Pierre Elliott Trudeau Foundation. Prior to joining the Trudeau Foundation, Dr Forest was Chief Scientist at Health Canada; he was also Health Canada's

G.D.W. Cameron Visiting Chair from 2003 to 2005. In 2002, he held the position of Research Director at the Commission on the Future of Health Care in Canada (Romanow Commission). Dr Forest is a Professor of Policy Analysis and Public Management with Laval University, where he received a master of political science. He also holds a PhD in history and sociology of science from University of Montreal.

Naomi Fulop is Professor of Health and Health Policy at the School of Social Science and Public Policy at King's College London, and Director of the King's Centre for Patient Safety and Quality Research funded by the National Institute for Health Research. Naomi's research interests are in the area of service delivery and organizational issues in health care. Recent and current topics include relationships between, and configurations of, health care organizations, and organizational aspects of IT implementation. Naomi also has a keen interest in the relationship between research and policy/practice.

John Gabbay is Emeritus Professor at the Wessex Institute for Health R&D at the University of Southampton, researching aspects of knowledge management and communities of practice.

Karen Golden-Biddle is Professor of Organizational Behavior at Boston University's School of Management. Her research examines the processes and symbolics of organizational change, with special emphasis on health system change and innovation, and the use of qualitative data in theorizing organizational phenomena. She has published numerous articles and is co-author of the book, *Composing Qualitative Research*, now in its second edition. She has served in numerous editorial roles and has received the Academy of Management's Advancement of Organizational Research Methodology Award. A member of the Academy of Management, she serves as Representative-at-Large of the Board of Governors.

Ian Greener is a Reader in Public Policy and Management at Manchester Business School. He has written extensively about NHS reform in journals such as *Public Administration, Governance, Policy and Politics*, and the *British Medical Journal*. He is particularly interested in the decentralization of health policy from the state to health organizations and to individual patients, and in trying to understand choice and citizenship agendas in public reform more generally. Ian lives in York and looks forward to the day when politicians read enough history to understand the lack of originality of their ideas.

Jeannie Haggerty, PhD is Assistant Professor, Département de Sciences de la Santé Communautaire, Université de Sherbrooke, and Canada Research Chair on Population Impacts of Health Services. Dr Haggerty's domain of research is the factors related to accessibility and quality of primary care both here in Canada and in developing countries, particularly the impact of clinical guidelines and health system policies and reforms. She has a special interest in profiling physician practice patterns, and understanding the impact of their decision-making on population health.

Larry R. Hearld is a Doctoral Candidate in the Health Services, Organization and Policy Program at the University of Michigan. He has a masters in business administration from Central Michigan University and a bachelors in science from University of Michigan. He is currently writing his dissertation which examines modes of physician control and their effects on clinical and organizational behaviour, and working on a number of research projects related to hospital offering of community benefits and organizational alliances for improving chronic care in local communities.

Donald Hindle, an applied mathematician, is currently Visiting Professor at the Faculty of Medicine, University of New South Wales, Sydney, Australia. Most of his research and consulting concerns health care financing and care provider payment, particularly emphasizing strategic planning. More recently, he has given attention to clinical work process control – specifically, to clinical teamwork and care pathways. He has consulted in over 30 countries on four continents during the last 15 years, mainly in Asia and Europe. He has published 250 papers in the last 10 years of which about half have been refereed book chapters and journal articles.

Lee Ann Hoff is a nurse-anthropologist, author of the award-winning book, *People in Crisis*, and other books, and founding director of the Life Crisis Institute in Boston and Ottawa. She is Adjunct Professor at the University of Ottawa, Visiting Professor at the Institute for Applied Psychology in Lisbon, Portugal, and was a Co-investigator with the PHASE research project at the University of Massachusetts Lowell. Her current focus is on international networking and the education of health and social service workers on crisis, violence, and human rights.

David J. Hunter is Professor of Health Policy and Management at Durham University, UK. He is Director of the Centre for Public Policy and Health in the School for Health located at the Wolfson Research Institute. A political scientist by background, he has researched and published widely in the field of health policy and management. Among his books are: *Desperately Seeking Solutions: Rationing Health Care* (1997), *Public Health Policy* (2003), and *Managing for Health* (2007). He is co-editor with Sian Griffiths of *New Perspectives in Public Health* (second edition, 2006). He is Chair of the UK Public Health Association.

Paula Hyde is Senior Lecturer in Leadership and Experiential Learning at Manchester Business School, University of Manchester. Her research concerns workforce modernization, human resource management, and psychoanalytic approaches to understanding organizational life. She has published on workforce development, role redesign, and organizational dynamics in health care.

Rick A. Iedema is Associate Dean (Research) and Professor of Organizational Communication, Faculty of Humanities and Social Sciences at the University of Technology, Sydney. Focusing on clinical communication in hospitals, he publishes his research in *Organization Studies*, *Social Science & Medicine*, and *Communication and Medicine*. His books include *The Discourse of Hospital Communication* (2007) and *Identity Trouble* (co-edited with Carmen Coulthard; in press), both with Palgrave Macmillan. Other books include: *Managing Clinical Processes* (co-edited with Ros Sorensen for Elsevier, 2008), and *Identity, Feeling and Sociality at Work: Affective Organizing*, co-authored with David Grant, Carl Rhodes, and Hermine Scheeres (2008, with Routledge).

Martin Kitchener, PhD MBA, is Professor at the University of California, San Francisco. His research concentrates on health care management and policy and he is currently directing a five-year, federally funded study of home care services. Martin has published widely in leading journals including: *Organization Studies*, *Organization*, *Health Affairs*, *Healthcare Management Science*, *Inquiry*, *Social Science & Medicine*, and *Journal of Health and Social Behavior*. He recently co-edited a special edition of the *Journal of Aging and Social Policy* (2007) on personal care services and is co-author of the book, *Residential Children's Care: A Managed Service* (Macmillan, 2004).

Ainat Koren – no biographical details are available for this contributor.

Mark Learmonth is Lecturer in Organizational Behaviour at the University of Nottingham. His interests include organizational ethnography, critical management studies, management education, and research methods. He has recently co-edited a book about critical perspectives on health services management, *Unmasking Health Management* (Nova Science).

Louise Locock is a University Research Lecturer in the Department of Primary Care, University of Oxford, working with the DIPEx Research Group (Personal Experiences of Health and Illness). She was previously a Research Associate at Templeton College, Oxford, and a Research Fellow at the Health Services Management Centre, University of Birmingham. She has published on health policy, change management, and quality improvement in the NHS, and patient perspectives on care.

Marion Macalpine has worked for many years as an organizational consultant in the public and voluntary sectors in the United Kingdom and internationally. She has co-developed and taught masters programmes on leadership/partnership development and on critical organizational theory. She focuses on surfacing issues of power and difference in order to reduce inequalities in organizations; on building confidence and involvement through participative approaches; and on using inquiry as a mode of development and change. With Sheila Marsh, she has published on whiteness in organizations, on gender, nursing and management, on managing paradox, and on supervision of action research.

Gail MacKean's interest in public participation in health services decision-making, initially grew from her own experience with the health care system as a parent of a child born with complex medical problems. Interested in working with health professionals to bring a client perspective to health services and policy development, Gail became a member of, and then chaired, a children's hospital parent advisory committee. With a health professional background, Gail went on to complete her PhD in health services research. Her research interests include public participation, patient and family centred care, organizational change, and knowledge exchange. Gail currently works with the Calgary Health Region's Knowledge into Action Department, and is an Adjunct Assistant Professor in the Department of Community Health Sciences at the University of Calgary.

Bretta Maloff is Director, Healthy Living, Calgary Health Region. In this role, she is responsible for developing and leading appropriate evidence-based strategies to address health issues for priority population groups and participating in applied research. Her work in health promotion focuses on promoting mechanisms to support citizen participation on issues that impact their health, and supporting alliances and promoting mechanisms for enhancing inter-sectoral coordination on health issues.

Russell Mannion is Director of the Centre for Health and Public Services Management at the University of York. His interests are in health care performance and quality, encompassing performance measurement and management, clinical governance, organizational culture and trust. He has published over 100 refereed articles and book chapters and was recipient of the Baxter Award from the European Health Management Association for the book, *Cultures for Performance in Health Care* (2005, Open University Press).

Sheila Marsh has been an independent organizational consultant for 20 years, working with the public and community sectors. She has in the last 10 years focused on leadership and partnership development with managers in health and social care, co-developing and teaching masters programmes at Thames Valley, Middlesex, and City Universities. Her work focuses on leading collaborative teams, projects, and services, including how leaders can really work with service users and embed issues of equality and diversity in what they do. Her PhD research concerned the consulting process in public sector work and how gendered discourses of consulting produce consulting interactions.

Martin Marshall – Professor Martin Marshall (CBE, BSc, MBBS, MSc, MD, FRCP, FRCGP) is Deputy Chief Medical Officer in the Department of Health, responsible for medical education, clinical engagement, IT, quality, and patient safety issues. Prior to joining the Department of Health, he was an academic general practitioner at the University of Manchester. He has been a principal in general practice for over 17 years. Falls off bicycles.

Andrée le May is Professor of Nursing, also in the School of Nursing and Midwifery at the University of Southampton, researching aspects of knowledge management and communities of practice.

Lorna McKee is Professor of Management at the University of Aberdeen Business School and is currently on secondment to the Health Services Research Unit. She is Programme Director of the Delivery of Care Programme and an Associate Director at the Centre for Research on Family and Relationships at the University of Edinburgh. Lorna studied social sciences at Trinity College, Dublin, and undertook her PhD work at the University of York. She has held research posts at the Universities of York, Aston, Warwick, and Aberdeen and also spent time as a NHS departmental manager. Lorna is Co-Vice Chair and a member of the Board of the NIHR Service Delivery and Organization. Current research interests include health care management and service delivery and the sociology of work and family life.

Rosalind McNally is a Chartered Librarian. She has spent most of her career supporting the research process, currently as Library and Information Services Manager at the National Primary Care Research and Development Centre. She has a first degree in social science from the University of Birmingham and studied for her masters degree in information management at the Manchester Metropolitan University. She also has a post-graduate certificate in education.

Karen Devereaux Melillo is Professor/Chair, Department of Nursing, University of Massachusetts Lowell. She earned her PhD from Brandeis University, 1990, and master of science degree in gerontological nursing from the University of Lowell, 1978. She is a Fellow in the American Academy of Nurse Practitioners. Her research involves the utilization of Nurse Practitioners in institutional long-term care, physical fitness and exercise activity of older adults, and the application of a wandering technology device for older adults with Alzheimer's disease. She was a Co-investigator on the study, 'Health Disparities among Healthcare Workers'. In 2005, she co-edited the book, *Geropsychiatric and Mental Health Nursing*.

Gregg Moor, BA is Project Coordinator, Centre for Clinical Epidemiology and Evaluation Vancouver Coastal Health Research Institute. Mr Moor has long been interested in disease prevention and wellness maintenance, particularly the role of mind and spirit in achieving and maintaining health. He brings a background in psychology, gerontology, business, communications, and non-profit management to his current work on the application of systems theory to facilitate multi-disciplinary and multi-organizational collaborations.

Richard Musto is Executive Medical Director for the Southeast Community Portfolio and a Deputy Medical Officer of Health for the Calgary Health Region. Programmes and services delivered for the 1.1 million residents of the Region by this portfolio include home care, rehabilitation and specialized clinical support, continuing care, environmental health, communicable disease control, aboriginal health, diversity services, health protection, and seniors' health, as well as the full range of integrated health services in the rural areas outside of Calgary. Dr Musto is also an Associate Professor in the Faculty of Medicine, University of Calgary.

Cameron D. Norman, PhD is Assistant Professor, Department of Public Health Sciences, University of Toronto, and Director of Evaluation, Peter A. Silverman Global eHealth Program. Dr Norman's research and practice is on the use of information technology to enable professional development, social engagement, knowledge translation, and health promotion. A focus of his work is on the formation and impact of social networks on knowledge transfer and exchange within public and population health.

Michael J. O'Sullivan joined the faculty of the University of Massachusetts Lowell in 1993, teaching graduate courses in health care management, organizational behaviour, health law and ethics, and leadership. He has served on the faculties of the University of New Hampshire, San Jose State University, and the University of California at Berkeley. Before coming to UMass, Dr O'Sullivan was Vice President and Regional Director of Medical Diagnostic, a mobile MRI services company which he co-founded. He has consulted with numerous health care delivery organizations, serves on the Board of Directors of the Avis Goodwin Community Health Centre, founded the In-Service Television Network in San Jose, CA, was the Health Coordinator for the Child Development Group of Mississippi, and served as the Administrator of the Bolivian National Leprosarium in Los Negros while a Peace Corps Volunteer. He is the author of numerous publications and reports on health care policy and management.

Catherine Pope is Reader in Health Services Research in the School of Nursing and Midwifery, University of Southampton and her research interests, besides the evaluation of health services, include professional practice and qualitative research. Previous research includes evaluations of advanced access, NHS walk-in centres, and studies of surgery and anaesthetic practice.

Trish Reay is an Assistant Professor in the Department of Strategic Management and Organization at the University of Alberta School of Business. Her research interests include organizational and institutional change, organizational learning, knowledge transfer, and dynamics of family enterprises. She has published articles on these topics in *Academy of Management Journal*, *Journal of Management Studies*, *Organization Studies*, and *Human Resource Management*.

Jill Schofield is the Somers Chair of Healthcare Management at the University of Edinburgh. Her research interests include the implementation of policy initiatives and the operation of the policy process across the not-for-profit and public sectors and in particular how managers learn to adopt new working practices. A second major strand to her research involves understanding the operation of intersectoral and inter-agency working, particularly around the organizational behavioural consequences of partnership and collaborative activity.

Rod Sheaff is Professor of Health Services Research at the University of Plymouth. His work focuses on the relationships between politics, organizational structure, and organizational processes in health organizations. He is also interested in the new public management and its relationship to neo-liberalism. At present, he researches mainly in the fields of primary and community services, but he has also published on the subjects of health system reform and its implementation, health care ethics, and marketing in health services.

C. Eduardo Siqueira is an Assistant Professor in the Department of Community Health and Sustainability at the University of Massachusetts Lowell. He holds a doctoral degree in work environment policy from UMass Lowell and a masters degree in public health from the Johns Hopkins University School of Hygiene and Public Health. Dr Siqueira graduated in medicine at the Federal University of Rio de Janeiro, Brazil.

Craig Slatin is an Associate Professor in the University of Massachusetts Lowell's Department of Community Health and Sustainability and Co-director of the Centre for Public Health Research and Health Promotion. His research interests focus on the political economy of the work environment and of environmental health. He has written about worker health and safety training programmes and health care worker health and safety issues. His recent research has addressed health disparities among health care workers in hospitals and nursing homes. Dr Slatin is an Associate Editor of *New Solutions*, a journal of environmental and occupational health.

Kathy Sperrazza – no biographical details are available for this contributor.

Peter Spurgeon has experience in a number of sectors (air traffic control, computing, and various Universities). He has worked in, and with, the NHS for the past 20 years, serving as Director of the Health Service Management Centre, University of Birmingham and more recently as Director, Institute for Clinical Leadership at the University of Warwick. He has particular interests in service reconfiguration, leadership development, and the preparation of doctors for management (leadership roles).

William K. Trochim, PhD is Professor, Department of Policy Analysis & Management, Cornell University. Dr Trochim's research is broadly in the area of applied social research methodology, with an emphasis on programme planning and evaluation methods. He is recognized for the development of a multivariate form of concept mapping, a method for mapping the ideas of a group of people on any topic of interest that integrates traditional group processes with state-of-the-art statistical methods.

Mary T. Westbrook is Conjoint Associate Professor in the Centre for Clinical Governance Research, University of New South Wales, following her retirement as Associate Professor in Behavioral Sciences at the University of Sydney. Her main areas of research are organizational behavior, the health professions, and the psychology and sociology of illness, disability, ageing, ethnicity, and gender. She has published over 100 research articles in peer reviewed journals. Mary is a Fellow of the Australian Psychological Society and a Member of the Order of Australia for 'services to people with disabilities and to education in the field of health sciences research'.

Edna M. White-O'Sullivan is a Mental Health Counselor with Market Square Counseling Associates in Portsmouth NH. As a licensed physical therapist, she conducted research on burn-out in hospital-based helping professionals. She teaches stress management skills to workers in the health care delivery system. Her current interest is extensive individual training and counselling in mind-body techniques for self-regulation of stress levels.

Acknowledgements

We would like to acknowledge all the participants of the Fifth International Conference on Organizational Behaviour in Health Care, held in Aberdeen, Scotland, in the spring of 2006. The editors are indebted to those who joined us on the conference planning committee and especially to Kate Ellis and Alexandra Gordon for their hard work in ensuring a successful conference. Thanks also to Jackie Kan for her help in preparing the manuscript and working with authors from around the world.

Introduction

Lorna McKee, Ewan Ferlie and Paula Hyde

This edition is the fifth in a series of texts published by Palgrave emerging from a linked series of international scholarly conferences held around the theme of organizational behavior in health care. These editions publish some of the best papers presented at these conferences which have survived editorial review. This latest edition continues the preoccupation with publishing recent high-quality organizational and managerial research on the delivery of health care and brings together a range of scholars with significant international expertise. The topics tackled are of enduring appeal and importance and will be of interest to health care professionals, managers, policy makers and the informed public as well as the community of health care management researchers.

The current text is based on proceedings from the most recent conference held at the University of Aberdeen in April 2006.The papers included were selected from over 60 presentations, including papers from North America, Australia, England and also the different devolved administrations in the UK. The high quality of the conference papers resulted not just in this text but also in the commissioning of a special double edition of the *Journal of Health Organization and Management*. The maturing of the field of organization behavior and health care is also reflected in the parallel development of the Society of the Study of Organizing in Health Care (SHOC) as a learned society which is linked to future OB in Health Care Conferences. These developments all suggest that this disciplinary field is now consolidating and having a cumulative, international presence and impact. More international delegates were attracted to the Aberdeen conference and to SHOC, especially from the USA, Canada and Australia, and we hope this internationalization will continue with the sixth OB in Health Care Conference to be hosted in Sydney, Australia, in March 2008.

The theme of the Aberdeen conference was 'Speaking Truth to Power' (using Wildavsky's, 1979, classic phrase). This topic was chosen to develop research-based insights around different interfaces: between researchers and the policy process and between the different communities of health care managers, practitioners and policy makers. A central theme was the development, use and status of evidence where some voices and types of data are privileged in decision-making and service delivery. Who listens to whom and why? Who is marginal and who is powerful? Do researchers have to compromise to be influential within the policy domain? Does organizational research itself have purchase and influence with decision makers and in what spheres?

The papers addressed this theme and the related questions in a varied way. We therefore grouped the papers in the edition around three recurring sub-themes which are reiterated across many chapters.

Organizing and reorganizing in health care: what does research tell us?

Many papers indicated that health care systems in diverse countries are in the continuing throes of repeated 'reform'. The picture presented is one of continuing cycles of reorganization with new models of care, new governance forms and formal organizational structures. But are the long-term outcomes of policy reform less transformational than the front-end political rhetoric suggests? These reforms may be sponsored by those at the top of the system (such as ministers and senior executives) who make their careers by acting as strategic change agents, or at least appearing to. Yet what is the impact of this reforming activity?

Sheaff's analysis of repeated cycles of policy reform in UK primary care suggested they moved from quasi-market to network-based modes of organization after the election of New Labour in 1997 (and we add then back again). Yet Sheaff concluded that 15 years of policy reform left organizational structures essentially unchanged (although the balance of power between doctors and managers did shift, as we explore below). Fulop et al.'s chapter on UK acute sector reconfiguration proposals also suggests severe implementation difficulties as interest groups reasserted themselves to block radical change. Braithwaite et al. suggest many organizational restructurings are futile, in the sense that they do not achieve the efficiency or performance gains claimed at the start. So the task of arguing that further restructuring is worthwhile should now fall to its proponents.

The papers paint major concerns about aspects of policy making in health care. These include the pattern of perpetual revolution minus evidence of desired impact (Fulop et al.; Braithwaite et al.) and (in)coherence and instability in policy. Exworthy and Greener's chapter on decentralization in UK health care remarks on potentially contradictory decentralizing and centralizing measures co-existing in the policy domain. They recall the limitations of an evidence-based approach where there is no settled evidence base to draw on (often the case in organizational research). For example, Schofield et al.'s overview of the literature on the relationship between organizational size and performance found it difficult to establish general conclusions which could guide policy.

Research/policy interface ('telling truth to power')

Many papers explored the challenges confronted by health services management researchers in linking to the different worlds of policy and practice and indeed in aligning to the wider discourse on evidence-based medicine. What is the status and significance of the evidence-based management or policy movement? Can or should it emulate the forceful advance in health services research in relation to the assessment of health care technologies and the methodological ascendance of systematic reviews and randomized control trials? Management, we are told, should be evidence based, develop robust methods of measurement and application and reflect 'what works'. But is it really so simple or indeed are the lessons from EBM transferable?

In a discursive chapter, Learmonth questions the extent to which evidence about managerial effectiveness within health care is uncontestable, neutral or value free or whether it is rather constructed and serves particular interest groups. Social science research is characterized by never-ending contest between different research methods, theories and agendas so that it is difficult to reach a simple 'overview' conclusion. Learmonth critiques the case of the influential and heavily cited NIHR SDO review (Iles and Sutherland 2001) of change management methods in health care arguing that it is overly influenced by the normative ideas of managerial gurus, and that it marginalizes more critical material on organizational culture. The implications here are that researchers can be captured by dominant or prevailing discourses or ideologies and thus need to be aware of how they construct their role vis-à-vis the policy system and whether there are (perhaps unconscious) biases in their research formulations, agenda and methods.

Hunter addresses this question head on in his chapter – based on a key note address – on the contemporary 'discomforts' of researching the UK health policy process. Despite a superficial rhetoric of evidence-based policy, there are severe difficulties in connecting research and policy. He raises a number of very serious concerns and challenges. In his view, researchers have a 'moral duty' to seek to speak truth to power and overcome the inevitable obstacles. He suggests the current style of UK policy making demonstrated by the New Labour regime suggests a number of pathologies. These lie not only in the domain of policy makers but also, it must be said, in the political naiveté or indifference of researchers and the inward-facing orientation of their host academic institutions (reinforced by the performance management metrics of the research assessment exercise which marginalizes applied research). Some health care management researchers are operating in highly politically charged fields (e.g., the effects of the private finance initiative) where their research may be seen as just another piece of bad news which has to be managed or indeed buried.

He argues that UK academics who do speak out may face subtle threats to future grants, advisory positions or even reputation as 'spin merchants' start to move into operation to close down bad news and rubbish critical or alternative narratives. In other words many of the wider deformations of the New Labour regime replicate themselves in the domain of health services research. The strong personal interactions needed to create a dialogue between research and policy may collapse under the cumulative pressure of these negative forces.

Another important question revolves around research agenda creation and the stance of the researcher. What does one research and why? Where is health service research located in the hierarchy of evidence and what types of research are respected and valued? Does research have a normative as well as an empirical agenda? Can health management research (like other forms of social science) ever really be value free? As well as research providing a critical lens on the decision makers and the integrity of policy, an invaluable role of the researcher can be to champion the marginal and the powerless and tell awkward truths to power. For example, O'Sullivan et al. explore why it is that American long-term nursing homes are such dangerous and unhealthy places for nursing aides to work. Their investigation was framed by social science concepts of organizational culture and management style. They found that assaults and injuries inflicted on staff by patients were common and often went unreported and uncorrected. Their research not only produced empirical findings but challenged the neglectful stance of the managerially powerful toward such untoward events. Such research could potentially move this issue up the policy agenda and help reverse current market-led policy reforms.

Other papers question the conventional model of evaluating 'an organizational innovation' for policy. Questions arise about measuring and defining new complex organizations which do not follow an organizational blueprint and whose design is elusive or in constant evolution. The task for researchers may be to question conventional models of evaluation and to uncover the empirical messiness of organizational transformation and in so doing to provide powerful new images and analogies for the policy system as well as surprising insights. Qualitative forms of evaluation in particular may provoke creative thought. Pope et al. use metaphorical terms as they seek to evaluate new independent treatment centers which they found to differ radically not just from the government master plan but from each other. How can one make sense of this highly pluralist world? They use the pictorial imagery of 'chameleons', 'chimera' and 'caterpillar' to sum up the very different modes of organization which emerged locally. Their paper reminds us that we need to understand what it is that is being evaluated and how innovations may take on a local life all of their own and reveals the power of methods which capture context.

One role of applied – and engaged – health management research is to reshape decision-making processes and even policy outcomes where the policy context is receptive. There may be an explicit value commitment by researchers toward uncovering different stories and thereby empowering unheard, repressed or marginal voices against elites. Casebeer et al.'s paper describes experiments in more ambitious public consultation processes in Canadian health care. These deliberative public consultation processes could expand the capacity of public voices to speak 'truth to power'. One site (Calgary) was particularly successful in linking 'good' process and subsequent action at the policy level and it is interesting to analyze why this linkage occurred. Macalpine and Marsh used a web site based resource to uncover different experiences and stories from participants in a partnership between health and social care in the UK public sector. Their research surfaced the often hidden concerns of different actors and this created a new discourse available to inform future policy making.

Handling organizational politics and change – developing a theoretical and empirical research base

Organizing and reorganizing in health care is revealed as an imperfect, messy and highly political process within the chapters, rather than one which is linear or rational. Indeed, some chapters explicitly develop new models to capture post-linear thinking in systems change (see the table in Chapter 12, Best et al., on three generations of research application models). Strong limits to policy rationality are found in such phenomena as: severe unintended consequences of change; mixed or contradictory policy messages; the power of local actors and contexts; the co-evolution of whole health care systems of which policy shifts are only a minor part.

Organizational power bases and power shifts are an important aspect of understanding the processes of health care reorganization. Here some chapters draw on fundamental social science concepts, applying them to the analysis of power inequalities and power shifts in health care organizations. What theories of power are in use? Sheaff's chapter on power shifts in UK primary care draws on political and social scientists as Lukes (1974) and Foucault (1977) for its theoretical orientation. Sheaff concluded that overall there has been a net strengthening of NHS managerial control and a reduction of GPs' professional autonomy, both individual and collective over time. So the old pattern of professional dominance has been eroded by a process of progressive managerialization.

By contrast, Fulop et al.'s comparative and case study based examination of the process of reorganizing UK acute hospital services – and their variable policy outcomes – utilizes a pluralistic analysis of power relations. A wide range of local stakeholders become involved in an essentially political process of decision-making. Reconfiguration is not a technocratic or purely evidence-based process, so approaches to policy making which ignore local politics fail. However, not all stakeholders retain equal power. Sheaff's chapter suggests that professional and managerial elites represent enduring alternative power centers jostling for dominance between them. Clinical elites retained an important role in the decision-making process described by Fulop with strong veto power.

The picture is therefore one of 'bounded' rather than pure pluralism as painted by Alford (1975) long ago in his study of health policy making in New York. So what has changed? Perhaps the 'corporate rationalizers' of management have gained rather more power vis-à-vis the dominant professionals, as Sheaff suggests, but again differences emerge across primary and acute contexts as illustrated by Fulop et al. The 'repressed community' interests (Alford 1975) may still appear to be largely repressed or nascent. They may not be mobilized directly but operate through MPs – especially from the governing party – who represent powerful community proxies able to block politically unpopular proposals for restructuring (Fulop et al.). Yet new consultation models as described by Casebeer et al. and alliances between researchers and the public may be mobilizing new power-based local action.

Reay and Golden-Biddle's chapter on the institutionalization of a novel nurse practitioner role in Alberta, Canada, accesses and develops the organizational change literature from a micro-perspective.

Its theoretical base is less conflictual and more developmental than some of the political science chapters. Individuals varied in the extent to which they were able to enact such a role in practice. What made for an effective organizational change agent? Drawing on a Weickian framework (Weick 1984), Reay and Golden-Biddle focus on the differential ability of novel post holders to negotiate new work practices. Engagement with micro-work practices at a local level and the achievement of 'small wins' was one effective method of role enactment.

Methods – a preference for qualitative modes of analysis

While there are various methods apparent in the chapters, the dominant methods are broadly process based, especially qualitative case studies, sometimes of a comparative nature. This 'orthodox' process-based methodology is clearly outlined in the chapter by Pope et al. on the evaluation of new treatment centers.

The level of analysis found within the case studies operates both at the micro- and macro-levels. At the macro-level, the Best et al. paper on systems dynamics draws on three case studies from different international health systems for empirical exemplification. At the micro-level, Reay and Golden-Biddle analyze how individuals enact a novel work role at local level.

While most of the chapters report primary data, there is also an interest in overview studies of substantial research streams. 'Meta analysis' and synthesis have emerged to be of greater importance in this field over the last 10 years, as in other branches of health services research. Schofield et al. report the (inconclusive) results of a literature review on the relationship between organizational form and performance. Fitzgerald et al. report an ambitious attempt to take an overview of results across a set of interrelated qualitative studies. These attempts at combining analyses to gain superior impact and abstraction mirror the fashion for systematic reviews in assessing the efficacy of clinical and health technologies. It is not clear if this trend will continue to gain momentum in organizational research but it is useful to reflect on what it tells us. It might be argued that the search for cumulative evidence is indicative of the mimetic nature of the research process (notions of evidence in social science imitating science). Or it may be more pragmatic with organizational researchers needing to assert political clout and resonance within an audit, evidence-based policy and managerialist environment/paradigm.

Within the edited volume we see relatively few quantitative, experimental or interventionist studies and this may be seen as a weakness in terms of the broad spectrum of research methods which could be employed. Braithwaite et al.'s use of DRG data is one important exception as is Banaszak-Holl et al.'s use of a large-scale postal survey and development of novel scales and regression analysis. This chapter uses a hypothesis-driven and deductive approach which contrasts with the formative and more inductive designs found in many other chapters.

The use of international and comparative methods within more ambitious studies is an interesting development. For example, Braithwaite et al.'s chapter on organizational restructuring brings together Australian and UK evidence. Kitchener and Exworthy undertake comparative theory building, refining an original theory based on American data within a UK context.

Social science theories and disciplines in use

We are pleased to report that many papers went beyond a narrow focus on performance management that might be expected in purely managerialist literature, but instead employed a broad range of social science theories as applied to the study of health care organizations. We regard this as a sign of the growing academic maturity of the field.

Which theoretical positions are most prevalent? Much work falls within an organizational analytic tradition but this tradition itself spawns a number of different approaches. The Schofield et al. paper used familiar contingency theory. Braithwaite et al. used and further developed institutionalist modes of analysis, drawing on classic work by Di Maggio and Powell (1983). Institutionalism is a theoretical framework that many find useful in the analysis of health care organizations, given the strong regulatory pressure of both the State and the professions, which are revealed as two core actors. The development of a typology of different modes of work control, such as a novel post-bureaucratic mode, was developed in the Kitchener and Exworthy paper. Basic work on the sociology of the professions – as applied to the ideal typical case of medicine – has been an influential theoretical source in a number of chapters (Scott 1982). The flow – or stickiness – of knowledge between different health care professions was highlighted in Fitzgerald et al., bringing in a concern for the knowledge management literature (Swan et al. 2002).

Political science has been an influential base discipline, as we have already noted. Hunter's discussion of different models of the policy process also draws on a political science based policy analytic literature.

The Best et al. paper on systems dynamics draws on a different literature base in complex adaptive systems theory allied with literature from community development, social ecology and social networks. The intellectual influence of the neighboring disciplinary community of public health is also evident in this chapter.

As already mentioned, Reay and Golden-Biddle used a different literature base which comes from organizational change and development. This is close to the diffusion of innovations literature and perspective utilized by Fitzgerald et al.'s keynote paper on the enactment of evidence in health care practice. This paper draws on actor network theory and a science policy literature (Callon et al. 1992), as well as accessing a literature stream which has developed in its own right on organizational change processes in health care organizations (Pettigrew et al. 1992).

Banaszak-Holl et al.'s paper on regulation in the increasingly important American nursing home sector uses concepts drawn from services marketing literature as well as more conventional organizational theoretic concepts.

On the other hand, we see little use of neo-Marxist perspectives, such as labor process theory, or of perspectives drawn from organizational economics, such as principal agent theory. Nor was there much use of postmodernist perspectives (as the Schofield et al. paper also remarks): instead we see a late modernist world of strongly institutionalized fields. More surprisingly, perhaps, the mainstream human resource management literature is only weakly present, despite the 'people-based' orientation of many of the chapters. There were no papers included drawing on more multidisciplinary insights or theories from the wider, more applied health services research traditions of health economics, health psychology or anthropology. Many of the papers were representative of single disciplines or research traditions.

Rising issues and concerns

Some of the chapters touch on upcoming health policy and management issues likely to be of increased importance in the future. The problems as well as possibilities of partnership-or network-based modes of working were explored by Macalpine and Marsh. The nature of possible long-term changes in the mode of governance and control in

UK primary care was explored by Kitchener and Exworthy and also by Sheaff. Network-based forms of health care organization are revealed as of growing importance so that it is increasingly important to access and develop basic organizational theory on network-based forms.

There are sometimes periods of policy transition when one long-established policy agenda gives way to another, creating a novel space for research. After a long period of centralizing and performance management based policy reforms in the UK, there has been at least a partial move away from a centralized approach. Exworthy and Greener's chapter addresses the impact of the novel 'post New Public Management' devolution and decentralization agenda on UK health care organizations. Internationally, the increasingly important voice and public participation agenda is explored in the Casebeer et al. chapter, based on Canadian data.

Concluding remarks

While there is a strong international flavor to the edition, we note that the authors are predominantly Anglophone, with little European presence, let alone papers from the BRIC (Brazil, Russia, India and China) or developing world countries. Is health care management a peculiarly Anglophone discipline or will it (hopefully) develop in other cultural and intellectual settings too?

We offer this edition as a further contribution to building an international and social science informed knowledge base on the theory and practice of health care management. We hope that readers will find the edition helpful in stimulating their own thoughts on current themes in health care management, both nationally and comparatively. It is also helpful at this stage after 10 years since the first conference not just to clearly distinguish the state of knowledge of organizational behavior research in health care but to differentiate the field from the more generic descriptor of health services research. This edited volume is aimed at both clarifying a boundary and a position.

References

Alford, R. (1975) *Health care politics*, London: University of Chicago Press.
Callon, M., Laredo, P., Rabehariosoa, V., Gonadr, T. and Leray, T. (1992) 'The management and evaluation of technological programs and the dynamics of techno economic networks', *Research Policy*, 21(3), 215–236.

Di Maggio, P. and Powell, W. W. (1983) 'The iron cage revisited: Institutional isomorphism and collective rationality in organizational fields', *American Sociological Review*, 48(April), 147–160.

Foucault, M. (1977) *Discipline and punish*, London: Allen Lane.

Iles, V. and Sutherland, K. (2001) *Organizational change: A review for health care managers, professionals and researchers*, London: LSHTM, NCCSDO.

Lukes, S. (1974) *Power: A radical view*, London: Macmillan.

Pettigrew, A., Ferlie, E. and McKee, L. (1992) *Shaping strategic change*, London: Sage.

Scott, W. R. (1982) 'Managing professional work – Three models of control for health organizations', *Health Services Research*, 17(3), 213–240.

Swan, J., Scarborough, H. and Robertson, M. (2002) 'The construction of "communities of practice" in the management of innovation', *Management Learning*, 33(4), 477–496.

Weick, K. (1984) 'Small wins: Redefining the scale of social problems', *American Psychologist*, 39, 40–49.

Wildavsky, A. (1979) *The art and craft of policy analysis*, Basingstoke: Macmillan.

1

Medicine and Management in English Primary Care: A Shifting Balance of Power?

Rod Sheaff

Policy re-cycling and organizational power

How power is distributed between managers and care professionals is a central question in social policy. Since 1990 English NHS primary care has had three main 'reforms' of organizational and governance structures and many smaller alterations. This chapter explores how they have altered the balance of power between the two most powerful occupational groups, managers and doctors, and some implications for organizational theory.

Weberian organizational sociology asserts that a group's power in an organization depends largely on its positional power, i.e. on the topology of the hierarchies which usually comprise an organizational structure and what place the group occupies within it. Individuals or groups occupying 'high' positions exercise 'position power' over subordinates. The wider the span of control an agent has over inferior levels and the more resources and discretion are delegated to him/her from higher levels in the hierarchy, the greater the superior's power. Despite disagreements as to the relative importance of different sources of power, most theories of power assume that power essentially consists in 'the probability that an actor in a social relationship will be in a position to carry out his own will despite resistance, regardless of the basis on which the probability rests' (Weber 1947; see also Blau 1964; Dahl 1986; Parsons and Shils 1951; Tawney 1938). The exercise of power is thus a zero-sum game whose prizes are the allocation of activities, technologies, economic rewards, formal position, status and other perquisites, and of the means of exercising power in future. Usually the main source of power given by a high 'vertical' position in an hierarchy arises from capacity to allocate the use of physical resources and budgets owned by the organization, which above all enables the superiors to appoint, promote or dismiss subordinates. In short, it derives from the property relations embodied in formal hierarchical structures. The exercise of power through any of these sources requires that the superiors monitor their subordinates' activity and apply these sources of power to reward compliance with the superiors' wishes and penalize non-compliance. The foregoing tenets imply that because of their positional power managers are the most powerful occupational group in hierarchical organizations.

The early 1990s was a zenith of neo-liberal policies towards the public sector in much of the Anglophone world. In Britain the NHS in 1990 was a 'Beveridge model' system in which the health ministry (Department of Health) and its subordinate local organizations directly managed the providers of NHS hospital services. In 1991 the Thatcher government began to 'reform' this system into a quasi-market one. One arm of the reform was to reconstitute secondary care providers as semi-autonomous 'public firms' which would work under contract to local organizations (Health Authorities) managed by the Department of Health. Commercial providers could also undertake NHS contracts. These measures were intended to promote competition between hospitals for patient referrals, thereby making NHS hospitals more responsive to patients' preferences (Department of Health 1989). The other arm – a belated addition to the reform – was to give primary care doctors the budgets and the responsibility for commissioning a large proportion of secondary care for their patients. Since in England the primary care doctors were (and mostly remain) independent general practitioners (GPs) working under contract to the NHS, this arm of the reform became known in England as 'GP fund holding', although similar reforms were attempted in parts of Sweden and Russia. This arm of the reform was intended to create incentives to minimize referrals to secondary, promote the substitution of primary for secondary care, and so moderate the workload pressures facing NHS hospitals and strengthen cost control.

Since then, the resulting organizational structures in the English NHS have undergone an almost circular evolution. Differentiating itself from the Thatcher government's health policies, the incoming 1997 'new Labour' government announced that 'partnerships' between public bodies would replace the quasi-market between hospitals and health authorities. Primary Care Trusts (PCTs), based on local networks of GPs, would take from individual general practices the 'fund holding' function of commissioning of secondary care. Insofar as they had a coherent programme theory, these changes in organizational structures were described as 'third way' policies (cp. Giddens 1998).

Like neo-liberalism, the 'third way' had followers in many countries besides the UK. By 2004, however, the English government appeared to be losing confidence in third way health policies and began restoring what are in essence (though not in name) the NHS organizational structures of the Thatcher period.

If formal organizational structures alone determined the balance of power between doctors and managers, one would predict that the circular evolution of NHS organizational structures would temporarily perturb the balance but in the end produce little net change in it.

Although some researchers argue that in England some elements of the medical profession gained and others lost power through such changes (e.g. McNulty and Ferlie 2002), others (e.g. Harrison 2002) argue that the net general tendency was to increase NHS non-medical management power over the medical profession and its clinical prac-tice. If so, the explanation for any shifts in the balance of power lies not in the topography of formal organizational structures and who occupies what places in them, but in the processes by which power is exercised within and through those structures. To hypothesize what changes in the non-positional factors might alter the relative power of two occupational groups (managers, doctors) involves summarizing an extensive literature. Leaving aside physical coercion (relevant to power relationships in mental hospitals, prisons and schools but not those between managers and doctors), the analysis of Sheaff et al. (2004a) suggests that the factors most relevant to the present topic appear to be changes in

1. *Environmental factors*: law and regulation; and the medical labour market
2. *A structural factor common to all health care organizations*: the techno-logical centrality of medicine to health care
3. *Specific organizational processes*: the negotiated order between managers and doctors, and medical resistance to management; professional 'discipline'; and ideological control.

To assess the balance of power between doctors and managers empiric-ally, one must therefore examine what changes (if any) have occurred in the above media by which power is exercised in NHS primary care. That is, one must assess what changes have been wrought, in NHS primary care, by changes since 1990 in the negotiated order between managers and doctors; professional 'discipline' and ideological control;

the medical Labour market; the 'technologies' of primary health care; and English law.

The foregoing outlines how occupational managers exercise power within a single organization. However, most health systems are not so much a single organization as a single governance structure within which are nested subordinate governance structures which include hierarchies, networks and quasi-markets through which the health ministry exercises governance, to varying degrees, over the actual providers of health services. The subordinate governance structures include contracts, often but not always special forms of contract peculiar to public sector quasi-markets, and 'arm's-length' governance through what might be called 'boundary-spanning hierarchies'. In England, for example, PCTs are managerially accountable to health authorities (HAs) through essentially the same hierarchical relations as obtained within a single organizational hierarchy, although the two organizations are structurally and legally separate. How far would the foregoing account of position power have to be supplemented or modified to apply to a health system comprised of diverse governance structures, such as English NHS primary care which is a particularly diverse system of small organizations (general practices) and larger ones (PCTs)?

Many of the factors mentioned above (and explained more fully below) operate as much at national level in a health system across all its constituent organizations as within each organization. Indeed, national-level events constrain the latter. For example, the market power conferred by scarcity of labour may be greater at whole-system level because whilst a single organization may recruit more than its proportionate share of scarce labour, such imbalances cancel out system-wide. Medical technological changes, or at least the knowledge they involve, are increasingly disseminated world-wide, let alone nationally. Conceivably an occupational group might be technologically central to a few providers (e.g. acupuncturists, in providers of traditional Chinese medicine), but these providers are atypical health system-wide. Governmentality through professional discipline is adapted to operate across as well as within formal organizational structures, and so are ideological legitimations of power. Thus the foregoing definitions of power and the accounts of the structures and processes through which power is exercised to all translate 'upwards' in generality from organizational to health system level. They apply, however, only in health systems like the NHS which contain a set of governance structures through which someone (government) attempts to exercise governance. (They would not apply in, say, a market.)

This chapter therefore enquires

1. In what ways has the balance of power between English NHS managers and doctors shifted since 1991?
2. How far can these changes be attributed to changed organizational structures and to what extent must other explanations be invoked?
3. What are the implications for theories of managerial and professional power in organizations?

In doing so the chapter focuses mainly but not exclusively on general practice, drawing upon published research, especially for the 1990–97 period, upon primary data from six post-1997 studies in which the author participated in from 1997, and upon the main policy and guidance documents for the whole period.

Negotiated order and resistance

Weber's definition of power mentions the possibility of resistance. If neither agent can dispense completely with the other's role in an organization or in society, the balance of power in organizations must be continuously re-negotiated, creating a 'negotiated order' (Strauss et al. 1963). In the NHS this negotiation occurs through two occupational sub-groups: doctors sufficiently senior to manage other doctors and negotiate with non-medical managers; and the latter group of managers. Indeed, some doctors (also) occupy managerial positions. The outcome, as in any negotiation, appears to depend partly upon how confident of success each party feels in the light of past attempts to apply sanctions; how far they regard it as legitimate to do so; how great they feel the threats to, or the opportunity to advance, their interests to be; and how they anticipate any powerful third party might respond.

Much of the English medical profession opposed the introduction of the NHS internal market and fund holding in 1991. Indeed the British Medical Association (BMA) ran a public campaign of advertisements, press conferences, lobbying of MPs and releasing research study findings supporting their standpoint shortly before the main parliamentary debates. Nevertheless, the reforms were implemented, including a revision of the GP contract to include the first measures of clinical activity and indicative prescribing budgets. The introduction of universal medical audit proceeded under the tacit threat that if the medical profession did not cooperate voluntarily, the government would find regulatory or legislative ways to compel them (NHS chief executive; personal communication). At national level, where it has long existed, the stratum of doctors mediating between other doctors and NHS management was thereafter on the defensive. Subsequently the English medical profession lacked confidence to take on the state (Armstrong 2002), conceding the stronger, more collective forms of disciplinary control described below.

On the management side, New Labour displayed less confidence than its predecessor. As the political price for participating in PCG/Ts, GPs were given a majority on PCG boards and PCT professional executives and guaranteed representation on PCT boards. The government preferred to 'buy out' GP objections to the closer monitoring of GP clinical work introduced under the 2004 GP contract and the *Quality and Outcomes Framework* (QOF) appended to it. Local medical committees (of the BMA) were generally passive or accommodating to PCG/T formation, clinical governance and successive forms of GP contract; at local level, sustained opposition has been rare. There is some evidence that a stratum of about 10–20% of GPs in most localities have consistently been early adopters of the new disciplines and organizational innovations (GP fund holding, PMS contracts, PCG committee membership). Successive widely publicized medical scandals (e.g. the Shipman, Ledward and Bristol cases) created a perception among GPs (Sheaff et al. 2004b) that if the profession did not adopt more rigorous and transparent forms of quality and safety control, national-level medical organizations, in particular the GMC, would be reformed, with the tacit threat of a stronger non-medical voice in them (Klein 1998). Soft coercion (Courpasson 2000) was also applied to the hospital half of the English medical profession. At local level there has emerged a stratum of doctors who mediate between the profession and NHS management (Sheaff et al. 2002) and who have acquired an interest in reforms which enhance their status, influence over other doctors and voice in NHS management.

Legitimation: ideology and 'discipline'

In both negotiating and managing an organizational 'order', power can also be exercised by an 'institutionalization of authority' legitimating the interests of (in the present case) one particular occupational group and defining the behaviour which they desire as 'binding obligations' (Parsons 1951). Lukes (1974) and Habermas (1976) argue that persuading others to do by means of rational argument is the exercise of authority or influence rather than of power. Conversely, persuading others to do what they would not do if they were fully informed prevents them from pursuing their own interests, with much the same effect as if sanctions were successfully applied, and is therefore an exercise of power. Many studies (e.g. Fairclough 2005) describe discursive, ideological and rhetorical devices used for these purposes, which include control of policy agendas (Bachrach and Baratz 1970) and insistence on discourse or ideology which does not even allow the formulation of certain topics (Lukes 1974) whilst insisting on others being 'problematized' in a way crafted to legitimate certain preferred 'solutions'. Insofar as an occupational group's working practices can be made transparent to other group members or outsiders or both, that knowledge also functions as 'power-knowledge', for it enables those who scrutinize the occupational group members' activities to apply whatever sanctions (moral, economic or physical) are at their disposal to promote practical compliance with that body of knowledge (Foucault 2004). It functions as a 'discipline' (Flynn 2002).

During the 1990s both managers and doctors have developed new 'disciplines'. Most influential were, respectively, the new public management (Ferlie et al. 2002; Flynn 1992) and evidence-based medicine (EBM) (Harrison 2002).

During the 1990s, and especially after 1997, NHS primary care management experienced a disciplinary shift towards the 'new public management' practices that NHS hospitals began using a decade earlier. PCTs were new organizations intended, unlike their predecessors, to manage rather than just reimburse GP activity. From 1999 PCTs were expected to implement national standards for services. Access targets were now applied to general practices, although 'advanced access' methods of appointment management were usually implemented through a national network of primary care 'collaboratives' rather than by PCTs alone. Above all, PCTs became responsible for ensuring that National Service Frameworks (NSFs) were implemented. To varying degrees NSF standards derived from EBM and the national bodies (above all, NICE) through which the NHS implemented it.

Apart from exceptional events such as gross malpractice or criminality, the topic of how doctors exercised their clinical autonomy was closed to NHS managers until the late 1980s. Since then, new management information and costing systems have gradually increased the transparency of medical practice. This trend began with incentives under GP funding for practices to install management information system (though to the practice's choice and specification). GPs came to record increasing amounts of data for NHS managers' use (Harrison and Dowswell 2002), a trend which QOF dramatically extended. The current

NHS informatics programme aims at comprehensive networking of patient and some administrative date by 2009. Regular independent surveys of patients and public views of NHS services began to be published, besides (according to anecdotal evidence) others which the Department of Health does not publish. Arrangements were introduced in 2002 for identifying and 'helping' doctors whose 'performance gives cause for concern' (Department of Health 2000). These systems were managerially instituted but still professionally operated and predominantly educational.

Within medicine EBM was the central medium for broader and closer disciplinary control over GPs' clinical work, a control that shifted from exception management towards governmentality over mainstream clinical practice and from an individual to a collective form of professional self-regulation and professional autonomy. The universal, but relatively weak, predominantly educational form of medical audit introduced in 1991 was from 1998 supplanted by two forms of disciplinary control based on EBM. Medical audit and local professional networks were reconstituted as clinical governance networks, of which GP membership was compulsory. Nevertheless clinical governance was often initiated by a core of 'early adopter' doctors, gradually involving other GPs through peer influence later. Other clinical professions, especially nursing, either had their own, more fragmentary clinical governance networks or participated *ad hoc* as semi-detached members of the medical networks on an issue-by-issue basis. QOF (see above) greatly extended the range of clinical quality standards to be implemented. Despite the contractual sanctions (financial rewards and penalties) attached to them, its standards were also largely evidence-based. These disciplinary changes also tended to re-medicalize general practice. EBM was more readily applied to, and legitimated, the biologically oriented aspects of clinical practice. Nevertheless EBM increasingly became a disciplinary tool common to both managers and doctors.

With decreasing lags the ideological climate in NHS management tended to follow that of the current government. Despite the change of party in government, the deepest policy difference between them (whether to contain or greatly expand the level of NHS spending) was not strongly reflected in the managerial ideologies of the period. Indeed the ideological continuities are more striking than the discontinuities, in particular the rhetoric of 'reform' ('change', 'modernization', 'new' policies) even though many of these changes (e.g. introduction of commercial and charitable providers) revert to pre-NHS policy. New Labour initially emphasized its ideology of 'no ideology' (the 'third way') and the slogan 'what matters is what works', which abstracts from the contentious question of precisely what the reformed working practices are meant to achieve, as though that point was already well defined and generally agreed. Its positive focus, though, is on day-to-day managerial and clinical work and innovations in both, with the implication of normalizing 'what works'. New Labour also accepts, indeed often states, the idea that health professionals, especially doctors, represent patients' interests. One rationale for each successive reform has been that it will allow clinicians to practice more freely and to influence the details of service management.

As for medical ideologies, the gradual GP uptake of salaried employment appears to suggest that GPs' hitherto powerful, near-universal aversion to it is weakening. English GPs have remained sensitive that new working methods be adopted voluntarily, not imposed by non-doctors. The emerging stratum of GP medical managers (see above), however, 'turns' this belief so as to legitimate their own new roles in terms of buffering general practices against the demands of (lay) NHS management. Closer regulation by fellow GPs remains a lesser evil for GPs than managerial control. Although a steady trickle of individual jeremiads have appeared in the professional press and researchers report certain GPs' passive resistance and scepticism towards the 'reforms', there have been few ideological challenges to the new disciplinary controls in medicine. The most coherent counter-argument contrasts the 'art' and 'holism' of general medical practice with EBM (Armstrong 2002). Yet it is also reported (Sheaff et al. 2003) that the argument that (say) NSFs are 'national policy' helps legitimate them to GPs, who reconcile this view with their preference for professional autonomy by saying that the policy coincides with local health needs. The tacit ideological outcome is that it is legitimate for national policy, represented by NHS management, to influence general practice *provided* this influence is mediated and buffered by local GP leaderships.

The labour market

An occupational group's market strength depends above all on how vulnerable managers are to that group disrupting production of the organization's main output. The greater the demand for its outputs and the more alternative providers exist, the more an organization stands to lose financially if an occupational group disrupts production, so the greater that group's power. The smaller the excess supply of labour in that occupation is, the harder it is for managers to replace non-compliant members and the weaker a sanction the threat of dismissal is. The limiting case is an organized monopoly in labour supply which managers cannot get individual members to defect from. The non-substitutability of members of an occupational group maximizes its power.

Demand for GPs' services increased, due to not only the expanding and ageing English population but also (from 1997) tightening targets for hospital waiting times, which increased demand for primary to replace secondary care at either end of the hospital episode. There were a few experiments with placing GPs in accident and emergency (A&E) departments, not widely copied. After 1997, GPs' increasing role in PCT management placed another demand on their time. Under the 1990 GP contract, GP cooperatives instead of commercial deputizing firms increasingly provided out-of-hours services, until the 2004 contract allowed GPs to relinquish responsibility for OOH services altogether, which many did. PCTs took over that responsibility.

Throughout the study period there was an intensifying shortage of GPs, especially in poor urban areas. No national data are collected on 'vacant' (doctor-less) general practice lists but the author has found the problem repeatedly discussed by NHS managers, reported in the professional and managerial press and in research (e.g. Gosden et al. 2000; Williams et al. 2001) evaluating possible solutions. The new medical schools opened too late to affect the shortage during the study period.

Technological centrality

There is also a technical sense in which a whole occupational group, rather than just its individual members, may or may not be substitutable. The Aston school argued that besides its place in the 'vertical' and 'horizontal' topography of an organizational structure, an occupational group's power depends on the group's relationship to the technology (physical equipment and processes) used for conducting the organization's core activity (Abell 1975). (Here the concept of 'technology' is taken widely to include, for instance, 'technologies of repression'; (Foucault 1977).) A group operating the technology possesses the potential sanction of disrupting the organization's capacity to pursue its objectives, that is, the power to determine whether those who formally control an organization actually can use its resources to pursue their particular objectives. This type of power depends on how far substitutes exist for

1. The occupational group which operates a given technology. The fewer are the alternative occupational groups that can do so, the more powerful is the occupational group who can.
2. The technology itself. The fewer the technologies which can replace it, the more powerful the occupational groups who can operate that technology.

Since this power derives from the productive process, it is not necessarily (indeed, typically not) reflected in the hierarchical position of the relevant occupational group. When it is collectively exercised, that typically happens through informal organization (trades union, unofficial action) or semi-detached (above all, professional) organizations. So, *pace* some claims (Fairclough 2005), not all social practices, and not even all technologies, are equally important in terms of power.

NHS management therefore explored whether other occupational groups were competent to substitute, at least partly, for GPs as points of first clinical contact for non-emergency patients. The main jurisdictional changes in occupational groups were introduction of nurse practitioners (Chambers 1998; Venning et al. 2000); nurse principals; Evercare nurses and their equivalents (EPIC nurses, community matrons etc.; Boaden et al. 2005); physician assistants; retail pharmacists (Hassell et al. 2001); and nurse triagers (Hanlon et al. 2005). The extent to which these could replace GPs varied but generally these new occupational groups' professionals took over the less complex elements of GP work and worked under medical (usually GP) clinical supervision and mentorship. The net effect was to make GPs' work more medical, reducing GP centrality for the less complex aspects of primary care 'technology' and maintaining it for the more complex.

These skill-mix changes were also partly a concomitant of substitute primary care technologies, developing for the same reasons. The main innovations were walk-in centres; NHS Direct (Hanlon et al. 2005); case management (e.g. Evercare, EPIC and similar projects, now promulgated nationally as the 'Community Matron' programme; and, more rarely, dedicated primary care clinics within or near hospital A&E departments. NHS Plus, established in 2000, provides OH services to non-NHS employers. Still relatively small, it nevertheless provides a service which by default general practice mostly provided. To provide for vacant lists and, after 2004, to provide out-of-hours services, PCTs gradually began directly employing salaried doctors and to a limited extent nurse practitioners. To a limited extent these new 'technologies' offered a substitute for independent GPs as providers of primary care, eroding the independent GPs' centrality.

Law and regulation

Whilst the everyday rule of law depends heavily on ideological legitimation, legal power is distinct in resting ultimately upon the state's greater capacity for physical coercion than any other organization or social group. What effect law, regulation, legally binding contracts and judicial interpretation have upon the balance of power between doctors and managers depends upon the normative content of the law and how it is enforced. The former can simply be 'read off' from the relevant documents, in the present case those which establish, define and enforce any limits to the roles, rights or substitutability of occupational groups. The sanctions can be discovered partly in the same way, but also by examining how law and regulation are in practice enforced, and to whose benefit.

In NHS primary care the most important legal and regulatory development was to make GP contracts more 'complete' and more contestable. The 1967 GP contract was little more than a reimbursement mechanism but from 1990 each revision introduced closer specifications of the clinical work expected from GPs. The 1990 contract introduced vaccination and immunization targets and delegated 'indicative' budgets for pharmaceutical spending. GP fund holding added responsibility for budgets for much of secondary and some primary care, though not for primary medical care itself except prescribing. From 1998 GPs had the option of taking a locally negotiated PMS contract rather than the standard national ('GMS') contract. PMS contracts set practice-specific targets, though usually broadly defined and weakly monitored (Sheaff and Lloyd-Kendall 2000). The QOF and 2004 GMS contract made general practice incomes depend on the degree of compliance with around 130 evidence-based indicators of clinical processes and, in a few cases, outcomes. PMS and the 2004 GMS contracts both defined the contract agent as the general practice (organization) instead of the general practitioner (named doctor) as before. Such a contract therefore survives changes in medical personnel including, in theory, the ousting of individual GPs for disciplinary or other reasons.

GP contracts have also been made more contestable through the introduction of organizational substitutes for the professional partnership model of general practice as small businesses. GP co-operatives providing out-of-hours services were first permitted under the 1990 GMS contract, gradually becoming more widespread (Hallam 1997) and, after 1997, wider in the range of services they provided although the 2004 GP contract precipitously reduced their number. The 1997

NHS Act also relaxed the conditions under which PCTs and general practices were permitted to employ salaried GPs. The Innovations in Primary Care Contracting policy creates a framework by which PCTs can contract other organizations to substitute for general practices in providing primary medical care. This policy is still at an early stage of implementation, but one attempt has already (2006) been made to replace a general practice (N. Derbyshire) with provision by a US for-profit HMO and then, when that failed due to local opposition, a British private provider. At the time of writing ten pilot site PCTs have been seeking and evaluating bids from providers other than existing general practices to provide primary health care.

What shifts in power between medicine and management in English primary care?

On the evidence of payment alone GPs would appear more powerful in 2006 than in 1991. They are highly paid by European standards and the 2004 contract considerably increased their incomes. The actual data are secret but GP remarks in the professional and national press point towards GPs' income typically being about 20–30% higher than before, and this for a workload reduced, in most cases, by ceasing out-of-hours work. GPs have a privileged role in PCT management compared with other clinical professions and, still, higher occupational status. With NHS managers, GPs are partners in a dominant coalition over NHS primary care.

However, the price for these gains has been that through the medium of professional discipline, the locus of control has clearly shifted (albeit from a low starting point) towards NHS management, who now exercise greater regulation and surveillance over GPs' work and are starting to normalize it on terms decided predominantly by management. Disciplinary changes in both medicine and management have led unidirectionally towards the greater regulation and surveillance of GPs' clinical practice. Ideological rationales for health reform and closer disciplinary control have largely won the day among GPs, in the absence of coherent alternatives.

As for labour market power, demand for services which GPs supply continues to increase. Yet this very trend has provoked skill-mix changes, the introduction of new forms of service (e.g. community matrons) and admitting new providers to NHS primary care. These changes create partial substitutes for general medical practice and attenuate its scarcity. A greater division of labour is slowly limiting GPs' technological centrality to a narrower range of more specialized work. Organizational substitutes for the self-employed partnership model of general practice have also begun to appear, eroding the bedrock of GP's financial and organizational autonomy. At critical junctures in NHS reform (1992, 2000–02) the English medical profession was on the defensive and made concessions to government, despite New Labour also buying GP support for their reforms with income and managerial influence. A layer of medical managers has emerged with an interest in disciplinary, and by proxy managerial, control over other doctors. Together these trends suggest a net strengthening of NHS managerial control and a reduction in GPs' professional autonomy, both individual and collective. Gradually power has been draining from medicine to management in NHS primary care. This effect, and the organizational processes which have brought it about, partly belie the similarities between the present-day NHS organizational structures and those of the 1990s.

Similar organizational structures, different power-relations

Fifteen years of successive organizational 'reform' have ended up leaving English NHS organizational structures essentially as they were in 1991, except for the addition of a minority of salaried GPs. Yet although the organizational structures have essentially returned to those adopted by the Thatcher government, the balance of power between doctors and managers has not.

This history provides further evidence that an occupational group's positional power is not defined purely by occupancy of a privileged or a 'high' position in an hierarchical organizational structure. Rather, the ability of an occupant of such a position 'to carry out his own will despite resistance' is exercised through the whole complex of organizational processes and technical conditions outlined above. Organizational, policy or technical changes generally involve some combination of re-negotiation of practical, everyday working activities; re-interpretation of laws and regulations; decision-making, to that extent legitimating managers' positional role as decision-makers; new activities to which technical and professional 'disciplines' are applied; redefining divisions of labour within and between occupational groups; and opportunities to introduce new production techniques ('technologies'). Such events present each occupational group with the question of whether it would be legitimate and feasible for them to resist or to exploit the changes under way. Reallocations of budgets, staff and physical resources are made through these processes in combination, making these processes the media through which positional power is reproduced, i.e. simultaneously both exercised and modified. Repeated changes to formal organizational structures are no exception to this pattern, so that at the end of them all the balance of power between managers and doctors is likely to have shifted even though in terms of formal organizational structures and roles the parties are almost back where they started. To that extent, Courpasson (1998) is right to say that 'change is a political tool'.

Exactly the same considerations apply, however, to the effects of such changes on the power of the non-managerial occupations. Furthermore, organizational change is sometimes not so much an occupational group's 'tool' as an accident which befalls them. Depending on the circumstances, unplanned changes in the development of natural sciences can alter the balance of power between (in this case) managers and doctors. So can unforeseen events which expose any half-truths, fallacies or inconsistencies in occupational and political ideologies. Since power is essentially contested, the outcomes of the processes through which it is exercised are liable to be uncertain. The interaction of these planned and unplanned changes is what defines and redefines the content and scope of 'positional' power in most organizations.

Such findings remind organizational researchers of the futility of attempting to understand organizational structures and organizational processes in isolation from each other when analysing power in organizations. It is through the organizational processes noted above that the property rights attached to a specific position in an organizational structure are exercised and in doing so the positional power which they give is reproduced, strengthen or weakened. Conversely, each occupational group's role in the organizational structure determines what resources the group brings to its participation in these organizational processes and what interests each group pursues in doing so. An organizational structure thus constrains the range of organizational processes that occur within it. For example, in England, attempts at monitoring policy implementation, disciplinary control and non-medical managerial control in general practice have long been constrained by the structural independence of general practices. This raises the research question of how far, and in what ways, the new organizational structures and property-relations recently created by the salaried employment of GPs by NHS PCTs and by the emergence of further organizational varieties of primary health care provider will accommodate or even produce changed organizational processes (e.g. for decision-making, resource allocation, management of clinical quality) within English primary care. This question is currently being empirically researched.

A policy lesson from English NHS primary care reform is that even without changes to health system organizational structures, changes in managerial – that is, disciplinary, ideological, negotiative and re-allocative – processes can produce at least modest shifts in the balance of power between independent-contractor doctors and managers. Yet in the minority of cases where the structural position of GPs has changed to that of salaried employee of the NHS, the balance of power, in the sense of degree of managerial control, appears little different to that where GPs remain independent contractors. One possible explanation is that the salaried GPs tend to hold hard-to-fill posts, making PCTs hesitate to exercise the power which this hierarchical relationship might in theory provide. However, there is also evidence that at least one of the newly contracted private providers of primary care, which also employs salaried GPs in similar settings, has no such reluctance. In England at least, a more thoroughgoing privatization of NHS primary care might constrain medical power more narrowly than incorporation into a public bureaucracy does.

References

Abell, P. (1975) *Organizations as bargaining and influence systems* London: Heinemann.

Althusser, L. (1969) *For Marx*, London: Penguin.

Armstrong, D. (2002) 'Clinical autonomy, individual and collective: The problem of changing doctors' behaviour', *Social Science & Medicine*, 55(10), 1771–1777.

Bachrach, P. and Baratz, M. S. (1970) *Power and poverty: Theory and practice*, London: Oxford UP.

Blau, P. M. (1964) *Exchange and power in social life*, London: Wiley.

Boaden, R., Dusheiko, M., Gravelle, H., Parker, S., Pickhardt, S., Roland, M., Sargent, P. and Sheaff, R. (2005) *Evercare evaluation interim report: Implications for supporting people with long term conditions in the NHS*, Manchester: NPCRDC.

Chambers, N. (1998) *Nurse practitioners in primary care*, Abingdon: Radcliffe Medical.

Courpasson, D. (1998) 'Le changement est un outil politique', *Revue Française de Gestion*, 120(Sept–Oct), 6–16.

Courpasson, D. (2000) 'Managerial strategies of domination: Power in soft bureaucracies', *Organization Studies*, 21(1), 141–161.

Dahl, R. A. (1986) *Democracy, liberty and equality*, Oslo: Norwegian UP.

Department of Health [England] (1989) *Working for patients*, London: HMSO.

Department of Health [England] (2000) *Protecting patients, supporting doctors*, Leeds: DoH.

Fairclough, N. (2005) 'Discourse analysis in organization studies: The case for critical realism', *Organization Studies*, 26(6), 915–939.

Ferlie, E., Fitzgerald, L. and Wood, M. (2002) 'Getting evidence into practice: an organisational behaviour perspective', Journal of Health Services Research and Policy, 5, 96–102.

Flynn, R. (1992) *Structures of control in health management*, London: Routledge.

Flynn, R. (2002) 'Clinical governance and governmentality', *Health Risk and Society* 4(2), 155–173.

Foucault, M. (1977) *Discipline and punish: The birth of the prison*, London: Allen Lane.

Foucault, M. (2004) *Naissance de la biopolitique: Cours au Collége de France (1978–1979)*, Paris: Gallimard and Seuil.

Giddens, A. (1998) *The third way: The renewal of social democracy*, Cambridge: Polity.

Gosden, T., Bowler, I. and Sutton, M. (2000) 'How do general practitioners choose their practice? Preferences for practice and job characteristics', *Journal of Health Services Research and Practice*, 5(4), 208–213.

Habermas, J. (1976) *Legitimation crisis*, London: Heinemann Educational.

Hallam, L. (1997) 'Out of hours primary care', *British Medical Journal*, 314(7075), 157–158.

Hanlon, G., Strangleman, T., Goode, J., Luff, D., O'Caithain, A. and Greatbach, D. (2005) 'Knowledge, technology and nursing: the case of NHS Direct', *Human Relations*, 58(2), 147–171.

Harrison, S. (2002) 'New labour, modernisation and the medical labour process', *Journal of Social Policy*, 31, 465–485.

Harrison, S. and Dowswell, G. (2002) 'Autonomy and bureaucratic accountability in primary care; what English general practitioners say', *Sociology of Health and Illness*, 24(2), 208–226.

Hassell, K., Whittington, Z., Cantrill, J., Bates, F., Rogers, A. and Noyce, P. (2001) 'Managing demand: Transfer of management of self limiting conditions from general practice to community pharmacies', *British Medical Journal*, 323(7305), 146–147.

Klein, R. (1998) 'Competence, professional self-regulation and public interest', *British Medical Journal*, 316, 1740–1742.

Lukes, S. (1974) *Power*, London: Macmillan.

McNulty, T. and Ferlie, E. (2002) *Reengineering health care*, Oxford: Oxford UP.

Parsons, T. (1951) *The social system*, London: Routledge.

Parsons, T. and Shils, E. A. (1951) *Toward a general theory of action*, Cambridge, MA: Harvard UP.

Sheaff, R. and Lloyd-Kendall, A. (2000) 'Principal–agent relationships in general practice: The first wave of English PMS contracts', *Journal of Health Services Research and Policy*, 5(3), 156–163.

Sheaff, R., Smith, K. and Dickson, M. (2002) 'Is GP restratification beginning in England?', *Social Policy and Administration*, xxxvi(7), 765–779.

Sheaff, R., Rogers, A., Pickhardt, S., Marshall, M., Campbell, S., Roland, M., et al. (2003) 'A subtle governance; 'soft' medical leadership in English primary care', *Sociology of Health and Illness*, xxv(5), 408–428.

Sheaff, R., Schofield, J., Mannion, R., Dowling, B., Marshall, M. and McNally, R. (2004a) *Organizational factors and performance: A review of the literature*, London: NHS-SDO.

Sheaff, R., Sibbald, B., Campbell, S., Roland, M., Marshall, M., Pickhardt, S., Gask, L., Rogers, A. and Halliwell, S. (2004b) 'Soft governance and attitudes to clinical quality in English general practice', *Journal of Health Services Research and Policy*, ix(3), 132–138.

Strauss, A., Schatzman, L., Ehrlich, D., Bucher, R. and Sabshin, M. (1963) 'The hospital and its negotiated order' in E. Freidson (ed.) *The hospital in modern society*, New York: Free Press, pp. 147–169.

Tawney, R. H. (1938) *Equality*, London: Allen and Unwin.

Venning, P., Durie, A., Roland, M., Roberts, C. and Leese, B. (2000) 'Randomised controlled trial comparing cost effectiveness of general practitioners and nurse practitioners in primary care', *British Medical Journal*, 320(7241), 1048–1053.

Weber, M. (1947) *The theory of social and economic organization*, London: Collier Macmillan.

Williams, J., Petchey, R., Gosden, T., Leese, B. and Sibbald, B. (2001) 'A profile of PMS salaried GP contracts and their impact on recruitment', *Family Practice*, 18(3), 283–287.

2
Processes of Change in the Reconfiguration of Hospital Services: The Role of Stakeholder Involvement

Naomi Fulop, Perri 6 and Peter Spurgeon

The process of reorganising acute hospital services provides an interesting case study of power and change in health care organisations. In addition to their other roles, hospitals appear to have a particularly important symbolic role with the public in terms of representing a strong welfare state (Healy and McKee 2002). It has also been argued that hospitals in the UK have a role in maintaining and improving trust in the NHS (IPPR 2007). Proposed changes to hospital services therefore often create high profile, contentious debates locally, and sometimes nationally. This study illustrates the range of complex interests which play out in the process of attempting to change the configuration of hospital services.

The term 'reconfiguration' has been used in the context of health policy in the UK to describe changes to hospital services. Earlier changes, for example in the 1980s, were referred to as 'rationalisation' or 'retrenchment' (Pettigrew et al. 1992). The use of language plays an important part here: these terms may be seen by stakeholders, such as the media and the public, as euphemisms for 'cutback management', changes driven by financial concerns. A recent Department of Health report describes reconfiguration as 'synonymous with major service change, service improvement and delivering value for money for the taxpayer' (Department of Health 2007). There is no one agreed definition, so for the purposes of the study on which this chapter is based, we have developed this one:

> A deliberately induced change of some significance in the distribution of medical, surgical, diagnostic and ancillary specialties that are available in each hospital or other secondary or tertiary acute care unit in locality, region or health care administrative area. (6 2004)

Although it may be associated with mergers, or the formation of structured networks, reconfiguration is that measure of change which directly addresses operational rather than structural change: hospitals may merge, form networks, or change their divisional or governance structures, without reconfiguring services.

The driving forces for these changes to hospital services are related to upward pressure on costs, as a consequence of new technologies and rising public expectations, colliding with downward pressure from economic recession and political unwillingness to increase taxes (McKee et al. 2002). The most frequent response to these pressures is to seek ways of limiting costs. With hospitals accounting for 40–60% of health expenditure in OECD countries, it is not surprising that the focus has been on acute hospitals and the way in which they are organised. These drivers are common across countries in Europe (McKee and Healey 2002), and other developed countries (Clark and Spurgeon 1999). Drivers have also included anticipated clinical gains, using arguments relating to improvements in clinical quality predicted through higher volumes of activity; better medical training; and easier recruitment and retention of staff (Ferguson et al. 1997). Evidence shows higher volumes are associated with improved clinical outcomes in some specialties, but gains are exhausted at relatively low thresholds (NHS Centre for Reviews and Dissemination 1997), and the mechanism for the relationship, if it is causal, is unclear (Halm et al. 2002).

The term 'reconfiguration' has tended to be used in the UK policy context in a way which suggests a problem to be solved by calculations of optimal design. The Department of Health and local health policy makers have often presented it as a technical matter of optimising bed to population ratios, or co-locating services that require close connections, and achieving 'rational' resource allocation (e.g. Department of Health 2004). However, the evidence base for these optimal ratios is slender, and much of it relies largely on rules of thumb endorsed by established professional clinical institutes, rather than on careful evaluations.

Many reconfigurations, particularly where proposals included closing or the 'downgrading' of a hospital, have produced major local political conflicts. One of the most high profile of these occurred during the 2001 General Election, where in one constituency, the election was fought on the issue of a proposed reconfiguration of Kidderminster hospital which many in the town and nearby region perceived as a 'downgrading' in favour of transferring and developing some services in Worcester. The local Labour MP, a junior minister in the government, lost his seat to a former medical consultant from Kidderminster hospital who stood under the banner of a local organisation called Health Concern (www.healthconcern.org.uk) established to 'save the hospital'.

This led to a change in government policy and publication of the white paper, 'Keeping the NHS Local' (Department of Health 2003), which aimed to strike a balance between pressures to centralise acute services and maintain patient safety, whilst maintaining local access. As part of this policy, an independent reconfiguration panel was established, which aims to adjudicate on controversial reconfiguration proposals to 'take the politics' out of such decisions. Further measures to incorporate the public's views in the development of reconfiguration proposals were developed including a strengthened statutory require-ment to consult the public over reconfigurations, and the extension of Local Authority Overview and Scrutiny Committee (OSC) powers to include local health services.

Subsequent policy changes, notably the introduction of 'payment by results' and patient choice, may increase pressures for reconfigura-tion as hospitals compete for activity. Stated policy aims to shift care from hospital into 'the community' (Department of Health 2006a). NHS Foundation Trusts have greater freedom to make service changes so reconfigurations may be more likely as more NHS Trusts gain Founda-tion status. The process of reconfiguration is currently widespread and has politically high profile. The Department of Health identified 77 NHS Trusts which are at risk of closing services (Guardian 8 November 2006), and in October 2006, the Guardian identified 50 areas where there were public protests at local reconfiguration proposals (Guardian 26 October 2006).

Government documents and policies have increasingly emphasised the role of 'evidence' and consultation with the public (e.g. Department of Health 2007) based on the assumption that if only the public are involved 'enough' and are presented with the 'right evidence' they will be convinced of the need to change.

What we know from the literature

While there is a substantial literature on the experience of closing long-stay psychiatric hospitals (e.g. Korman and Glennerster 1990; McKee 1988), there is a paucity of empirical studies on the recon-figuration process in the acute sector. There were some studies of 'rationalisation' of acute hospitals in the 1980s (Pettigrew et al. 1992) and, more recently, there have been a few studies published on partic-ular local struggles over closure proposals such as in Kidderminster

(Brown 2003; Harris et al. 2005; Parkinson 2004). There are also a number of normative and prescriptive papers which develop modelling tools to help decision-making (e.g. Congdon 2001; Department of Health 2004, 2006b; Stummer et al. 2004). There is a literature on mergers of hospitals, although these have not always resulted in service reconfigurations (Fulop et al. 2005; Kitchener and Gask 2003), and studies on other types of relationships between hospitals, such as networks (Goodwin et al. 2004)

The current study

In the light of 'Keeping the NHS Local' (Department of Health 2003), the Department of Health funded three pilots of 'reconfiguration' in different parts of England. They commissioned an evaluation of these pilots through the NIHR Service Delivery and Organisation Programme. The objectives of the study are as follows:

1. How has each site 'performed' in terms of sustaining the delivery of acute services:

   - *what* changes were proposed?
   - *what* changes have been implemented?

2. Identify factors associated with 'success' and 'failure' at each site

   - *how* have changes been implemented?
   - *which* stakeholders are involved and *how*?
   - identify *processes* of change over time

3. Develop a generic framework to help future reconfiguration options.

In this chapter, we focus on what changes have been proposed and implemented, analyse what part is played by various stake-holders (individuals, groups, organisations) in these reconfiguration processes, and how their involvement affects these processes. Our study is based on the ideas of 'stakeholder analysis', which has been used both as a management tool and as a method to understand policy processes (Brugha and Varvasovzky 2000). This assumes a pluralist approach to policy-making and implementation, emphasising the importance of interest groups, such that although there are elites (for example, professional or technocratic elites), no one elite dominates at all times. This approach is useful in a study of policy-making and implementation in the context of a health care system funded through tax system where particular types of stakeholders will be important, and others less important. For example, in the USA, hospitals frequently reconfigure services with little or no public involvement in the process, whereas shareholders are important stakeholders in the process.

Methods

We combined qualitative and quantitative methods to address our objectives. The qualitative study consists of semi-structured interviews with internal and external stakeholders over two periods of time, as well as the documentary analysis, to study the proposed changes and the implementation process, including consultation and involvement of stakeholders. The first round of interviews was conducted between February and August 2005, and 52 interviews were conducted across the three sites. The second round of interviews was conducted two years later. This chapter reports findings from the first round of interviews and analysis of documentary data.

A core group of 'internal' and 'external' stakeholders were interviewed in each of the three case study sites as shown in Table 2.1. By 'internal', we mean internal to the organisation. However, this is not a homogeneous group, with different interests playing different roles in the reconfiguration process. For example, clinicians may or may not perceive their interests as aligning with those of management. Similarly, 'external' stakeholders are those outside the Trust, but again, this is not a homogeneous group, with Local Authority stakeholders having very

Table 2.1 Stakeholders interviewed in all three case studies

Internal stakeholders	External stakeholders
Chair of Board	Strategic Health Authorities
CEO	Primary Care Trusts
Director of Nursing	Social Services
Medical Director	Overview and Scrutiny Committees
Project Manager	MP
Financial Director	Local media
Director of Modernization/Service Re-Design	

different interests to NHS stakeholders such as Strategic Health Authorities. Interviewees were identified through a combination of an initial
review of documents and use of 'snowballing'.

The case studies

The three case studies (here called Trusts A, B, and C) are in different
areas of England (one urban, one mixed urban/rural, one rural). The sites
share some important factors in terms of the context for reconfiguration,
for example, two (Trusts A and B) have experienced merger; and the
same two have new buildings funded by the private finance initiative
(PFI), whereas Trust C does not. The context for each case is summarised
in Table 2.2.

The 'high' political context differs between sites. Two trusts have had
political influence at various times: Trust A was known as the Prime
Minister's favourite Trust in the early days of the new Labour Government, while Trust B has some very influential MPs in the government's
party. Trust C, however, has not had any particular political influence
and, because of its location, might be perceived as being on the 'peri-
phery' of any national political influence.

The drivers for reconfiguration also differ between each site. At Trust A,
the main drivers were to provide an improved model of care for patients,

Table 2.2 Context of case studies

Trust A

- Merger of two DGHs, 1999 (500,000 pop)
- Urban, inner city
- PFI funded new buildings
- Significant financial issues

Trust B

- Merger three DGHs, 2002 (570,000 pop) – hospitals X, Y, and Z
- New PFI's at hospital Z (2001) and Y (2002)
- Largely rural area, pockets of deprivation (esp round hospital Y)
- Sustainability issues

Trust C

- Two hospitals covering remote rural area – one much larger than the other (400,000 pop, large temp tourist pop)
- Geography important: smaller hospital based on peninsula
- Issues of patient safety for smaller hospital

increase the volume of patients seen by the hospital, and address financial issues.

At Trust B, a key driver was to maintain a safe service as the Royal College of Surgeons had withdrawn support for emergency surgery at hospitals X and Y, whilst maintaining access to services for all communities. Sustainability of services, with new PFI buildings at hospital Z and Y, was also a factor. Financial issues were not reported as a key driver.

At Trust C, the drivers were about how best to provide health care across a remote geographical area whilst maintaining clinical standards and financial sustainability.

Proposed changes

The original proposed changes at each site are summarised in Table 2.3. These are three very different reconfigurations, reflecting the different drivers and contexts.

Consultation processes

The consultation processes at the three sites also differed in terms of which stakeholders were involved, to what degree, and in what ways.

At Trust A, stakeholder involvement was almost exclusively internal to the organisation. There was very little involvement of external

Table 2.3 Proposed changes

Trust A

- Separation of elective and emergency care, and redesign of emergency care
- New building (PFI), decreased length of stay, greater integration of primary and secondary care, simplification of patient pathway

Trust B

- Y to focus on elective surgery and emergency medicine
- Transfer emergency surgery and trauma from Y to X
- Centralize maternity and paediatrics at X (move from Y)

Trust C

- Cessation of 24 hour medical-led emergency admissions to small hospital
- Development of medical assessment unit working in collaboration with larger hospital

stakeholders, partly because the new building meant 'reconfiguration' was not perceived as services being 'downgraded'. The proposed changes were to be implemented on one site, not across two or more sites where local populations may perceive they are 'losing out'. An important factor was that clinicians supported the proposals because they perceived that the main driver for the changes was strongly related to improved patient care. Finally, the new model of care was developed by a longstanding executive team of the pre-merger trust who were committed to change:

> I think that any organization needs to have its share of mavericks...I think you need some independent people within the organization who are not answerable for the deliverables around targets, who are just there to ask the questions 'Why are you doing it in this way? Could we do it in another way?' (Clinician, Trust A)

At Trust B, there were two consultations on each of the two main proposed service changes (i.e. changes to location of emergency and elective services, and centralisation of maternity and paediatric services). The consultations were perceived by interviewees as 'successful' in terms of process. People leading the consultation were perceived as 'decent', and clinicians were involved in external consultation process:

> there's a guy called Fred, a northern guy, very straightforward...and I was impressed by the way he addressed the mob because he was simply explaining that it would no longer be safe. I mean, he is an obstetrician and I think he convincingly made the case that it was not viable...I was convinced. There were still some people who were saying, you know 'We don't agree with this.'...And there was also...Sally who was from midwifery...and they were quite impassioned really...they were aware how much it meant to people'. (External stakeholder, Trust B)

The consultation was perceived as being based on values of listening and openness, and took care to find the 'right' people to consult with. The process was also praised for its use of 'evidence':

> I think we were able to allay fears in the sense that we'd done a very comprehensive review by telephone of all the midwifery-led units and they hadn't had adverse outcomes... (Clinician, Trust B)

However, this consultation 'failed' as the Primary Care Trusts did not feel able to sign up to taking maternity services out of hospital Y as originally proposed. As a result, an independent consultant was brought in and a compromise solution was 'agreed' with a midwife-led obstetric unit and paediatric service to be located at hospital Y, although this was despite opposition from the local patient group. The proposal was then referred to the Department of Health which agreed that the changes should be implemented.

The context for Trust C included a long history of debates about changing services. A local campaign group in the area served by the small hospital had formed during the 1990s. In 2002, proposals for change had met with strong local resistance with a march of 20,000 local people against the proposals. Following this, a stakeholder steering group was established as a way of attempting to seek agreement. The Trust, supported by the Royal Colleges, proposed to end emergency admissions at the smaller hospital. The local campaign group continued to argue for full district general hospital services in their town. The two groups became increasingly polarised, as the following two quotes show:

we made it clear from day one 'We want to look at all the options' but I said, 'I'm going to be completely honest with you, if anybody is saying you think you're going to create another district general hospital in XX: it's pie in the sky, When you talk about a full DGH you're talking about a fully blown accident and emergency department that requires an intensive care unit, orthopedics on site, ... So we made it quite clear from day one that that wasn't on – not just from my perspective ... The SHA are saying it's not on, the Royal Colleges, all of my staff are saying it's not on ... the learning point from this is there are some individuals who will not be open to rational debate or persuasion.' (Senior manager, Trust C)

there's been a catalogue of broken promises. There's certainly a perception in the public and it's certainly an opinion that I hold, that things are taken away and promises are made that other things will be put in their place, which will make things better, but we still wait to see them. (External stakeholder, Trust C)

The steering group ended after three years with the two sides failing to agree. An external consultant was brought in to help develop a local emergency medical unit. There was a proposal to use telemedicine and other digital links between the two hospitals in order to implement this model of care, but it was not taken forward.

What has been implemented?

At the time of the first round of fieldwork, it was striking how little had been implemented in relation to the original proposed changes. This was in part at least due to the role of different stakeholder groups acting as barriers to implementation, particularly at Trust B and Trust C.

At Trust A, the new building opened in spring 2006. Some aspects of the new model were implemented prior to the new building opening, but it was not clear yet if the full, original plans had been implemented. However, the Trust were keen to claim a number of early successes, for example, the lowest rate of admissions and shortest length of stay in region; increased community care/earlier discharges reported as being popular with patients; 'improved' clinical decision-making and use of beds.

Given that one of the main drivers for this redesign of services was to improve the experience of receiving health care for patients, it is not surprising that clinicians were hopeful that patients would be happier and healthier after reconfiguration. One clinician already working on the new model said:

> our very rough data suggests that patient satisfaction is enormous. Patients absolutely love being managed at home ... having someone to call on who will come in and see them straight away [chronic disease practitioners] rather than dealing with a GP ... instant access to a consultant is very much appreciated (Clinician, Trust A).

Over time, however, the reconfiguration process was perceived to distract the organisation from the Trust's performance on key targets:

> they were seen to be off on a tangent and not supporting the day to day or the short term ... Day to day operationally the trust is under significant pressure ... The project management structure was not seen to support the operational running of the hospital. (Manager, Trust A)

This failure to perform on key targets led to an almost wholesale change in the senior management of the Trust subsequent to the first round of fieldwork.

At Trust B, although most of the proposed service changes appear to have been implemented, the sustainability of services was questioned: hospital Y, a new PFI building opened in 2002, had been significantly under-utilised. Clinicians from hospital Z were reluctant to transfer elective surgery to hospital Y, raising issues of patient safety. These were questioned by managers attempting to implement the change who speculated that their reluctance was more related to their concerns about the negative effect on their private practice as hospital Y is located in a poorer socio-economic area:

> They'll use patient safety as an issue to get what they want... I'm not a cynical person by nature but I've learned over the years that if a consultant says something is not in the patient interest you need to look very, very closely at the argument because what he or she may well be saying is that it's not in their interest. (External stakeholder, Trust B)

Interestingly, the Trust has been held up as 'flagship' example of how to prevent closure of small, rural hospitals by the Department of Health (2004).

At Trust C, no major service reconfiguration had been implemented. There was very little joint working between the two hospitals in the Trust, and emergency surgery was still in place at the small hospital at the time of our first round of fieldwork, despite clinical governance concerns.

Conclusions

This study illustrates the way different stakeholders with different interests play a role in reconfiguration processes in different contexts. From our study, and other studies of hospital reconfigurations, it seems that both class and geography may play an important part in the process. Smaller towns, with a large middle class population, are more likely to produce conflict between the public and the hospital on reconfiguration. In our study, this is illustrated by the history of Trust C compared with Trusts A and B, and other examples of reconfiguration in Kidderminster and East Kent (Harris et al. 2005; IRP 2003). The way stakeholder interests play out differently in different contexts is also illustrated by the importance of the configuration of local politics: local MPs from the governing party can play a much greater role in the reconfiguration process than those from other parties.

The type of reconfiguration is an important factor. Where reconfiguration is perceived as a 'downgrading' of service provision, there is more active internal (professional) and external stakeholder involvement as illustrated in Trusts B and C, whereas in cases where changes are not perceived as 'downgrading' because services are not being moved from one site to another or closing, as in Trust A, there is less conflict. Clinicians' interests will play out differently according to how they perceive the changes. In Trust A, there was strong clinical support for the changes as they were based on clear objectives to improve patient care. In Trust B, however, changes were not supported and not fully implemented where some clinicians, in this case surgeons, were concerned about the impact on their private sector work.

Great store has been placed on stakeholder involvement and the use of 'evidence' to persuade reluctant stakeholders both at national (e.g. Department of Health 2007) and local levels. However, a consultation process in Trust B which was perceived as 'good' did not seem to lead to a more straightforward process of implementation. In Trusts B and C where there was active stakeholder involvement, the original plans were less likely to be implemented.

From our study, it is evident that complex relationships between the interests of a range of stakeholders influence reconfiguration processes. Our findings support the pluralist approach to understanding the policy process whereby different interest groups with different public interest claims and power resources will influence policy and its implementation. Reconfiguration is not just a technocratic process, as has often been assumed both by those developing the policy and those implementing it. Their response, therefore, has been to undertake technical analyses as described above of, for example, the numbers of beds required or where specific services should be sited and then share these analyses with stakeholders. The role of hospitals in symbolising public entitlement to public services and maintaining trust in the NHS has been underplayed, or even misunderstood. The role of professionalised interests has been underestimated, particularly in the implementation process. Even in cases where professional interests appear to have agreed with proposals, they can delay or scupper implementation (e.g. in Trust B).

So what is the future for reconfiguration? With current policies of 'payment by results', 'choice', and a proposed increasing role for community services, the pressure to reconfigure hospital services is likely to increase. Pressures on trusts to become Foundation Trusts (FT) may lead to more reconfigurations as current FTs are encouraged to take over trusts less able to achieve FT status. Local conflicts are likely to increase if the 'market' is allowed to work and destabilise providers. The key question is how these conflicts between policies of maintaining local service provision and those creating a market will be resolved. From the findings of our study, we would predict that a technocratic solution will not be successful.

Acknowledgements

We are very grateful to the three Trusts for agreeing to participate in the study, and to individual interviewees for their time and interest. We would also like to thank Alice Mowlam for assistance with fieldwork.

Funding

This study was funded by the NIHR Service Delivery and Organisation Programme (SDO/63/2003).

Ethical Approval

NHS London Multi-centre Research Ethics Committee and NHS Trust Local Research Ethics Committees.

References

6, P. (2004) *Hospital reconfiguration: Issues arising from the available recent literature* (Unpublished paper).

Brown, T. (2003) 'Towards an understanding of local protest: Hospital closures and community resistance', *Social and Cultural Geography*, 4(4), 489–506.

Brugha, R. and Varvasovsky, Z. (2000) 'Stakeholder analysis: A review', *Health Policy and Planning*, 15(3), 239–246.

Clark, J. and Spurgeon, P. (1999) *International critique of integrated clinical services*, Paper for Metropolitan Health Services Board, Western Australia.

Congdon, P. (2001) 'The development of gravity models for hospital patient flows under system change: A Bayesian modelling approach', *Health Care Management Science*, 4(4), 289–304.

Department of Health (2003) *Keeping the NHS local: A new direction of travel*, London: DH.

Department of Health (2004) *The configuring hospitals evidence file*, London: DH.

Department of Health (2006a) *Our health, our care, our say: A new direction for community services*, London: The Stationery Office.

Department of Health (2006b) *Strengthening local services: The future of the acute hospital*, NHS National Leadership Network Local Hospitals Project. London: DH.

Department of Health (2007) *Service improvement: Quality assurance of major changes to service provision*, London: DH.

Ferguson, B., Sheldon, T., and Posnett, J. (1997) *Concentration and choice in healthcare*, London: Royal Society of Medicine.

Fulop, N., Protopsaltis, G., King, A. et al. (2005) 'Changing organisations: A study of the context and processes of mergers of health care providers in England', *Social Science & Medicine*, (6), 119–130.

Goodwin, N., 6, P., Peck, E., Freeman, T. and Posaner, R. (2004) *Managing across diverse networks of care: Lessons from other sectors*, www.sdo.lshtm.ac.uk/studyinghealthcare.htm.

Guardian, 26 October 2006 [http://www.guardian.co.uk/medicine/story/0,,1931714,00.html].

Guardian, 8 November 2006 [http://www.guardian.co.uk/medicine/story/0,,1942697,00.html].

Halm, E., Lee, C. and Chassin, M. (2002) 'Is volume related to outcome in healthcare? A systematic review and methodologic critique of the literature', *Annals of Internal Medicine*, 137(6), 511–520.

Harris, M., Raftery, J. and Spurgeon, P. (2005) *Evaluating the effects of the reconfiguration of Kidderminster hospital, 2001–2004*, Birmingham: Health Services Management Centre, University of Birmingham.

Healy, J. and McKee, M. (2002) 'The role and function of hospitals' in M. McKee and J. Healy (eds) *Hospitals in a changing Europe*, Buckingham: Open University Press.

Independent Reconfiguration Panel (2003) *Advice on NHS service changes in East Kent*, London: DH. Available at http://www.irpanel.org.uk/lib/doc/eastkentreptjun03.pdf.

IPPR (2007) *The future hospital: The progressive case for change*, London: IPPR.

Kitchener, M. and Gask, L. (2003) 'NPM merger mania: Lessons from an early case', *Public Management Review*, 5(1), 20–44.

Korman, N. and Glennerster, H. (1990) *Hospital closure*, Milton Keynes: Open University Press.

McKee, L. (1988) 'Conflicts and context in managing the closure of a large psychiatric hospital', *Bulletin of the Royal College of Psychiatrists*, 12(8), 310–319.

McKee, M. and Healy, J. (eds) (2002) *Hospitals in a changing Europe*, , Buckingham: Open University Press.

McKee, M., Healy, J., Edwards, N. and Harrison, A. (2002) 'Pressures for change' in M. McKee and J. Healy (eds) (2002) *Hospitals in a changing Europe*, Buckingham: Open University Press.

NHS Centre for Reviews and Dissemination (1997) 'Concentration and choice in the provision of hospital services. The relationship between hospital volume and quality of health outcomes', *CRD Report no. 8, part I*, University of York, Centre for Reviews and Dissemination.

Parkinson, J. (2004) 'Hearing voices: Negotiating representation claims in public deliberation', *British Journal of Politics and International Relations*, 6(3), 370–388.

Pettigrew, A., Ferlie, E. and McKee, L. (1992) *Shaping strategic change*, London: Sage Publications.

Stummer, C., Doerner, K., Focke, A. and Heidenberger, K. (2004) 'Determining location and size of medical departments in a hospital network: A multiobjective decision support approach', *Health Care Management Science*, 7(1), 63–71.

3
Hospital Sector Organisational Restructuring: Evidence of Its Futility

Jeffrey Braithwaite, Mary T. Westbrook, Donald Hindle and Rick A. Iedema

Introduction

Restructuring is a prevalent managerial strategy, favoured by those who say they seek to create improvements by merging organisations, streamlining organisational hierarchies or rationalising reporting arrangements (Brocklehurst 2001; Lathrop 1993; Relman 2005; Sen 2003). Proponents tend to argue that they will create through their restructuring efforts greater efficiency, i.e. more benefit for the same or less cost. Restructuring is typically sponsored by those in political or executive positions with capacities to enact such change and assume responsibility for leading efficient and effective services.

In healthcare, this means ministers for health, bureaucrats running health departments, managers responsible for regional health services (trusts or boards in the United Kingdom's NHSs; area health services, regions or districts in Australia and elsewhere) or local heads of individual health facilities such as hospitals or general practices. At issue is what they conceptualise as structure, how they go about restructuring and what they achieve in practice by doing so.

In this chapter we discuss some of the parameters of this issue and assess international evidence for restructuring, particularly in NHS trusts and Australian teaching hospitals. Evidence is provided that restructurings are often futile. Many do not achieve the efficiency claimed and can lead to adverse consequences (Braithwaite et al. 2005a). But first, restructuring as a phenomenon has been undertheorised amongst healthcare organisational scholars, and it is important to reflect on some underlying theoretical accounts to conceptualise the empirical work discussed.

Theoretical themes on structure and restructuring

What is structural? What does it mean to restructure? And, if efficiency is the aim, has this been achieved by those who restructure, and when it has, under what circumstances? In relation to the first two questions, we could think about organisational structure and restructuring through the lens of neo-institutional theory and contingency theory, alternate conceptualisations of organisations.

Neo-institutional theory

Neo-institutional theorists argue that there are normative, mimetic and coercive demands for structural homogeneity (Di Maggio and Powell 1983). This means organisations are under pressure from various internal and external sources to look like others in their field and to structure in similar ways to peers. This predicts that sets of teaching hospitals will look structurally alike at any one time, as will sets of banks and steel mills. Once a structure is accepted, alternative ways of organising become neglected, even dismissed a priori as unimaginable. Accordingly, once an organisational form becomes legitimised in an organisational field, organisations within that field tend to move to that sanctioned way of organising, and stay there. Extending this further, some neo-institutionalists argue that, as a result of internal and external institutionalised pressures, organisational agents collectively project formal structural images and conceptualisations in order to achieve stakeholder recognition, ratification and legitimacy (Kamens 1977; Lee 1971; Meyer and Rowan 1977).

In contrast to formal structure, social structure refers to on-the-ground, ethnographically observable patterns of recurrent and habituated behaviours. Social relations are characterised as being busy, restless, chaotic and ambiguous. Contrary to stakeholder projections of formal structural stability, the organisation is seen as inchoate and emergent; and continuously enacted, framed and reframed by the agents who constitute it (Silverman 1971; Strauss et al. 1963). Structure is hammered out through chaotically – yet repetitively – anchored routines brought into being via continuous flows of action. People within organisations create through their actions the social forces which both enable and constrain them (Giddens 1979, 1984; Strauss 1978).

For neo-institutional theorists, then, at the centre of the complex weave of organisational myth and ceremony lies the formal prescribed structure, and this may have little generalised effect on social structuring. It has been argued that there is no relationship between formal structure and efficiency (DiMaggio and Powell 1983). For healthcare this means that trusts and hospitals will be likely to look structurally similar and will tend to restructure in concert, although time lags may occur. This helps explain how for decades hospitals worldwide were structurally alike. Then, when clinical directorates emerged and caught on, they radiated across health systems until hospitals looked similar again. It also suggests that organisational structures are not really functional – they tend to be isomorphic (copied from each other, and similar) and a façade. An organisational structure – say, depicted by the boxes on an organisation chart – is merely a representation of how some organisational players think the world should be rather than a concrete entity (Braithwaite et al. 2005b).

Structural contingency theory

The organisation looks different from the point of view of structural contingency theory. Structure tends to be conceptualised in concrete terms and is amenable to scientific empiricisation (Clegg and Hardy 1996). For Donaldson (1985) organisational structure is the sum of the formal and informal relationships and interactions between individuals and groups, and reflects authority and control mechanisms. These are often depicted in organisationally sanctioned normative documentation like organisational charts, job descriptions and standard operating procedures.

Structural contingency theory holds that organisations adapt to their environment as a consequence of moderating variables known as contingency factors (CFs) that typically comprise organisational characteristics such as strategy, size, environment, growth and innovation. CFs and structure must be fit for good performance. When in misfit, an organisation will alter its structure in response to CFs to find a better fit (Chandler 1962; Lawrence and Lorsch 1967) rather than accommodate its CFs to the extant structure.

Donaldson (1987) has advanced the structural adaptation to regain fit (SARFIT) model and demonstrated the phases of the underlying mechanisms of structural contingency theory. The initial condition can be hypothesised as an organisation in fit with its environment, i.e. its structure and the CFs are congruous. When CFs change resulting in misfit, as a corollary, performance reduces. Misfit is corrected when the structure is changed adaptively towards a new fit, and performance is regained. Thus accommodation is structural, and this occurs adaptively, perhaps over a considerable time. Accommodation is also deterministic and there is less scope for strategic choice than alternative theories suppose (Donaldson 1997). There is some empirical support for the claim that organisations in fit achieve better financial performance (e.g., Donaldson 1987; Hamilton and Shergill 1992; Hill et al. 1992). Structural contingency accounts suggest that in the case of healthcare restructuring, organisations moved into misfit as a result of external or internal CFs and that restructuring is an attempt to regain fit and enhance performance. If this is so, it would be expected that restructuring would improve performance, i.e. produce more streamlined, productive service delivery.

Conceptualising efficiency

Conceptually, efficiency can be understood in terms that would be of interest to investigators in fields as different as biomechanics, biology, engineering or economics. At a general level efficiency relates to the conversion of energy or effort from one thing to another. In the language of operations research it refers to the transformation of inputs to outputs. Efficiency gained by merging trusts, or hospital efficiency gained by restructuring, measured by costs saved or reduced expenditure, are analogous to notions of efficiency in other disciplines.

In this sense efficiency is a measure of benefit over cost. Diagnosis-related groups (DRGs) provide a measure of weighted inpatient episodes produced by a hospital compared with inpatient budget allocated in the production of those services. The DRG classification was developed by Fetter (1990) for the purpose of investigating quality of care (Duckett 1994). However, funders of acute services quickly realised they were an ideal tool for costing and reimbursing hospital products. An excellent Australian variant (AR-DRG) developed after 1990 has been adopted by other countries including New Zealand, Slovenia, Singapore and Germany. Although DRGs do not represent a complete description of a hospital's outputs (Braithwaite and Hindle 1998; Hindle and Braithwaite 1998), DRG costs per case provide a common metric and a robust measure of relative efficiency (see Fetter 1990). Proponents of DRGs have persuasively suggested that acute admitted patients are the dominant and most costly component of a hospital's work (Hindle et al. 1996), thus capturing the majority of a hospital's performance.

It follows that neo-institutional theory suggests that although new organisational charts are produced and various changes are invoked through restructuring, to a large extent any particular restructuring may be unrelated both to efficiency and changes to the social structure. Structural contingency theorists might argue differently, holding that restructuring is an adaptive change from misfit to fit, i.e. the regaining of improved performance. For a neo-institutional account to be convincing, we might expect restructuring to lead to reactive feelings and beliefs. For structural contingency theory to explain the data we might expect to see improved efficiency or another performance improvement as a result of the adaptive structural change.

Surveying the research evidence: exemplar studies from the NHS and Australia

Past research evidence accounting for healthcare restructuring has been patchy and inconclusive, despite the frequency with which restructuring occurs and the possibly accelerating propensity to restructure (Smith et al. 2001). Recent work has begun to illuminate the phenomenon.

Mergers in the NHS

Cereste et al. (2003) surveyed 457 senior NHS managers following earlier work by Garside (1999) and Weil (2000). Their results confirmed that while mergers were occurring at a rapid rate, and could be disruptive, the aims for some mergers were not merely efficiency but also enhanced services and patient care. Respondents were equivocal about whether these were or could be achieved through mergers. Less than half of respondents believed mergers would secure these benefits. Cereste et al. concluded that buy-in of multiple stakeholder groups to a restructure was a determinant of successful merging.

Fulop and her colleagues (Fulop et al. 2002, 2005) examined the mergers of different NHS trusts in a range of contexts. They found that NHS mergers specifically and structural change more generally were underpinned by simplistic conceptualisations of organisational change management, and failed to understand the nature of complex systems and cultures. Fulop's work showed that the overt forces and stipulated rationale for mergers were mainly cost efficiencies, quality and service improvements, and staff morale, well being and productivity. Below-the-surface reasons for merging were to resolve managerial, financial and local shortcomings. She argued that the merging strategy is a relatively blunt, even crude organisational change process which fails to account for the complexities of systems dynamics and organisational cultures and sub-cultures. Typically, mergers set organisations back 18 months, and on balance led to more negative than positive outcomes; efficiency and clinical objectives were not largely achieved. A serious question from this research is whether mergers can realise these objectives.

Restructuring Australian teaching hospitals

Braithwaite et al. (2006) investigated the restructuring activity of the 20 adult tertiary referral hospitals in the Australian states of New South Wales (NSW) and Victoria diachronically over a five to six year period. They compared hospitals' efficiency, measured by AN-DRGs adjusted for inflation, with their structural type each year. Structural types were categorised as traditional-professional (TP), clinical-divisional (CD) or clinical-institute (CI). No structural type was more efficient than any other. Restructuring did not yield any efficiency benefits, and the restructuring year was no more or less efficient than any other. Restructuring more than once in the study period was associated with reduced efficiency.

To explore these data further, we invoke the idea, borrowed from biology, of the fitness landscape. Organisms adapt to the landscape – the environment – by scaling the peaks. At the peaks we find organisms that are fitter, better adapted and more efficient than their counterparts. Under this scenario, drawn from population ecology concepts (Burgelman 1996; Young 1988), and in particular the work of Kauffman (1995), the acute health sector environment is viewed as a fitness landscape within which a set of organisations is found. Although biologists might apply such ideas to individual organisms vis-à-vis populations, and strictly speaking the theory might be more appropriately applied to populations of hospitals than individual hospitals, we suggest the analogy is a useful one. Each hospital in the sample would be located somewhere within the fitness landscape. The landscape itself will be characterised by peaks and troughs. At the peaks is fitness, and the efficient hospitals, and in the valleys and the foothills lie the less well adapted. The terrain may be rugged and multi-peaked, or relatively flat. In the former, it is harder to travel and become more efficient: there are limited resources, and others have already scaled and occupied the peaks. Flatter landscapes are easier to traverse. As Kauffman said of rugged landscapes: 'the rate of improvement slows exponentially as one clambers uphill'. Wherever an individual hospital fits in the landscape, its relative efficiency can be compared to its structural type, and those in the set, over time.

A hospital within a set which exhibited higher levels of efficiency than its rivals, measured by cost per case of producing casemix-weighted inpatient separations, will be considered better adapted – fitter – than its counterparts. It will be at higher levels on the fitness landscape.

The graph (Figure 3.1) illuminates the comparative performance of the set of NSW teaching hospitals. We measured efficiency by relative performance on AN-DRGs, a measure of costs of hospitals. Peaks of efficiency are evident in the early part of the period for Hospitals B, G and F, all of which were developing teaching hospitals in the outer regions of metropolitan Sydney in the early 1990s. The lower valleys of inefficiency are occupied by more established teaching hospitals. These were Hospitals A and I in the earliest period, A and J briefly in the middle period and by I, L and E in the later period. Hospital A nestled in 1991–92 and 1993–94 in the lowest valleys of inefficiency. The remainder of the map shows intermediate levels of efficiency.

Figure 3.2 shows the comparative performance of the Victorian teaching hospitals. In the early part of the period the dominating feature of the set was relative inefficiency and in the case of the Hospitals M, S, R and Q, valleys of greater inefficiency. This state-of-affairs was recognised by the Victorian State government, and a one-off cost reduction in hospital budgets and a funding system based on outputs were introduced in 1992–93. The improved efficiency across the set was attributed to these policy changes (Duckett 1994). There is a general pattern of

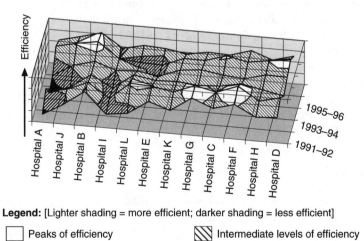

Legend: [Lighter shading = more efficient; darker shading = less efficient]

☐ Peaks of efficiency   ⧄ Intermediate levels of efficiency

▨ Lower levels of efficiency   ■ Valleys of inefficiency

Figure 3.1 A fitness landscape for NSW principal teaching hospitals, 1991–92 to 1996–97

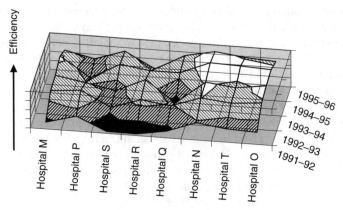

Legend: [Lighter shading = more efficient; darker shading = less efficient]

☐ Peaks of efficiency   ▨ Intermediate levels of efficiency

▨ Lower levels of efficiency   ■ Valleys of inefficiency

Figure 3.2 A fitness landscape for Victorian principal teaching hospitals, 1991–92 to 1995–96

increasing efficiency since 1992–93 (with the exception of P and R). The newer teaching hospitals, located outside the inner metropolitan area (N, T and O), exhibited peaks of efficiency in the latter period of the data review, especially during 1994–95 and 1995–96.

However, having said that, in both the NSW and Victorian settings, despite considerable individual and group variation in efficiency, the overall efficiency of hospitals was unrelated to any particular structural type. It did not matter where the hospital fitted in the efficiency landscape, structure did not predict efficiency and was unrelated to it ($p = 0.571$).

Discussion

The data from both the NHS and Australian studies do not support a contingency explanation. In neither case has restructuring led to improved performance or efficiency, at least on the measures selected for study by Fulop et al. and Braithwaite et al. On this argument, restructuring is futile, and it would be better to use the energies, time and expertise devoted to it to focus on alternative managerial activities or strategies to change cultures rather than structures.

Although we should discard a structural contingencies account of the data, we can advance an explanation based on neo-institutional theory, particularly for the teaching hospital study. Di Maggio and Powell (1983) argued that there are inexorable forces towards homogeneity, regardless of whether this leads to improved efficiency. Once the clinical directorate model emerged as a pre-institutional possibility for many early adopters, perhaps through coercive means, mimetic and eventually normative pressures began to build. The clinical directorate model diffused as an innovation across Western healthcare. Although efficiency was heralded as one major consequence of organising this way, a clear conclusion from the Australian hospital study, as neo-institutional theory predicts, is that no greater efficiency prevails.

Thus after decades of functional TP isomorphism, teaching hospital structures changed in many countries to another type of structure. The stages of habituation (pre-institutionalisation), objectification (semi-institutionalisation) and sedimentation (full institutionalisation) put forward by Tolbert and Zucker (1996) seem to have occurred in relatively rapid succession. Clinical directorates have become the privileged rationalised form, but do not, on our findings, produce superior efficiency.

The processes of changing the structure of teaching hospitals from a neo-institutional standpoint can be explained as follows. The normative myths in the institutional environment espouse that teaching hospitals ought to be more efficient, effective, patient-focused, team-based and concerned about patients (see, for example, Braithwaite et al. 2006; Lathrop 1993; Leatt 1994; Taft and Pelikan 1990). By implication, TP teaching hospital structures are associated with poor quality, inefficiency and ineffectiveness, and impersonal and uncompassionate care (Braithwaite 1995; e.g., Fitzgerald and Sturt 1992). TP hospitals are viewed as being functionally organised around the needs of professionals, not patients, and as fragmented and political (Allen 1995; e.g., Guinn 1993; Rivers et al. 1997).

The imbalance between the normative myths in the institutional environment and the criticism of TP isomorphism represents a kind of structural dissonance. This seems to have led to pressure to change to a CD or CI structure. Clinical directorate hospitals, pre-institutionally and once they have emerged, are said to be organised, in contrast to the older TP version, to have the capacity to deliver more efficient, effective care. They are said to be more personal, caring, patient- not profession-focused and organised around patients. The new rationalised logic says that clinical directorate structures are less fragmented, more integrated and better managed than their predecessors (Disken et al. 1990; Packwood et al. 1991; Smith and Chantler 1987). Because of these accounts, CD or CI hospitals are advanced as more legitimate, and performing better, than were TP hospitals. In this way the structural dissonance seems to have been overcome. However, there is no satisfactory evidence to support this new picture of organisational well-being.

Independent of performance effect, the adoption of clinical directorates explicitly displays a commitment to care, a dramatic pledge to patient-focused, efficient and effective services. Our data fit with the suggestion that these accounts of clinical directorates are little more than a rationalised myth, a socially reconstructed signifier of care and compassion. The comparative evidence from our hospital study provides insights into structural institutionalisation at the time when it emerges. Organisational agents inhabit a social world created by their own actions that is non-linear, disequilibrious, reverberating, messy and sometimes unfathomable, but they offer a summarised, preferred prescription of it, a ritualised, sacred script. Generically, this gilded account has come to be called 'the formal structure' and in the specific case of the study hospitals, 'the clinical directorates'.

A final institutional question centres on the finding that there are two main kinds of clinical directorate. We may thus have found duomorphism, and this discovery does not sit comfortably with one proposition of neo-institutional theory, specifically to the effect that heterogeneity of structure will give way to isomorphism (Di Maggio and Powell 1983). To the contrary, we have found functional isomorphism preceding a shift to one of two alternatively differentiated structural types. It may be that a unique example of duomorphism has surfaced in large hospitals. Or it could be that either CD or CI is an intermediate type, and the shift across time will be towards isomorphism of one of these two options, or to an as yet unidentified prescribed structure. Either of these possibilities will require further theorising and empiricising.

Conclusion

There are theoretical implications here for health services researchers. We need to go beyond past debates about the merits of any one theory and indulge in theoretical pluralism. Our work suggests that comparing theoretical paradigms, and reasoning between them, based on convergent forms of organisational evidence, may serve to illuminate some facets of our field.

There are practical implications for health service executives and poli-cymakers. Merging and restructuring in these studies did not lead to efficiency, despite this being a key expressed aim of proponents. In this respect restructuring activities were futile. The task of arguing the case for restructuring, and refuting these findings by adducing evid-ence in favour of the benefits of restructuring, now falls heavily to its proponents. Our data ask: how defensible are restructuring behaviours? The clear alternative to structural change is cultural change, but this seems a much more long-term enterprise, and runs counter to short-run political and executive time-frames. The battle between the proponents of structural change and the advocates of cultural change may have only just begun.

References

Allen, D. (1995) 'Doctors in management or the revenge of the conquered: The role of management development for doctors', *Journal of Management in Medi-cine*, 9, 44–50.

Braithwaite, J. (1995) 'Organisational change, patient-focused care: An Australian perspective', *Health Services Management Research*, 8, 172–185.

Braithwaite, J. and Hindle, D. (1998) 'Casemix funding in Australia', *Medical Journal of Australia*, 168, 558–560.

Braithwaite, J., Westbrook, J. and Iedema, R. (2005a) 'Restructuring as gratifica-tion', *Journal of the Royal Society of Medicine*, 98, 542–544.

Braithwaite, J., Westbrook, M. and Iedema, R. (2005b) 'Giving voice to health professionals' attitudes about their clinical service structures in theoretical context', *Health Care Analysis*, 13, 315–335.

Braithwaite, J., Westbrook, M., Hindle, D., Iedema, R. and Black, D. (2006) 'Does restructuring hospitals result in greater efficiency? An empirical test using diachronic data', *Health Services Management Research*, 19, 1–12.

Brocklehurst, M. (2001) 'Power, identity and new technology homework: Implic-ations for 'new forms' of organizing', *Organization Studies*, 22, 445–466.

Burgelman, R. A. (1996) 'Intraorganizational ecology of strategy making and organizational adaptation: Theory and Field Research' in J. R. Meindl, C. Stub-bert and J. F. Porac (eds) *Cognition within and between organizations* Newbury Park: Sage.

Cereste, M., Doherty, N. F. and Travers, C. J. (2003) 'An investigation into the level and impact of merger activity amongst hospitals in the UK's National Health Service', *Journal of Health Organisation and Management*, 17, 6–24.

Chandler, A. D. (1962) *Strategy and structure: Chapters in the history of the industrial enterprise*, Cambridge: MIT Press.

Clegg, S. R. and Hardy, C. (1996) 'Introduction: Organizations, organization and organizing' in S. R. Clegg, C. Hardy and W. R. Nord (eds) *Handbook of organiz-ation studies*, London: Sage.

Di Maggio, P. and Powell, W. W. (1983) 'The iron cage revisited: Institutional isomorphism and collective rationality in organizational fields', *American Soci-ological Review*, 48(April), 147–160.

Disken, S., Dixon, M., Halpern, S. and Shocket, G. (1990) *Models of clinical management*, London: Institute of Health Services Management.

Donaldson, L. (1985) *In defence of organization theory: A reply to the critics*, Cambridge: Cambridge University Press.

Donaldson, L. (1987) 'Strategy and structural adjustment to regain fit and performance: In defense of contingency theory', *Journal of Management Studies*, 24, 1–24.

Donaldson, L. (1997) 'A positivist alternative to the structure–action approach', *Organization Studies*, 18, 77–92.

Duckett, S. J. (1994) *Reform of public hospital funding in Victoria*, Sydney: Australian Studies in Health Service Administration No 80, School of Health Services Management, University of New South Wales.

Fetter, R. B. (1990) *DRGs: Design, development and application*, Ann Arbour: Health Administration Press.

Fitzgerald, L. and Sturt, J. (1992) 'Clinicians into management: On the change agenda or not?' *Health Services Management. Research*, 5, 137–146.

Fulop, N., Protopsaltis, G., Hutchings, A., King, A., Allen, P., Normand, C. and Walters, R. (2002) 'Process and impact of mergers of NHS trusts: Multicentre case study and management cost analysis', *British Medical Journal*, 325, 246–249.

Fulop, N., Protopsaltis, G., King, A., Allen, P., Hutchings, A. and Normand, C. (2005) 'Changing organisations: A study of the context and processes of mergers of health care providers in England', *Social Science & Medicine*, 60, 119–130.

Garside, P. (1999) 'Evidence based mergers?' *British Medical Journal*, 318, 345–346.

Giddens, A. (1979) *Central problems in social theory*, London: Macmillan.

Giddens, A. (1984) *The constitution of society: Outline of a theory of structuration*. Berkeley: University of California Press.

Guinn, R. M. (1993) 'Operational restructuring for patient focused care: The facility implications', *World Hospitals*, 29, 21–30.

Hamilton, R. T. and Shergill, G. S. (1992) 'The relationship between strategy–structure fit and financial performance in New Zealand: Evidence of generality and validity with enhanced controls', *Journal of Management Studies*, 29, 95–113.

Hill, C. W. L., Hitt, M. A. and Hoskisson, R. E. (1992) 'Cooperative versus competitive structures in related and unrelated diversified firms', *Organization Science*, 3, 501–521.

Hindle, D. and Braithwaite, J. (1998) 'Product costing, managerialism and organizational learning: Some insights from a case study from the Tasmanian health sector', *Australian Journal of Public Administration*, 57, 36–45.

Hindle, D., Degeling, P. J. and Braithwaite, J. (1996) *An introduction to casemix*, Sydney: Centre for Hospital Management and Information Systems Research, University of New South Wales, School of Health Services Management.

Kamens, D. H. (1977) 'Legitimating myths and educational organization: The relationship between organizational ideology and formal structure', *American Sociological Review*, 42, 208–219.

Kauffman, S. (1995) *At home in the universe: The search for the laws of complexity*, London: Penguin.

Lathrop, J. P. (1993) *Restructuring health care: The patient focused paradigm*, San Francisco: Jossey-Bass.

Lawrence, P. R. and Lorsch, J. W. (1967) *Organization and environment: Managing differentiation and integration*, Boston: Harvard University, Graduate School of Business Administration.

Leatt, P. (1994) 'Physicians in health care management: 1. Physicians as managers: Roles and future challenges', *Canadian Medical Association Journal*, 150, 221–242.

Lee, M. L. (1971) 'A conspicuous production theory of hospital behavior', *Southern Economic Journal*, 38, 48–58.

Meyer, J. M. and Rowan, B. (1977) 'Institutionalized organizations: Formal structure as myth and ceremony', *American Journal of Sociology*, 83, 340–363.

Packwood, T., Keen, J. and Buxton, M. (1991) *Hospitals in transition: The resource management experiment*, Philadelphia: Oxford University Press.

Relman, A. S. (2005) 'Restructuring the U.S health care system', *Issues in Science and Technology Online*, Summer http://www.issues.org.

Rivers, P. A., Woodward, B. and Munchus, G. (1997) 'Organizational power and conflict regarding the hospital–physician relationship: Symbolic or substantive?' *Health Services Management Research*, 10, 91–106.

Sen, K. (2003) *Restructuring health services: Changing contexts and comparative perspectives*, London: Zed Books.

Silverman, D. (1971) *The theory of organizations*, London: Heinemann.

Smith, N. and Chantler, C. (1987) 'Partnership for progress', *Public Finance and Accountancy*, 6 November, 12–14.

Smith, J., Walshe, K. and Hunter, D. J. (2001) 'The "redisorganisation" of the NHS', *British Medical Journal*, 323, 1262–1263.

Strauss, A. L. (1978) *Negotiations*, San Francisco: Jossey Bass.

Strauss, A., Schatzman, L., Ehrlich, D., Bucher, R. and Sabshin, M. (1963) 'The hospital and its negotiated order' in E. Freidson (ed.) *The hospital in modern society*, New York: Free Press of Glencoe, 147–169.

Taft, S. H. and Pelikan, J. A. (1990) 'Clinic management teams: Integrators of professional service and environment change', *Health Management Care Review*, 15, 67–79.

Tolbert, P. S. and Zucker, L. G. (1996) 'The institutionalization of institutional theory' in S. R. Clegg, C. Hardy and W. R. Nord (eds) *Handbook of organization studies*, London: Sage.

Weil, T. (2000) 'Horizontal mergers in the United States health field: Some practical realities', *Health Services Management Research*, 13, 135–151.

Young, R. C. (1988) 'Is population ecology a useful paradigm for the study or organizations?' *American Journal of Sociology*, 94, 11–24.

4

Decentralization as a Means to Reorganize Health-Care in England: From Theory to Practice?

Mark Exworthy and Ian Greener

Introduction

Decentralization provides graphic illustrations of many of the recurrent themes in contemporary health policy and management as power and control are re-located within health-care systems (Pollitt 2005). This oscillating balance of power – a 'perpetual struggle' (Pollitt 2005) – involves the formation and dissolution of new organizational forms, the re-location of health-care managers and a commensurate shift in their roles and responsibilities. Whilst it is possible to suggest that this process of organizing and reorganizing has a marginal impact on service delivery, decentralization (and centralization) affects the ways in which organizations are managed and in which they relate to other local and national organizations. As the current wave of health-care reforms in the UK appears now to be leaning toward decentralization in the form of localism (such as mutual ownership) and new freedoms (from central government) aimed to create high performing organizations, it is instructive to examine how this process of organizing, reorganizing and potentially disorganizing health-care is played out in the English National Health Service (NHS).

Decentralization is, also once again, fashionable in the health policy arena. The waxing and waning of managerial fads and fashion (Marmor 2004) has, in recent years, alighted on decentralization in England and elsewhere (Pollitt 2005; Saltman et al. 2007a). Although the current decentralist wave has been dominant (Pollitt 2005), there are some notable exceptions (such as Norway and Denmark) (Saltman et al. 2007b). As all countries are at different points on the policy pendulum between decentralization and centralization, it is nonetheless instructive to learn from the UK's recent experience.

Though manifest in various guises, the decentralization of power (however defined) has become a notable feature in recent English NHS policies, viz. Foundation Trusts (FTs), budgetary devolution to PCTs, earned autonomy and payment by results, amongst others. However, at the same time, an under-current of (re-)centralization has also been apparent. The shift of power to the center has been promoted through new inspection and performance regimes but power has not always been 'returned' to the same central location. New agencies (such as the UK's Healthcare Commission and Monitor (for FTs)) have powers which might formerly have been retained by the ministry (English Department of Health). A unitary center is no longer apparent.

It is timely to re-examine decentralization in health-care settings in order to aid academic and practical understanding of the new forms and functions of decentralization initiatives, and because Mintzberg (1979) has described decentralization as 'probably the most confused topic in organization theory' (p.181). Using the English NHS as an exemplar, this chapter thus focuses on a hitherto neglected area of decentralization studies in the health-care sector, *viz.* aspects of organizational behavior such as staffing and managerial capacity. It will contribute to understanding of the design and implementation of decentralization from conceptual and practical perspectives. It will also demonstrate the ways in which policy can benefit from conceptual developments as well as policy and practice informing such concepts.

The chapter is divided into two main sections. First, the policy landscape is mapped, with particular attention being paid to the revival of the decentralization (and its concomitant centralization) among contemporary health policy in England. In the second section, the current NHS policy is analyzed in terms of emergent organizational responses, managerial and policy compromises and their likely outcomes.

Decentralization in the English NHS: an old concept in a new context

This chapter focuses specifically on decentralization in the NHS in England. Given its political saliency in delivering local health services, the NHS offers, as usual, a compelling case-study of the tensions of policy debates (Klein 2006) – here, between centralization and decentralization.

A crucial point of understanding in the decentralization debate in the NHS is that, as a policy, it is not the first time it has been proposed or implemented (Burns et al. 1994; Exworthy 1994). For example, the major reforms of 1974, 1979 and 1983 as well as the introduction of the quasi-market of the 1990s placed significant emphasis on decentralization and led Klein (2003b) to describe the latest version as another turn of the 'revolving door.'

As the Labour government's health policy has undergone 'three moments' (Greener 2004b), their approach to decentralization has also waned, then waxed. The first term of the Labour government (1997–2001) was marked by a significant shift in power toward the center; legislation underpinned the authority of the health minister (the Secretary of State for Health) as the de facto 'executive chairman' of the NHS and the introduction of performance regimes was widespread (Greer and Jarman 2007). The moment at which the policy pendulum began to shift (back) toward decentralization is uncertain but two events seemed to encapsulate (not least, for ministers) the limitations of this centralist approach.

The first was the case of Bedford hospital where the chapel was being used as a temporary morgue. In 2001, the media reported that bodies were being stored on the floor of the chapel as part of the hospital's mortuary was undergoing maintenance. An inquiry found the hospital's management at fault, and the Chief Executive (Ken Williams) subsequently resigned (BBC 2001). The then Secretary of State (Alan Milburn) maintained that the issue was a local management issue:

> it was a management problem in the hospital – a failure to implement clear national guidelines and resolve a clear local problem immediately. (*Hansard*, 16 January 2001, col.201)

This blaming of local managers for their failure to implement central policy is a clear form of decentralization.

The second spur for decentralization was a series of events in 2001. During the UK General Election campaign, many voters complained about the pace of health reform despite increased government funding (Stevens 2004). The inquiry into the Bristol Royal Infirmary (where there had been excessive mortality following pediatric cardiac surgery) was also published in 2001. The Bristol event and subsequent inquiry had a

> double ideological impact: as a testament to the putative failings of local provider competition as the sole driver of improvement, and as a warning about the dangers of leaving doctors entirely free to set and enforce their own standards. (Stevens 2004:19)

Although Alan Milburn was to write much of the NHS Plan (Secretary of State for Health 2000) (which many saw as a retrenchment of central power), this was followed by 'Shifting the balance of power' (Department of Health 2002b) a short while later, which appeared to move policy in the opposite direction.

In the wider international policy context, arguments in favor of decentralizing public policy and management made considerable headway. Osborne and Gaebler (1993) had a considerable impact on the Clinton government with their suggestions for allowing greater scope for public sector entrepreneurship (Saint-Martin 2000). This was followed by Mark Moore's (1997) notion of creating 'public value', in which policy-makers were encouraged to allow local contractual markets to flourish to allow a new public ethic based around customer service. Introducing reforms to decentralize control in the NHS therefore had a fashionable American lineage (Klein 2003b; Marmor et al. 2007) but one that has been spread by aid of international institutions such as the World Bank, UN agencies (e.g., WHO) and management consultants (Premfors 1998; Saint-Martin 2000).

In short, the re-emergence of decentralization as a policy theme within English health policy forms part of both a wider international trend of reorganization and a response to a specific national context. Since 2001 and especially in the last couple of years, NHS policy has favored decentralization across a variety of policy fronts (in England):

- Earned autonomy (performance-based freedoms) (Secretary of State for Health 2000, para. 6.29)
- Foundation Trusts (FT) (Department of Health 2002b)
- Payment By Results (PBR) (Department of Health 2002a)
- Practice-based commissioning (Department of Health 2004a)
- PCT funding (Department of Health 2003b)
- Patient choice (Department of Health 2003a)
- Diagnostic and treatment centers (run by private sector agencies) (Department of Health 2004b)
- Political devolution to Scotland and Wales (Jervis and Plowden 2000)
- Discussions about the notion of an independent NHS board (Health Service Journal 2006).

Crucially, at the same time, a range of centralizing tendencies has also been evident:

- Inspection and regulatory agencies (e.g., Healthcare Commission, National institute for Health and Clinical Excellence, NICE)
- Performance regimes (e.g., explicit national targets)

- National standards (e.g., National Service Frameworks)
- Re-location of some national competencies to supra-national agencies (e.g., EU).

It is apparent that this 'portfolio' of policies may act in opposition to each other. This is likely to create the potential for ambiguity and uncertainty amongst health-care managers and policy-makers (Vancil 1979), as they 'lose' some powers, gain other powers and see some other powers 'by-pass' them altogether (either upward (centralization) or downward (decentralization)) (Peckham et al. 2005b). Both features denote the importance of assessing both the properties being decentralized and the source and destination of such re-location in short, the 'what' and 'where' of decentralization (Vrangboek 2007). Understanding the multiple layers of health policy explains why claims of decentralization and centralization often appear ambiguous, if not contradictory (Peckham et al. 2005a).

Implications of organizing and reorganizing by decentralization

A thematic analysis can afford greater insight into the processes and consequences of both the inevitable tension between decentralization and centralization and, as a result, the continual ebb and flow of organizing and reorganizing health-care.

Equity and responsiveness

Greater responsiveness has often been claimed as a primary objective of decentralization (Pollitt 2005), clearly linking with American ideas from Osborne and Gaebler and Moore. Such responsiveness can be accompanied by improved accountability (downward) to the public, as well as a more explicit customer-driven ethic into public service. This has underpinned many arguments in favor of FTs. However, this enhanced responsiveness must be weighed against the potential negative effects on equity. By allowing greater local 'freedom', diversity (of access, provision, quality, etc.) is a natural by-product of decentralization. Such diversity can be seen as a form of intra-area/group inequality (Powell and Exworthy 2003). Reforms made in the name of increasing patient choice (Department of Health 2001, 2003a; Greener 2003b) rely upon not only being able to create competition on the supply side, but the ability and capability of individuals to make choices in the demand side. Evidence from choice-based reforms in other areas of the public sector is that they benefit the middle classes disproportionately (Exworthy and Peckham 2006; Propper et al. 2006), leading to public services often diverging in quality rather than converging at the highest level.

Managerial capacity

Decentralization is supposed to give managers the freedom to manage. However, many public sector managers can be inured to centralization, deferring to superiors, accustomed to not taking risks, being rule-bound and cost-conscious (Hales 1999). Indeed, in a pluralist NHS with a reformed center, it may well be in the public interest to have formal processes which ensure equity in terms of waiting times and clinical audit (Schofield 2001) or professional accountability (Gray and Harrison 2003). In such a view of the world, managers appear to regard themselves as guardians of the public interest instead of service entrepreneurs. As such, decentralization policy may struggle to shift attitudes and behavior of managers despite formal institutional re-arrangements. That said, the Department of Health has become increasingly dominated by NHS managers (Greer and Jarman 2007), with a stronger vertical (managerial) ethos from the ministry to the individual organization.

Another factor may be a simple lack of available management talent. By creating a larger number of (decentralized) semi-autonomous units, local competition is increased, but fewer, larger organizations might be better able to recruit and retain senior managers, compromising decentralization's ability to realize (previously untapped) managerial potential. The decision to reduce from 303 PCTs to 152 in October 2006 was partly based on the premise that so many individual PCTs had weak management, as the available talent had been spread so thinly.

Centralization

Many commentators claim that decentralization is inevitably accompanied by some form of (re-)centralization (De Vries 2000). As the constraints of organizations are 'loosened' locally, the commensurate effect at the center is for a tighter regime, notably in terms of performance management, inspection and regulation. This accords the notion that the modern state has 'more control over less' (Rhodes 1997). One implication of this under-current is that the roles, functions and mind-sets of central stakeholder need to change from a 'command-and-control' approach to one of steering (Osborne and Gaebler 1993). Traditionally, (central) government has been ill-equipped to steer such governance networks (Day and Klein 1997). Setting the rules of the game must mean that policy-makers cannot be active players of the game as well. Many managers and policy-makers whose careers have, until now, been developed with reference to the center often lack the skills to deal with the new challenges that this form of governance brings. Debates about the dual or separate role of the NHS Chief Executive and DH Permanent Secretary, the scope of regulatory regimes and the possibility of an 'independent' NHS board amply illustrate the need for reform at the center, wrought by decentralization.

Discussion

The type and nature of decentralization (and by implication, centralization) will depend on the specific organizational and policy context within which such policies are being implemented. Moreover, the rhetoric of decentralization policies (at the center) may not match its implementation (in local organizations) which signifies that such policies may be legitimating wider discourses rather than meeting specific objectives (Pollitt 2005). In the English NHS, there are specific nuances to the application of this latest round of reorganization which will shape the impact of current reforms.

First, decentralization to date has been largely an organizational focus (cf. an individual one). Government policy has always trod a fine line between autonomy and control, especially in relation to health-care professionals. However, recent decentralization seeks to augment the organization as the local focus. The introduction of the 'Patient Choice' policy (whereby patients can select a hospital to which they would be referred by their GP, from a list of four or five) extends organizational decentralization to the individual – a form of personalization of public services. Patients, despite their apparent 'choice' of hospital, will still be influenced by GP opinion, reputation of providers and distance (Coulter et al. 2005). Similarly, FTs are founded on the basis of the mutuality and social ownership of patients (Klein 2003a). This form of responsiveness extends decentralization 'further' than previous reorganizations by attempting to improve responsiveness through individual participation. Whilst mutual membership of FTs may be unduly influenced by interest groups, it is also unclear how far the Governors of FTs will participate in the Trust's strategic decision-making (Lewis 2005). Such an extension might, in future, open the possibility of other forms of 'individualized' decentralization such as the use of vouchers or patients selecting the PCT with whom they enroll. At this stage, however, it is unclear how far either represents a radical change in the distribution of power, though it is likely that the implications for organizing and reorganizing care will be significant (Exworthy and Peckham 2006; Ferlie et al. 2006).

From an organizational perspective, patient choice represents a number of significant challenges. First, it offers the opportunity for organizations to market health services in a way that has not been possible in the past. If patients are to make choices between local health providers, this creates the need for the active promotion of local elective services in order to attempt to raise the profiles of providers. Yet, marketing in a second sense may be even more significant. If we are to treat seriously the idea that patient choice represents a decentralization of decision-space to individual users of health services, then we must also accept that they may demand a greater voice in the services they receive (Newman and Vidler 2006). The customer-focused ethic of US ideas from Moore (1997) suddenly becomes far more relevant.

Second, the growing involvement of the private sector is manifest in primary and secondary care. This has been justified in terms of the increase in capacity it offers to the NHS, allowing waiting times to be reduced, and greater choice for patients. But it also introduces a clear competitive element in many areas of elective care, presuming that greater competition has the capability of initiating reform in the delivery of health services including greater patient responsiveness. Whilst some see 'privatization' as a form of decentralization (Atun 2007; Rondinelli 1981), this is a lateral policy shift (rather than vertical/hierarchical) , illustrating the multiplicity of public, private and independent sector organizations and the multiple strands of relations between them.

Third, the decentralization to PCTs and FTs, among others, has necessitated a redefinition of the role of the Department of Health (Greer and Jarman 2007). Perhaps most apparent is the role of inspectorates and regulations. The separation of steering and rowing functions was deemed ineffective by Day and Klein (1997) but recent institutional re-configurations have made more formalized this separation. However, the proliferation of regulatory agencies in the late 1990s has now been tempered by their amalgamation. Monitor (the regulator of FTs) is merging with other regulators (notably the Healthcare Commission) as all NHS Trusts had been scheduled to become FTs within the next few years. The Commission on Social Care Inspection is being dismembered, with its children's work being re-located to the Office of Standards in

Education (OFSTED) and its work with adults to the Healthcare Commission (*Public* February 2006:26–27). This rationalization of health-care-related regulators will generate a significant counter-balance of power to the DH at the 'center.'

We can interpret these reforms several ways. In one sense (and from the perspective of the Department of Health), they are decentralizing, because they pass both control and resource from the organizational center of the NHS to semi-autonomous bodies. They literally 'decenter' the control of health-care. This can be seen as a progressive attempt to depoliticize health policy through the use of independent organizations, or a more cynical view is that politicians appear to be actively attempting to pass potential blame accruing from health reform failure away from them. From the perspective of health organizations, however, these reforms are centralizing because they require far more accountability to regulatory and inspectorate bodies than in the past. The obverse to 'divide and rule' also applies; whilst blame is decentralized (as the failure of local managers), credit is centralized. Yet, the desire (if not always the ability) to intervene in an electorally popular and media-sensitive service (such as health-care) is, as many generations of politicians have found, almost irresistible.

Fourth, there is evidence that, as a result of reform fatigue (Smith et al. 2001), health managers do not necessarily become engaged in reforming their organizations, but instead in complex forms of game-playing in which they learn which reforms they need to pay attention to and which they can safely ignore (Greener 2004a). Performance indicators which are not attached to star-ratings, in this view, can be ignored (Greener 2003a; Talbot 2000), whilst others, the so-called 'P45 targets', have to be complied with or managers might face the ultimate sanction now available for 'failing' health organizations, the franchising of their management to either the private sector or to public managers from more successful trusts. The form in which decentralization has taken in English health policy suggests that game-playing is possibly more significant than before.

Fifth, the form of decentralization, implemented in the NHS, has been conditional upon performance (Mannion and Goddard 2002). The performance-based freedoms have enabled 'successful' Trusts to have less monitoring by the center, to have more freedom over their staff and to make certain financial decisions without recourse to higher authorities. Such 'earned autonomy' was closely linked to the 'star ratings' awarded to Trusts based on their performance (Mannion et al. 2005). Judgments about the relative performance between apparently similar Trusts had led to much criticism and hence the subsequent replacement of a more rounded 'health check', to be undertaken by the Healthcare Commission. Decentralization has not been applied uniformly but selectively, based upon compliance with particular performance targets on the basis of the data returns that have been assessed as of extremely poor quality (Audit Commission 2003), and with the differences between high and low performers no greater than we might expect within statistical confidence intervals (Street 2000). However, the determinants of organizational performance are multi-faceted and not wholly determined from 'above' (Scott et al. 2003). A concomitant aspect is that this further underlines the enhanced power of the center in determining what constitutes 'performance' (Greener 2003a).

Conclusion

By virtue of its pivotal position in current English health policy debates and its ability to link with many wider health policy debates (Pollitt 2005), decentralization raises issues which strike at the heart of healthcare organization and reorganization, and hence the nature of the NHS itself. The type of decentralization being advanced, the way in which it is being implemented and the under-currents of (re-) centralization may have profound implications for the central and local agents if it is translated into practice. Alternatively, the multiple meanings and motives of decentralization may confound implementation and provide an opportunity for re-labeling extant practices and/or re-playing former struggles (Exworthy 1994; Pollitt 2005). This chapter has sought to help understand and explain better the effect of decentralization upon organizing and reorganizing processes.

Furthermore, the particular type of decentralization we are seeing at the moment is significant because it creates such considerable uncertainty in the planning and organization of health services. Decentralizing elective care decisions to individual patients, as the patient choice reforms attempt to do, introduce an emergent and bottom-up element into the workings of local health economies on a scale that we have not seen before. This, coupled with the roll out of practice-based commissioning, means that health service decisions have never before been made on such a local scale. The trade-offs inherent in any organizational reform are, as yet, uncertain, to say nothing of the ways in which they might be handled. Whilst such tensions may never fully be resolved in a system with so many competing stakeholders and the oscillation between organizational tiers, the process by which decentralization policies are articulated and manifest will largely denote the outcome of this latest round of organizing and reorganizing. In sum, how much local autonomy and innovation we will see in practice, and how much politicians and policy-makers will allow the reforms to work themselves out without interference, remains to be seen.

Acknowledgements

We are grateful to our collaborators on this research (Francesca Frosini, Lorelei Jones, Stephen Peckham and Martin Powell) and for funding from the NHS Service Delivery and Organisation (SDO) programme (http://www.sdo.lshtm.ac.uk/sdo1252006.html).

References

Atun, R. (2007) 'Privatization as decentralization strategy' in R. Saltman, B. Bankauskaite, and K. Vrangboek, K (eds) *Decentralization in health care*, Buckingham: Open University Press, Chapter 14, pp. 246–271.
Audit Commission (2003) *Waiting list accuracy: Assessing the accuracy of waiting list information in NHS hospitals in England*, London: Audit Commission.
BBC (2001) *Hospital chapel used as mortuary for years*, http://news.bbc.co.uk/1/hi/health/1147266.stm.
Burns, D., Hambleton, R. and Hoggett, P. (1994) *The politics of decentralization*, Basingstoke: Macmillan.
Coulter, A., le Maistre, N. and Henderson, L. (2005) *Patients' experience of choosing where to undergo surgical treatment: Evaluation of London Patient Choice Scheme*, Oxford: Picker Institute.
Day, P. and Klein, R. (1997) *Rowing, but not steering*, Bristol: Policy Press.
Department of Health (2001) *Extending choice for patients*, London: Department of Health.
Department of Health (2002a) *Reforming NHS financial flows: Introducing payment by results*, London: Department of Health.
Department of Health (2002b) *Shifting the balance of power within the NHS: Securing delivery*, London: Department of Health.
Department of Health (2003a) *Building on the best: Choice, responsiveness and equity in the NHS*, London: Department of Health.
Department of Health (2003b) *Resource allocation: Weighted capitation formula, FID resource allocation*, Leeds: Department of Health.
Department of Health (2004a) *Practice based commissioning – engaging practices in commissioning*, London: Department of Health.
Department of Health (2004b) *The NHS improvement plan: Putting people at the heart of public services*, London: Department of Health.
De Vries, M. (2000) 'The rise and fall of decentralization: A comparative analysis of arguments and practices in European countries', *European Journal of Political Research*, 38, 193–224.

Exworthy, M. (1994) 'The contest for control in community health services: General managers and professionals dispute decentralization', *Policy and Politics*, 22, 17–29.

Exworthy, M. and Peckham, S. (2006) 'Access, choice and travel: Implications for health policy', *Social Policy and Administration*, 40, 267–287.

Ferlie, E., Freeman, G., McDonnell, J., Petsoulas, C. and Rundle-Smith, S. (2006) 'Introducing choice in the public services: Some supply side issues', *Public Money and Management*, 26, 63–72.

Gray, A. and Harrison, S. (2003) *Governing medicine*, Buckingham: Open University Press.

Greener, I. (2003a) 'Performance in the NHS: Insistence of measurement and confusion of content', *Public Performance and Management Review*, 26, 237–250.

Greener, I. (2003b) 'Who choosing what? The evolution of "choice" in the NHS, and its implications for New Labour' in C. Bochel, N. Ellison and M. Powell (eds) *Social Policy Review 15*, Bristol: Policy Press.

Greener, I. (2004a) 'The drama of health management' in M. Learmonth and N. Harding (eds) *Unmasking Health*, New York: Nova Science.

Greener, I. (2004b) 'The three moments of new labour's health policy discourse', *Policy and Politics*, 32, 303–316.

Greer, S. and Jarman, H. (2007) *The department of health and their civil service: From Whitehall to department of delivery to where?*, London: Nuffield Trust.

Hales, C. (1999) 'Why do managers do what they do? Reconciling evidence and theory in accounts of managerial work', *British Journal of Management*, 10, 335–350.

Health Service Journal (2006) 'Scepticism greets plans to take politics out of the NHS',28 September 2006, **http://www.hsj.co.uk/nav?page=hsj.news.story& resource=5687223.**

Jervis, P. and Plowden, W. (2000) *Devolution and health: First annual report*, London: Constitutional Unit, UCL.

Klein, R. (2003a) 'Governance for NHS foundation trusts', *British Medical Journal*, 326, 174–175.

Klein, R. (2003b) 'The new localism: Once more through the revolving door?', *Journal of Health Services Research and Policy*, 8, 195–196.

Klein, R. (2006) *The new politics of the NHS: From creation to reinvention.* Abingdon: Radcliffe Publishing.

Lewis, R. (2005) *Putting health in local hands*, London: Kings Fund.

Mannion, R. and Goddard, M. (2002) 'Performance measurement and improvement in health care', *Applied Health Economics and Health Policy*, 1, 13–24.

Mannion, R., Davies, H. and Marshall, M. (2005) 'Impact of star performance ratings in NHS acute trusts', *Journal of Health Services Research and Policy*, 10, 18–24.

Marmor, T. (2004) *Fads in medical care management and policy*, London: Nuffield Trust.

Marmor, T. R., Freeman, R. and Okma, K. G. H. (eds) (2007) *Learning from comparison in health policy*, Yale University Press. Forthcoming.

Mintzberg, H. (1979) *The structuring of organizations: A synthesis of the research*, London: Prentice Hall.

Moore, M. (1997) *Creating public value: Strategic management in government*, Harvard: Harvard University Press.

Newman, J. and Vidler, E. (2006) 'Discriminating customers, responsible patients, empowered users: Consumerism and the modernisation of health care', *Journal of Social Policy*, 35, 193–209.

Osborne, D. and Gaebler, T. (1993) *Reinventing government*, New York: Addison Wesley.

Peckham, S., Exworthy, M., Greener, I. and Powell, M. (2005a) *Decentralisation as an organisational model in England*, London: NCCSDO.

Peckham, S., Exworthy, M., Greener, I. and Powell, M. (2005b) 'Decentralizing health services: More local accountability or just more central control,' *Public Money and Management*, 25, 221–228.

Pollitt, C. (2005) 'Decentralization: A central concept in contemporary public management' in E. Ferlie et al. (eds) *Oxford handbook of public management*, Oxford: Oxford University Press, Chapter 16, pp. 371–397.

Powell, M. and Exworthy, M. (2003) 'Equal access to health-care and the British NHS', *Policy Studies*, 24, 51–64.

Premfors, R. (1998) 'Reshaping the democratic state: Swedish experiences in a comparative perspective', *Public Administration*, 76, 141–159.

Propper, C., Wilson, D. and Burgess, S. (2006) 'Extending choice in English health care: The implications of the economic evidence', *Journal of Social Policy*, 35, 537–557.

Rhodes, R. (1997) *Understanding governance*, Buckingham: Open University Press.

Rondinelli, D. (1981) 'Government decentralization in comparative perspective: Theory and practice in developing countries', *International Review of Administrative Science*, 47, 133–145.

Saint-Martin, D. (2000) *Building the new managerialist state: Consultants and the politics of public sector reform in comparative perspective*, Oxford: Oxford University Press.

Saltman, R., Bankauskaite, B. and Vrangboek, K. (eds) (2007a) *Decentralization in health care*, Buckingham: Open University Press.

Saltman, R., Bankauskaite, B. and Vrangboek, K. (2007b) 'Introduction: The question of decentralization' in R. Saltman, B. Bankauskaite and K. Vrangboek (eds) *Decentralization in health care*, Buckingham: Open University Press, 1–6.

Schofield, J. (2001) 'The old ways are the best? The durability and usefulness of bureaucracy in public sector management', *Organization*, 8, 77–96.

Scott, T., Mannion, R., Davies, H. and Marshall, M. (2003) *Healthcare performance and organisational culture*, London: Radcliffe Medical Press.

Secretary of State for Health (2000) *The NHS plan: A plan for investment, a plan for reform*, London: HMSO.

Smith, J., Walshe, K. and Hunter, D. (2001) 'The "redisorganisation" of the NHS: Another reorganisation leaving unhappy managers can only worsen the service', *British Medical Journal*, 323, 1262–1263.

Stevens, S. (2004) 'Reform strategies for the English NHS', *Health Affairs*, 23, 37–44.

Street, A. (2000) 'Confident about efficiency measurement in the NHS?', *Health Care UK*, 47–52.

Talbot, C. (2000) 'Performing "performance" – A comedy in five acts', *Public Money and Management*, 20, 63–68.

Vancil, R. (1979) *Decentralization: Managerial ambiguity by design*, Homewood, Ill.: Dow Jones-Irwin.

Vrangboek, K. (2007) 'Towards a typology for decentralization in health care' in R. Saltman, B. Bankauskaite and K. Vrangboek (eds) *Decentralization in health care*, Buckingham: Open University Press, Chapter 3, 44–62.

5
Va Va Voom, Size Doesn't Matter: Form and Function in the NHS

Jill Schofield, Rod Sheaff, Russell Mannion, Bernard Dowling, Martin Marshall and Rosalind McNally

Introduction

This chapter presents a synthesis of a research project funded by the British National Health Service (NHS) Service Delivery and Organization (SDO) R and D Programme of Research on Organizational Form and Function that addresses the relationship between organizational form and performance (Sheaff et al. 2004) using a meta-analysis of the literature. Readers are referred to the full report for a comprehensive coverage of all sections. This chapter describes briefly the structure of the overall project paying particular attention to one analytical element – namely, what the evidence says about the nature of organizational structure and healthcare. The discursive focus concerns the issue of organizational size as a specific element of organizational structure.

The organizational forms established in the NHS in 1948 were based more on what could be negotiated with the medical profession than on an informed judgment about creating the most effective structures to perform the functions of the new service (Ham 1992). Although these initial organizational forms remained practically unchanged until 1974, since that date there has been an assumption in UK health policy that structural, managerial and cultural changes are key levers for improving the performance of NHS organizations.

Yet the existing evidence base for such changes is limited. Apart from a few earlier studies (Forsyth and Logan 1960; Georgopoulos 1986) little research linking healthcare organizations' form (structure) and function (processes or behavior) with performance (outcomes) was carried out prior to the 1990s, and systematic reviews of such research have only recently become possible (Ferlie 1997; Mitchell and Shortell 1997). The purpose of the overall study was to indicate where the evidence base could be expanded and to inform future empirical studies about the relationship between organizational form, function and performance.

A four-level analytical frame was designed to assist our understanding of the relationship between organizational factors and performance and was expressed as follows:

1. The context or *environment* within which organizations function
2. The formal *structures* which make up the organization
3. The *processes* or activities which go on within the organization
4. The *outcomes* or consequences of these processes categorized as outcomes for patients, staff satisfaction, equity, efficiency, process quality, humanity and adherence to external performance targets.

The evidence from the literature – both theoretical and empirical – was then further classified by expressing the four levels of analysis in the form of dyadic relationships to each other and subsequently mapped around six sets of relationships and shown in Figure 5.1:

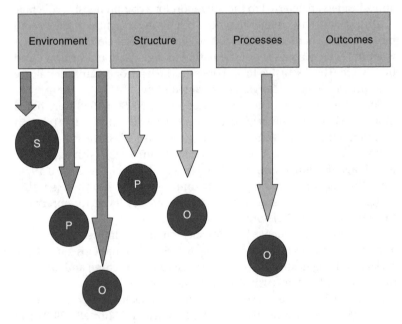

Figure 5.1 Study method and approach

1. How environment influences organizational structure ('form')
2. How environment influences organizational processes
3. How environment influences organizational outcomes
4. How organizational form influences organizational processes ('organizational behavior')
5. How organizational processes influence organizational outcomes ('function')
6. How organizational structure ('form') influences organizational outcomes.

At the outset the project sponsors stipulated the seven outcomes which the review should focus on. The combination of seven outcomes with three categories of organizational factors (environment, structures, processes) that might produce these outcomes implies the 21 relationships shown in Table 5.1. However, for the purposes of bibliometric analysis it was necessary to have a series of definitions of these outcomes, these are listed below

1. Outcomes for patients: to apply studies from outside the health sector, the terms 'users' or 'consumers' had to be taken as analogous to 'patients'. These outcomes were taken to include users' preferences and satisfaction.
2. Process quality: was defined to include clinical quality, perceived care or standards of care, emotional support to patients and carer.

Table 5.1 Levels of organizational analysis and policy outcomes

	Environment	*Organizational structure/form*	*Organizational processes/behaviour*
Outcomes for patients			
Process quality			
Humanity			
Staff satisfaction			
Equity			
Efficiency			
Adherence to external performance targets			

Favourable staff attitudes to patients, provider–user interaction, speed of service (waiting times), product differentiation, product quality, physical environment, quality of ancillary services.

3. Humanity: substantially overlaps with process quality (quality of social interactions which users experience, staff attitudes to patients or other service users) and patient outcomes (response to user preference, waits). What was added under this head were therefore quite narrow outcomes: patient influence over what treatments they receive, service responsiveness to users, user participation in decision-making.

4. Staff satisfaction and morale: job stress and psychological (as opposed to organizational) climate; worker alienation, commitment, need satisfaction, health and safety and conversely workplace violence. Absenteeism, burnout and staff turnover are known correlates of job dissatisfaction, and therefore counted as 'negative morale', as are worker cynicism, resistance, anger, distress, anxiety and stress.

5. Equity: is defined in terms of equal access for equal needs, and probity (with criminality as its obverse). It therefore includes access and redistributions between workers, shareholders and consumers. Probity includes ethical sensitivity, conscientiousness, transparency, whistle-blowing and reduction of sex discrimination among staff and/or patients.

6. Efficiency: was defined in terms of cost and effectiveness. Effectiveness was defined to cover clinical effectiveness, productivity-related outcomes such as evidence-based practice, technical and service innovations and 'performance', unless the context clearly implies defining performance in other terms. Performance was defined in 'real' (i.e. non-financial) and in financial terms, such as transaction costs and budgetary control.

7. Adherence: to external performance targets was defined to cover two broad areas. The first was public policy targets. The other area was profitability such as return on investment, dividends and shareholder value.

The literature review methods drew on the established systematic review guidelines (Khan et al. 2001) as a source of best practice but these were adapted according to constraints of time and the particular requirements of a diffuse and ill-defined subject. The heterogeneity of the literature meant that the bibliographic indexing systems were far from robust, so less systematic approaches needed to be adopted. The project's conceptual framework was used to categorize the studies that met the inclusion criteria. One of the aims of the study was to identify which issues key stakeholders in the service regarded as of greatest practical relevance to aid their decision-making and what sort of evidence would assist them. The stakeholder consultation included key NHS decision-makers from a 'diagonal slice' of NHS organizations. Data were collected using one-to-one telephone interviews, a focus group and participation in national meetings focused on organizational change in the NHS.

The study team involved five academics, two PhD students and one librarian. Ten bibliographies were searched across a range of disciplines and subjects relevant to the topic. These included medicine, health-care management, organizational science, nursing, social sciences and psychology. A broad search strategy for scoping the topic was used, with adaptations for each database to allow for indexing and the nature of the literature. Analysis of the literature searching for the project is reported elsewhere (Sheaff et al. 2004) including copies of the search strategies employed and list of databases searched. The bibliography handling system used was Reference Manager V10. The results of each database search were merged and duplication eliminated. This gave 14,314 records each with a unique record identifier from 1990 onwards. Ongoing journal alerts were created and search strategies saved for continuous updating of the evidence base in this area.

The initial scan of the literature identified 14,314 studies of potential relevance. On the basis of the title, key words and in most cases the abstract, 2171 references were considered to be relevant, reduced to 1568 references by tightening the inclusion criteria. The inter-rater reliability of this reduction process was low (Cronbach alpha 0.34) reflecting the heterogeneity of the literature. Survey and case study methodologies were most frequently employed. Only 19% of studies used any kind of comparative group; 4% employed a longitudinal design, 1% a quasi-experimental design and just one study a randomized controlled trial. Studies meeting the inclusion criteria were equally likely to be conducted in health and non-health-related organizations, but more likely to be conducted outside the UK (86%). Forty-six per cent of the papers addressed the relationship between organizational processes and outcomes. Most of these examined efficiency, and only a small proportion explored issues relating to equity or humanity. Fifty-five per cent of the papers addressed organizational structures and seventeen per cent the environment within which organizations operate.

Organizational size

The results from the meta-study on the relationship between organizational size and process are numerous. They generally associate organizational size with complexity, formalization, specialization and hence economies of scale in supervision despite the presence of taller hierarchies (Marsden et al. 1994). Together, they suggest that for each of the multiple functions which a health organization might have, a different size may be optimal. The pursuit of a single 'ideal size' appears illusory for all except the most narrowly specialized organizational structures (e.g. an ambulance crew). Economies of scale and scope appear to set in at quite moderate levels in healthcare planning organizations (Bojke et al. 2000) and larger organizations may have greater bargaining power with governments. Against this, smaller organizations appear to give staff and patients greater psychological satisfaction (Issel et al. 2003; Zinn and Mor 1998), and to solve problems and implement change more rapidly (Hannan and Freeman 1989; Hetherington and Hewa 2000).

Similarly, size is perhaps the feature of structure that has most pervasively occupied researchers' attention when examining the impact of organizational form on organizational performance (Child and Mansfield 1972; Gooding and Wagner 1985). Far more research papers were evident on organizational size than on organization age. Such research has often focused on economies of scale by examining the optimum organization size (or the size of an organization's subunit) to result in the lowest cost per unit of production (Gooding and Wagner 1985; Stigler 1958). However, there is very little evidence to support the view that economies of scale result from having bigger organizations, either from recent empirical research (for example, see Wilkin et al. 2003) or from meta-analytic reviews of the longer-term literature (see Gooding and Wagner 1985). Moreover, hospital mergers have had no apparent impact on the satisfaction of patients with the care they received (Ljunggren and Sjoden 2001) or on hospital efficiency (Meyer and Tucker 1992).

Neither have American HMO mergers reduced prices for consumers (indeed, the short-term effect in some places has been to increase prices, Feldman et al. 1996); similarly, the evidence that hospital mergers in the USA have promoted efficiencies is divided (Kralewski et al. 1988). Ferguson and Goddard (1997) were sceptical but Lee and Alexander's meta-study (1999) did find economies, although mainly for small hospitals with duplicate facilities. However, HMOs do show some economies of scale (Wholey et al. 1996), as do US nursing homes (Smith et al. 1979). Innovations compatible with the interests of lower level decision-makers seem more readily adopted in large but decentralized hospitals (Moch and Morse 1977). Support for this view that large organizations tend to be more innovative also came from Subramanian and Nilakanta (1996). For the NHS, Fulop et al. (2002) record that the process of merging exacted a cost in terms of service delivery and delaying other changes, but without obvious improvements in staff recruitment or retention or economies of management costs. There is evidence for a volume – quality relationship, but only for specific modes of hospital treatment and this seems to be attributable to the fact that larger organizations facilitate specialization, formalization, quality management (Germain and Spears 1999) and innovation (Damanpour 1991; Kimberly and Evanisko 1981; Rogers 1983). Urbach and Baxter (2004) attribute it to specific hospital structures (on-site support services, teaching status, multiple related services) not the volume of work per se. Lee and Wan (2002), however, found a positive relationship between (US) hospital size, mortality and complications.

Results from the stakeholder survey

There was a threefold focus to the interviews with stakeholders with regard to organizational structure and therefore indirectly to size. Firstly, what did respondents see as the most problematic structural characteristics within their organizations; secondly, what positive outcomes might they expect from structural change; and thirdly, what type and form of research evidence could assist them.

One set of answers concerned the lack of adequate structures to enable planning to occur. Strategic Health Authority (SHA) and Primary Care Trusts (PCT) informants alike stated that their organizations were increasingly focused on short and medium-term operational and 'modernization' objectives which diverted them from longer-term perspectives. Both groups agreed that PCTs were very stretched, had capacity issues, were too small, lacked skills and faced a vast agenda. With specific reference to size even NHS trust informants, wondered whether trusts were too big. Size was conceptualized in these responses in terms of how it would impact upon issues such as monitoring clinical competence, achieving collective objectives and maintaining the inherent cohesiveness of long-term objectives.

Three desired outcomes of structural change predominated: there was a desire to move away from occupationally demarcated structures towards multi-professional structures organized around specific activities or services and make the delivery organizations 'less of a coalition, more a cohesive body'. A second main desired outcome was to satisfy higher-level bodies, which for NHS trusts meant the SHA and DH rather than the PCT, except with regard to income, to maintain which, PCTs had also to be kept 'confident' about NHS trust restructuring. Another theme was to promote flexibility and teamwork, whilst retaining clear communication and lines of accountability.

The characteristics of a good organizational structure were very much phrased in terms of how structure could enhance better communication and direction – both at an operational and strategic levels. Thus, clarity in terms of goals, accountabilities, chains of command were highly valued as a positive outcome of structural change, although one respondent added that this clarity was sometimes an emergent property; organizational structures did not necessarily have to emerge fully defined from their first day. Scope for teamwork was next most frequently mentioned, with an emphasis on flexibility and allowing teams to learn and to innovate. 'Fit for purpose' was also referred to, although different respondents interpreted it in different terms; one respondent in terms of making NHS services intelligible and accessible to users; a second in terms of supporting clinical practitioners in developing good quality services; and several in terms of achieving current NHS policy objectives. Overall, there was little sense of what an ideal or even a right size for healthcare organizations should be, except where there could be serious economies of scale for example, the provision of NHS payroll services at a national level.

With regard to the helpfulness of evidence a number of respondents commented on the form as well as the content of the evidence they wanted. Several mentioned the fragmented character of what organizational data the NHS does collect. One suggested that researchers should produce a synthesis of all such results for each individual NHS organization, drawing out the practical implications. Nevertheless, case studies were more often mentioned as the preferred format for research into organizational structures, because this approach was felt better able to expose the connections between organizational structures and particular local contexts; and to show concretely what other NHS organizations had done. They also helped managers to see beyond their own particular local circumstances and personalities.

Nobody thought that researchers should seek one optimal structure for each type of NHS organization but several respondents thought that research should try to identify a number of preferred structures, each suited to a specific kind of setting, for example, urban versus rural, London. In any event, managers disliked 'bumph' and 'large reports on websites'; they preferred concise summaries of research results. The two most frequently mentioned desirable but (allegedly) unavailable evidence was that showing what organizational structures (including what degree of size and centralization) were conducive to 'best practice', 'joined-up', high-quality, cost-effective healthcare, especially at the level of service provision itself. These interests focused particularly on team structures and upon what organizational frameworks for informatics, HRM, controls assurance, organizational development and transport are necessary to support the clinical team itself; and how to restructure NHS trusts to produce quicker, more effective decision-making.

Discussion: conceptualizing and measuring size

A number of meta-analyses have attempted to bring order to the vast amount of literature relating to organizational size and in so doing addressing the reasons for the contradictory evidence from the literature in respect of its effect. Three of the most comprehensive are Camisón-Zornoza et al. (2004), Damanpour (1991) and Gooding and Wagner (1985), but we were unable to find a similar analysis that related to public services, yet alone healthcare. Indeed the most consistent results from the literature are that the evidence about the effect of size is inconsistent. This alone supports an argument for the design and commissioning of some empirical work to not only scope out measures of health and size, but in particular to model and understand at least something of the nature of the direction, stability and intensity of the relationship between size and other organisational variables.

Tables 5.2 and 5.3 describe how size has been conceptualized in the more general management literature and early but enduring papers that established the relationships between size and other organizational variables.

'These relationships seem to have remained consistent over time as has the problem of the direction of causality and whether size should be viewed as a dependent or independent variable. In part, this may be because size is a difficult area to study in an integrated way because of (i) the complexity of measurement; (ii) the highly contingent nature of

Table 5.2 Size variables

Productive capacity	Assets
Number of employees	Capital value
Budget	Capital spread/physical capacity
Transactions/volume of work done	Output–throughput
	Density, configuration and spread, distribution

Table 5.3   Relationships between size and organizational variables

Size/variables	Authors	Size/variables	Authors
Structure	Pugh et al. (1969)	Innovation	See Damanpour (1991) and Camisón-Zornoza et al. (2004) for meta-analysis
Structure (via moderating effect of technology as the independent variable)	Aldrich (1972), Child (1973)		
Division of Labour, Specialisation	Durkheim (1933)		
Differentiation (Labour) (Subunits)	Blau (1970), Meyer (1972)	Resource control + access;	Pfeffer and Salancik (1978),
		Economies of scale	Stigler (1958)
Centrality increased hierarchy formalisation	Parkinson (1957), Hickson et al. (1971), Hall (1977)	Performance and productivity	(see Gooding and Wagner's Meta-Analysis 1985)
Stress	Khan (1964), Toffler (1980)		
Success Failure	Greiner (1972), Hannan and Freeman (1977)		

See Kralewski et al. (1985) and Wholey and Christianson (1992) for an application of some of the above 'classic' theories to healthcare.

its role; and (iii) the importance of moderating factors. It is within this latter area that there is potential for a greater illumination of the role that organizational size may play in healthcare organizations and why the importance of size as one variable may be diminishing.

That size is so important, as both a dependent and independent variable in organizational life can be supported by six decades of social science and organizational sociology literature. What might fruitfully be explored in the future for healthcare organization is the effect of what could be called 'modern moderating' influences that are specific to the context of healthcare. Within the literature the following factors are normally presented as moderators: type of organization (particularly within the size and innovation literature); its niche and age; the level of analysis; the importance of the subunit (particularly in respect of size and performance); the actual measurement of size and above all how it is operationalized (see Kimberly 1976 for a comprehensive review); the below subunit size, particularly group size (which in turn is subject to the influences of all that we know about group dynamics, West 2002; West and Anderson 1992); the environment that the organization resides in, in particular its related density and the wider moderating effect of sample and measurement characteristics.

Overall, the literature is relatively silent with regards to a more refined set of health-specific, moderating factors. Describing and measuring the effect of these may actually be more helpful as a set of guidance for policy. We would suggest that such factors are: the skills and expertise of employees and their subsequent access to 'hyper' expertise and knowledge; new types of inter-organizational linkages and inter-organizational structures whether they be 'collaboratives', networks or virtual gatherings. The technology in use, especially ICT together with an understanding of the impact of the intensity and velocity of transactions on work processes and outcomes. The relationship between healthcare and technological innovation is so strong that technology in itself can have a structuring effect.

Conclusion: does size matter?

In the project as a whole, not one paper addressed the issues of form and function from a post-modern perspective, not even from a critical or interpretive perspective. Indeed, the whole approach was one of functional, material measurements of size rather than any consideration of the perception of size and its consideration in a relative way. Thus, from the classic papers of 50 years ago to the present day meta-analyses made possible through information technology the story is one of contingency and mostly of situational contingency. Contingency theory suggests that a match between the organization's strategy for the achievement of goals, its structure and the environment or context it operates in is necessary for high performance (Drazin and Van de Ven 1985; Priem 1994). However, perhaps the biggest contribution of contingency theory is that it posits organizational structure as one contributor towards organizational performance alongside many other factors that include the environment, organizational processes and decision-making, but not as the sole determinant of performance (Priem 1994). In other words, structure may well affect performance to an extent, but other factors also do, giving the researcher the problem of identifying and evaluating these multiple causalities.

From this perspective it looks distinctly probable that there is no one organizational structure that is best for achieving all organizational goals (Zinn and Mor 1998), especially in the case of a healthcare system like the NHS that has so many different and complex aims. As such, the view that flexible organizations that are able to adapt their structures to changing circumstances tend to perform better (see Jennings and Seaman 1994; Masten 1993) looks persuasive. Nonetheless, one is left with the feeling that as far as the evidence is concerned, it provides only limited decision-making guidance for dealing with such complexity.

Although the main purpose of the overall project was to indicate ways of strengthening the evidence-base for future policy decisions about NHS organizational structures, it has the potential to also assist in evidence-basing a few of the current policy decisions in UK healthcare. A whole series of recent policy initiatives in the British National Health Service (NHS) has been introduced and justified on the basis of size. However, they appear to be using the evidence in contradictory ways. On the one hand, there are proposals for independent treatment centres (ITCs) for radiotherapy and chemotherapy that will be physically separated from the knowledge base of a broader oncology unit. On the other hand, the economies of scale, size and collection of expertise argument is being used to support proposals for the restructuring of primary care provision, District General Hospitals, Ambulance trusts, Strategic Health Authorities and to justify the move towards AGHs – acute general hospitals with major accident and trauma units planned around catchment populations of over 500,000–750,000 people.

Mergers of NHS bodies are another current policy issue. The present review suggests that it is probably misguided to search for the 'one right size' for each kind of NHS body. Different advantages accrue to relatively small organizations (flexibility, scope for 'charismatic' management) and relatively large ones (specialization, formalization). At most there may be a threshold 'floor' or 'ceiling' for the scale for each organizational process that produces a desired outcome, but most organizations have many such functions with, it may be, different thresholds. Indeed, the relevant studies imply that it misses the point to conceptualize mergers in healthcare in terms of organizational size. What matters is whether working processes can be made more effective by concentrating on expertise and assembling complementary sets of skills and technologies, or cheaper by removing duplication. Mergers which simply federate organizations that otherwise retain separate core working activities and physical resources are likely to make little practical difference to their constituent organizations' productivity or efficiency.

The account of causation used in our conceptual framework and the subsequent review draw attention to the complexity of links between policy decisions and their effects (McNulty and Ferlie 2002). To find evidence of a 'relationship' between organizational structures and policy outcomes is one thing; to assume that changes in organizational structure therefore provide a trusty mechanism for producing such outcomes is quite another. The history of successive NHS reorganizations is a caution on that point.

Acknowledgement

This project was made possible by funding from:

- NHS Service Delivery and Organisation R&D Programme
- Programme of Research on Organisation Form and Function
- Organisational Factors and Performance (Reference number: WS15).

References

Aldrich, H. E. (1972) 'Technology and organisational structures: A re-examination of the findings of the Aston Group', *Administrative Science Quarterly*, 17, 26–43.

Blau, P. C. (1970) 'A formal theory of differentiation in organisations', *American Sociological Review*, 35, 200–208.

Bojke, C. Gravelle, H. and Wilkin, D. (2001) 'Is bigger better for Primary Care Groups and Trusts?' *British Medical Journal*, 322, 599–602.

Camisón-Zornoza, C., Lapiedra-Alcanu, R., Segera-Cipres, M. and Boronat-Navaro, M. (2004) 'A meta-analysis of innovation and organizational size', *Organisation Studies*, 25(3), 331–361.

Child, J. and Mansfield, R. (1972) 'Technology, size, and organisation structure', *Sociology*, 6, 369–393.

Child, J. (1973) 'Predicting and understanding organisations structure', *Administrative Science Quarterly*, 18, 168–185.

Damanpour, F. (1991) 'Organizational innovation: A meta-analysis of effects of determinants and moderators', *Academy of Management Journal*, 34, 555–590.

Drazin, R. and Van de Ven, A. (1985) 'Alternative forms of fit in contingency theory', *Administrative Science Quarterly*, 30(4), 514–539.

Durkheim, E. (1933) *The division of labour in society*, Free Press.

Feldman, R., Dowd, B. E., Coulam, R., Nichols, L. and Mutti, A. (1996) 'Effect of mergers on health maintenance organization premium', *Health Care Financing Review*, 17(3), 171–90.

Ferguson, B. and Goddard, M. (1997) 'The case for and against mergers' in B. Ferguson, T. Sheldon and J. Posnett (eds) *Concentration and choice in healthcare*, London: Royal Society of Medicine.

Ferlie, E. (1997) 'Large-scale organizational and managerial change in health care: A review of the literature', *Journal of Health Services Research and Policy*, 2(3), 180–189.

Forsyth, G. and Logan, R. (1960) *The demand for medical care: A study of the caseload in the Barrow and Furness Group of Hospitals*, London: Nuffield Provincial Hospitals Trust.

Fulop, N., Protopsaltis, G., Hutchings, A., King, A., Allen, P., Normand C. and Walters, R. (2002) 'Process and impact of mergers of NHS trusts: Multicentre case study and management cost analysis', *British Medical Journal*, 325, 246–249.

Georgopoulos, B. (1986) *Organisational structure, problem solving and effectiveness: A comparative study of hospital emergency services*, San Francisco: Jossey Bass.

Germain, R. and Spears, N. (1999) 'Quality management and its relationship with organizational context and design', *The International Journal of Quality & Reliability Management*, 16(4), 371.

Gooding, R. and Wagner, J. (1985) 'A meta-analytic review of the relationship between size and performance: The productivity and efficiency of organizations and their subunits', *Administrative Science Quarterly*, 30, 462–481.

Greiner, L. (1972) 'Evolution and revolution as organisations grow', *Harvard Business Review*, 50, 37–46.

Hall, R. H. (1977) *Organizations, structures and process*, 2nd ed., Englewood Cliffs, NJ: Prentice-Hall.

Ham, C. (1992) *Health policy in Britain*, Basingstoke: Macmillan.

Hannan, M. T. and Freeman, J. H. (1977) 'The population ecology of organizations', *American Journal of Sociology*, 82(5), 929–964.

Hannan, M. T. and Freeman, J. (1989) *Organizational ecology*, Cambridge : Harvard UP.

Hetherington, R. W. and Hewa, S. (2000) 'The structural correlates of climate for change in a multi-hospital system', *International Journal of Contemporary Sociology*, 27, 26–50.

Hickson, D. J., Hinings, C. R., Lee, C. A., Scneck, R. E. and Penning, J. M. (1971) 'A strategic contingencies' theory of intraorganizational power', *Administrative Science Quarterly*, 16(2), 216–229.

Issel, L. M., Anderson, R. A. and Kane, D. J. (2003) 'Administrative characteristics of comprehensive prenatal case management programs', *Public Health Nurse*, 20(5), 349–360.

Jennings, D. and Seaman, S. (1994) 'High and low levels of organizational adaption: An empirical analysis of strategy, structure, and performance', *Strategic Management Journal*, 15(6), 459–475.

Khan, R. L. (1964) *Organizational stress: Studies in role conflict and ambiguity*, New York: Wiley.

Khan, K. S., Riet, G., Glanville, J., Sowden, A. J. and Kleijen, J. (2001) *Undertaking systematic reviews of research on effectiveness. CRD's guidance for those carrying out or commissioning review*, 2nd ed. York: NHS Centre for Reviews and Dissemination [CRD Report Number 4].

Kimberly, J. R. (1976) 'Organizational size and structuralist perspective – review, critique and proposal', *Administrative Science Quarterly*, 21(4), 571–597.

Kimberly, J. R. and Evanisko, M. J. (1981) 'Organizational innovation – the influence of individual, organizational, and contextual factors on hospital adoption of technological and administrative innovations', *Academy of Management Journal*, 24(4), 689–713.

Kralewski, J. E., Pitt, L. and Shater, D. (1985) 'Structural characteristics of medical group practices', *Administrative Science Quarterly*, 30, 34–45.

Kralewski, J., Gifford, G. and Porter, J. (1988) 'Profit vs. public welfare goals in investor-owned and not-for-profit hospitals', *Hospital and Health Services Administration*, 33(3), 311–329.

Lee, S. Y. D. and Alexander, J. A. (1999) 'Consequences of organizational change in U.S. hospitals', *Medical Care Research and Review*, 56, 227–276.

Lee, K. and Wan, T. T. H. (2002) 'Effects of hospitals' structural clinical integration on efficiency and patient outcome', *Health Services Management Research*, 15, 234–244.

Ljunggren, B. and Sjoden, P. (2001) 'Patient reported quality of care before vs. after the implementation of a diagnosis related groups (DRG) classification and payment system in one Swedish county', *Scandinavian Journal of Caring Sciences*, 15(4), 283–294.

Marsden, P. V., Cook, C. R. and Kalleberg, A. L. (1994) 'Organizational structures: Coordination and control', *American Behavioral Scientist*, 37, 911–929.

Masten, S. (1993) 'Transaction costs, mistakes, and performance: Assessing the importance of governance', *Managerial and Decision Economics*, 14, 2, 119–129.

McNulty, T. and Ferlie, E. (2002) *Reengineering health care*, Oxford: Oxford UP.

Meyer, M. (1972) 'Sizes and the structure of organisations: A causal analysis', *American Sociological Review*, 37, 434–440.

Meyer, P. G. and Tucker, S. L. (1992) 'Incorporating an understanding of independent practice physician culture into hospital structure and operations', *Hospital & Health Services Administration*, 37, 465.

Mitchell, P. H. and Shortell, S. M. M. (1997) 'Adverse outcome and variations in the organization of care delivery', *Medical Care*, 35 (suppl.), NS19–NS32.

Moch, M. and Morse, E. (1977) 'Size, centralization and organizational adoption of innovations', *American Sociological Review*, 42(5), 716–725.

Parkinson, C. N. (1957) *Parkinson's law*, Boston: Houghton Mifflin.

Pfeffer, J. and Salancik, G. R. (1978) *The external control of organisations: A resource dependence perspective*, New York: Harper and Row.

Priem, R. (1994) 'Executive judgment, organizational congruence, and firm performance', *Organization Science*, 5(3), 421–437.

Pugh, D. S., Hickson, D. J., Hinings, C. R. and Turner, C. (1969) 'The context of organisational structures', *Administrative Science Quarterly*, 14, 91–114.

Rogers, E. (1983) *The diffusion of innovations*, New York: Free Press.

Sheaff, R., Schofield, J., Mannion, R., Dowling, B., Marshall, M. and McNally, R. (2004) *Organisational factors and performance: A review of the literature* (Reference Number: WS15), NHS Service Delivery and Organisation (SDO) Research and Development Programme of Research on Organisational Form and Function.

Smith, H. L., Shortell, S. M. and Saxberg, B. O. (1979) 'An empirical test of the configurational theory of organizations', *Human Relations*, 32(8), 667.

Stigler, G. (1958) 'The economies of scale', *The Journal of Law and Economics*, 1, 54–71.

Subramanian, A. and Nilakanta, S. (1996) 'Organizational innovativeness: Exploring the relationship between organizational determinants of innovation, types of innovations, and measures of economic performance', *International Journal of Management Science*, 24(6), 631–647.

Toffler, A. (1980) *The third wave*, New York: William Morrow.

Urbach, D. R. and Baxter, N. N. (2004) 'Does it matter what a hospital is "high volume" for? Specificity of hospital volume–outcome associations for surgical procedures: analysis of administrative data', *British Medical Journal*, 328, 737–740.

West, M. (2002) 'How can good performance among doctors be maintained?' *British Medical Journal*, 324(7366), 669–670.

West, M. A. and Anderson, N. (1992) 'Innovation, cultural values, and the management of change in British hospitals', *Work and Stress*, 6, 293–310.

Wholey, D. R., Christianson, J. B. and Sanchez, S. M. (1992) 'Organization size and failure among health maintenance organization', *American Sociological Review*, 57, 829–842.

Wholey, D., Feldman, R., Christianson, J. D. and Engberg, J. (1996) 'Scale and scope economies among health maintenance organizations', *Journal of Health Economics*, 15(6), 657–684.

Wilkin, D., Bojke, C., Coleman, A. and Gravelle, H. (2003) 'The relationship between size and performance of primary care organisations in England', *Journal of Health Services Research and Policy*, 8(1), 11–17.

Zinn, J. and Mor, M. (1998) 'Organizational structures and the delivery of primary care to older Americans', *Health Services Research*, 33(2), 354–380.

6
Evidence-Based Management: The Power of Evidence or Evidence of Power?

Mark Learmonth

Introduction

Evidence-based health care (EBHC) has now enjoyed over 10 years of popularity in many clinical fields across the globe. Today, it seems axiomatic that all health care practice can, and should, be evidence-based – that is to say, practice should integrate individual clinical expertise 'with the best available external clinical evidence from systematic research' (Sackett et al. 1996:71). But whilst EBHC can 'work' – at least when work means (quite specifically) that aggregate clinical outcomes are improved – its overall successes are overdrawn (evidence-based medicine rarely provides categorical, recipe-style answers for individual clinical situations). Indeed, much optimistic hype is accumulating about EBHC with some unintended consequences.

For example, the question of whether or not clinical practice can be said to be evidence-based is taking on a significance that is wider than its mere effectiveness. As Morse suggests, today, '[e]vidence and *evidence-based practice* have become the new mantras for health care' (2006:80; italics in original). To be able to claim practice is 'evidence-based' provides a significant source of prestige and legitimacy that contributes to the construction of professional identity (Green 2000; Traynor 2004). Furthermore, the same ideas that underpin evidence-based medicine have become central, not merely in guiding individual clinicians' practice, but also in shaping research agendas, formulating health policy and allocating resources (Lambert et al. 2006). Evidence-based practices are taking on a legitimatory and symbolic role which create a cultural environment in health care in which *any* problematization of using 'evidence' – virtually regardless of context – can be constructed (and dismissed) as reminiscent of early arguments against evidence-based medicine.

The aim of this chapter, therefore, is to encourage critical reflection upon the uses (and abuses) of 'evidence' in health care. Following Tenbensel , it will draw attention to the claim that 'any understanding of the role of knowledge and evidence... requires an understanding of how knowledge is articulated through relations of power' (2004:190). This is especially important in the debate about evidence in health care because most proponents of the evidence-based movement assume that by recourse to science and evidence they can escape the taint of politics and ideology (Donovan 2005) an assumption that is, to say the least, problematical. Indeed, a central concern of this chapter is to reveal the unobtrusive but constraining operation of power associated with the dominant ways evidence tends to be constructed – and through which alternatives are typically disregarded or rendered invisible (Deetz 2003).

Evidence-Based management

These arguments are developed through a critical exploration of evidence-based management – about which there is now a large body of appreciative literature (for example, Axelsson 1998; Briner 2000; Davies et al. 2000; Dopson 2006; Hewison 1997; Kovner et al. 2000; Ozcan and Smith 1998; Stewart 2002; Tranfield et al. 2003; Walshe and Rundall 2001). Most recently, evidence-based management has been advocated in particularly high-profile ways – ways that have taken it well outside a health care domain. For example, at the 2005 Academy of Management Conference (the world's largest academic management conference), Rousseau, the outgoing President of the Academy, entitled her presidential address: 'Is there such a thing as "evidence-based management"?' (Rousseau 2006). A few months later, Pfeffer and Sutton (two very prominent US-based management scholars) published *Hard Facts, Dangerous Half-Truths and Total Nonsense: Profiting from Evidence-Based Management* (2006). Their work exemplifies the arguments made by most of the proponents of evidence-based management.

Rousseau's address was aimed principally at the academic community, Pfeffer and Sutton's book at practicing executives. What they share, however, is the aim of convincing their respective audiences of the benefits of evidence-based management, and they both do so by providing virtual panegyrics upon evidence-based management for managerial practice. As panegyrics, however, neither discussed the contestation surrounding the nature of 'facts', 'evidence' and so on within the social sciences (for an introduction to this debate, see, for example, Potter 1996). Furthermore, both share an unremittingly pro-top management tone – to the exclusion of any 'evidence' that might cause us to reflect in a serious and sustained manner on the legitimacy of conventional management goals (profitability, control and so on). Thus, for Rousseau, evidence-based practice is a (theoretically unproblematic) 'paradigm for making decisions that integrate the best available research evidence with decision-maker expertise and client/customer preferences to guide practice toward more desirable results' (2006:258).

To be clear, I am not contesting that 'evidence' can (and should) inform practice in organizations – indeed, the implications of this point will be developed later in the chapter. But the assumptions made about the nature of 'evidence' by Rousseau, Pfeffer and Sutton and many other advocates of evidence-based management are particularly problematic in a social science like organization studies. In this discipline, 'evidence' can never be just there, waiting for the researcher to find as they imply. Rather it is necessary to construct evidence in some way – a process that is inherently ideological and always contestable – not merely a technical, 'scientific' task (Alvesson and Deetz 2000).

This means that questions such as what counts as evidence; what organizational practices the evidence might (ethically and politically) inform; what interests different constructions of the evidence support and deny (and so on) are questions that, for most major issues in the field, are the subject of radical dispute. That is to say, the grounds on which the disputes can be conducted are themselves contested (Burrell and Morgan 1979; Grey 2004; Learmonth 2006). Indeed, if we take ideas about the fragmentation of knowledge in organization studies seriously, then as Jack and Westwood argue, 'research must become reflexive and aware of its ontological and epistemological assumptions, political positioning and ethical obligations' (2006:481). But where, one might ask, is any reflexivity concerning the political positioning of research and evidence in this statement from Rousseau's speech to the Academy?

Through evidence-based management, practicing managers develop into experts who make organizational decisions informed by social science and organizational research – part of the zeitgeist moving professional decisions away from personal preference and unsystematic experience toward those based on the best available scientific evidence. (2006:256)

If we were to speculate about the absence of reflexivity in evidence-based management, part of the explanation has to do with politics and power. For as Grey argues, 'the ideological nature of management is obscured by the way in which it appears to be based upon objective knowledge independent of political or social interests and moral considerations' (1996:601). To illustrate this point, let us turn to other academic literature concerned with promoting evidence-based management. In this literature, whilst *some* of the problems with management 'evidence' are acknowledged, in my reading, there is always an attempt to *de-radicalize* dispute in one way or another. Disputation cannot be acknowledged to be over fundamentals, or it would represent a threat to the coherence of the evidence-based movement in management.

De-radicalizing dispute

For some proponents of evidence-based management such as Axelsson (1998), radical dispute in organization studies can simply be ignored because it occurs outside the domains of traditional science. For Axelsson, much management research is becoming 'more and more esoteric and largely dissociated from the problems of manage-ment ... [having come] to a scientific dead-end, where nothing can be proved or disproved any longer' (1998:307). He commended instead the evidence that he believed to be legitimate – as he put it, manage-ment research 'inspired by the practical and scientific developments of Evidence Based Medicine' (1998:308).

Perhaps more realistically, given the amount of management research that relies upon evidence from work other than quantitative experi-mental designs, Walshe and Rundall (2001) discuss the *problems* asso-ciated with adapting from medicine an evidence-based approach for management. For example, compared to doctors, 'managers make rather fewer but larger decisions [which] ... may take years to be made and implemented, and it can be difficult even to discern or describe the decision-making process or to pin down when a decision is actually made' (2001:444–445). Also, in terms of the research base, they acknow-ledge 'the loosely defined, methodologically heterogeneous, widely distributed, and hard-to-generalize research base for health care manage-ment is much more difficult to use in the same way [as medicine's research base]' (2001:444). And furthermore, managers' attitudes to applying research in their jobs is also problematical – compared to medi-cine: '[p]ersonal experience and self-generated knowledge play a much larger part in determining how managers approach their jobs, and there is much less reliance on a shared body of formal knowledge in decision making' (2001:439). Nevertheless, Walshe and Rundall still believe that efforts should be made in 'outlining an agenda for action to promote the development of evidence-based management' (2001:430).

The magnitude of the problems for developing such an agenda can be further illustrated by Scott et al. who attempts '[t]o review the *evidence* for a relationship between organizational culture and health care performance' (2003:105; italics added). At the start of their essay, they highlighted their 'striking finding' (2003:105): the absence of consensus in the organizational theory literature about definitions for either culture or performance. Indeed, from their discussion, it is reasonable to infer from this absence of consensus that a search for 'evidence' in these areas would introduce *more* ambiguity and uncertainty, thereby seriously reducing (rather than promoting) the possibilities for rationality enhancing decision-making. As they put it,

> Once we accept that performance is as contested a domain as culture, and that culture and performance are likely to be mutually constituted, then the difficulties of reconciling the two domains through simplistic equations such as 'strong culture equals superior performance' begin to seem insurmountable. (2003:115)

But, perhaps surprisingly, and in spite of the theoretical problems to which they draw attention, Scott et al. do not draw the conclusion that a consideration of the evidence introduces more ambiguity (though some of their comments hints at such a possibility). Rather their explicit suggestion to deal with the divergent nature of management evidence posits a methodological solution: '[c]onsiderably greater methodological ingenuity will be required to unravel the relationship(s) between organizational culture(s) and performance(s)' (2003:105). I interpret this statement as an attempt to de-radicalize dispute. But methodological ingenuity cannot resolve disagreements in management studies because there are no universally accepted parameters and limits that allow for certain 'methodologies' to be axiomatic and beyond dispute.

So why do many health management commentators play down dispute to make evidence-based management seem plausible? This is where power becomes important. The popularity of evidence-based management in health care is due not so much to its utility in addressing effectiveness problems nor to its theoretical coherence, but rather to the intellectual climate in health care and the management interests that are served by dominant beliefs about 'evidence' in such an environment. This is the theme to which we now turn.

Evidence-based management and unobtrusive power

The intellectual climate of health care today is dominated by the natural science assumptions of medicine. Among many with influence in and around health services, there is a sustained optimism in the ability of scientific experts to find technological solutions for physical ills. And these technological solutions are assumed to be applicable in principle to social fields as well – including management. Thus all aspects of health care have become environments in which 'evidence' is saturated with positive cultural valences.

Particularly in a management context, this kind of intellectual and emotional environment is likely to be interest-serving. Indeed, Alvesson and Willmott have argued that the sort of applied management research necessary for producing management evidence could well have the effect of 'creating and legitimizing an image and ideal of managers as impartial experts whose prerogative is associated with, if not founded upon, scientifically respectable bodies of knowledge' (1996:27).

In health care such an effect may be especially strong because the production and use of evidence in management suggests that management is associated with similar sorts of evidence to that which health care professionals are being encouraged to use in their practice. This represents a significant shift for doctors, who, as Llewellyn shows, have not generally regarded '[m]anagers ... as possessing abstract, scientific knowledge, and any craft experience that they have is depicted as being derived from careers that started as "office boys"' (2001:605). But evidence-based management might suggest to doctors that management *is* in some way abstract and scientific – informed by the research of academics from prestigious institutions.

I want to emphasize the unobtrusive nature of these processes. I am not suggesting that the introduction of the discourse of evidence into management has been a planned managerial intervention; indeed, given the taken-for-grantedness of dominant beliefs about evidence in health services, most managers no doubt understand the incorporation of evidence into their practices as a politically innocent way to help deal with effectiveness problems. The problem is that the natural science ideal of a-social evidence has (perhaps accidentally) elevated *managerialist* evidence as the only form. This a-social ideal has shaped the format that evidence can take and constrained the questions that might be asked, a process that has, paradoxically, caused problems for those whose experience of the complexity of the everyday world of health care does not conform to the model presumed in evidence-based approaches.

To illustrate the processes involved, let us turn to a report by Iles and Sutherland (2001). The authors were commissioned by the National Health Service (NHS) Service Delivery and Organization (SDO) Programme to review popular management ideas for their applicability to managing change in health care in a way that would be accessible and relevant to health care managers and professionals. It is similar in tone to other work aimed at communicating the benefits of evidence-based management to a practitioner audience. This report is important for two reasons. First, it is well known within UK health services, having been widely distributed by the SDO without charge amongst health service managers and health practitioners (Cranfield and Ward 2002). Second, it was the first major report commissioned by the SDO and has formed the basis for further work (see for example, Iles et al. 2004).

The SDO specified that the review should include a consideration of the following:

> re-engineering; the business excellence model; Total Quality Management; Continuous Quality Improvement; the learning organization (e.g. Peter Senge's *The Fifth Discipline*); the Mckinsey 7S model; the Theory of Constraints; as well as theories set out by management writers such as Peters and Waterman, and Kanter. (SDO 2000:no page number; in Learmonth 2003:111)

Such authors and ideas have enjoyed much optimist hype from management consultants over the last two decades, so it is possible to represent these ideas, following Clark and Salaman (1998), as *guru theory*. Indeed, Clark and Salaman's list of gurus and associated ideas (p.138) included almost all those appearing in the SDO's brief. But for Clark and Salaman most of these ideas would not count as theory in conventional academic settings – for them, guru 'theories' are important to consider, not for their intellectual content, but because they provide a window on:

> managers' values, and ... describe what [managers believe] organizations are like, how they work and how they must be managed ... [they therefore] offer a conception of management itself in virtuous, heroic, high status terms. Guru activity ... not only constitutes organizational realities, it constitutes managers themselves. (1998:157)

However, and in sharp contrast to Clark and Salaman, Iles and Sutherland (2001) were concerned to provide a broadly sympathetic reading of the intellectual content of these theories. They never used the term *guru*, and rather than understanding these ideas as (at least potentially) partial and managerialist representations of organizational realities, they universalized them by examining merely the empirically testable claims these writers made about organizational life. Significantly, this empirical emphasis was in the (ostensibly apolitical) tradition of evidence-based clinical practices. Ignored therefore was the possibility that this kind of work may have constitutive effects or that it might proceed from managers' values.

For example, commenting on Peters and Waterman's (1982) excellence ideas, Iles and Sutherland noted criticisms such as the lack of supporting empirical studies; that five years after publication, two-thirds of the excellent companies had slipped from the pinnacle of success; and that the conflict and dissension that also shapes an organization's culture is ignored by the work. But much more radical, politically orientated critique of Peters and Waterman has been voiced. Willmott (1993), for example, has offered an extended and widely cited critique of the instrumental use of culture by Peters and Waterman, which he suggested has gained popularity because it 'aspires to extend management control by colonizing the affective domain...by promoting employee commitment to a monolithic structure of feeling and thought' (1993:517). Other commentators in similar traditions, Linstead and Grafton-Small (1992); Parker and Dent (1996) or Strangleman and Roberts (1999), might also concede Iles and Sutherland's empirical point that Peters and Waterman's ideas on culture have produced ways in which managers might influence change in their organizations. But for them, as for Willmott, the impact would be interpreted as domination rather than an appropriate extension of managers' legitimate functional authority.

Yet this more critical 'evidence' on organizational culture (along with Clark and Salaman's work) is absent from Iles and Sutherland's report. The absence allowed Iles and Sutherland to opine that in spite of the (presumably relatively minor) acknowledged problems with the approach, Peters and Waterman's (1982) teaching

> is considered important by many commentators because of its dual emphasis on 'soft' organizational components...as well as the 'hard'...popularizing the notion of organizational culture as the 'normative glue' that holds together the organization. (2001:28–29)

Citing unnamed 'many commentators' gives the (misleading) impression that management scholars broadly agree about the positive ways in which Peters and Waterman's work is 'considered important'; we were not told that a significant number of prominent academics consider it important for rather darker reasons. And it is submitted that the plausibility of this misleading impression is enhanced when it is given in the broad context of EBHC. Radical or political disagreements are much rarer among scholars in medicine and other clinical fields; but after reading Iles and Sutherland's report it might be assumed by people accustomed to health care research that management academics are as ideologically united as commentators in scientific health care disciplines.

So, why was this material omitted? Perhaps, had Iles and Sutherland discussed the more critical material on the work of the gurus they examined they might have produced an unacceptable report, one that implied that a rational consideration of the evidence is not enough to resolve questions of how managers should manage change, because the 'evidence' shows that the desirability of the outcomes of these management interventions is disputed. Also, had their report included alternative evidence, it might not have gained the favorable appraisal the report received from National Health Service staff (Cranfield and Ward 2002). Moreover, as guru theories were already officially sanctioned and widely in use within the UK National Health Service at the time, critiquing these theories on ideological and ethical grounds may well have been interpreted as an attack on current practices and government policy. And as Fuller has noted, client-centered researchers are careful not to 'draw undue attention to the client's role in maintaining the power relations revealed in the ... report' (2000:11).

Concluding comments

How, then, could things be different? To start with, researchers should not be so aligned with managers' agendas. After all, most organizational topics have no necessary connection to questions of how health care might be managed and controlled – nor are they the exclusive concern of those who have management responsibilities.

The greater use of research traditions that consider organizational themes in ways that are (often explicitly) divorced from questions of how to manage would be a positive development. Such work typically focuses on groups with little conventional prestige and finds inspiration in social and political theories that offer sharp counterpoints to traditional managerialist ideas on these matters. Even Pfeffer and Sutton, in their book that celebrates evidence-based *management* (though they 'hesitate to recommend' (2006:230) it), discuss the value of what they say 'might be called *evidence-based misbehavior*' (2006:230; italics in original). More researchers should develop their suggestion – and with less hesitancy!

It is important to concede that this sort of work tends to be messy and contradictory – different papers have different theoretical underpinnings and serve contrasting interests. It is therefore hard to read and use such a body of literature (if we can allow it to be put together as a 'body') to provide answers to the difficulties and dilemmas of people in organizations. Nevertheless, if such evidence were to be introduced within the mainstream of other evidence-based approaches, it *could* become a means to unsettle and destabilize what otherwise might comfortably be assumed about organizational life and policy-making in health services. Whilst such destabilizing *could* involve paralyzing action, such risks are not inevitable and may be worth it for bringing more creativity to policy-making and encouraging more open debates that represent wider constituencies and interests.

The practical difficulties faced in adopting the position advocated are considerable – not least the resistance that the powerful groups with an interest in evidence-based management might offer. Governments and public managers usually look to academics to give them straightforward answers to their difficulties and dilemmas; they may well be reluctant to fund research that does not provide these answers – or that explicitly opposes them! But should academics acquiesce to pressures to produce work that simply serves management purposes, then we risk failing the interests of everyone in health care. Such acquiescence, in the longer term, could remove incentives to comment outside institutionally approved discourses. And if it were to do so, academic work would ultimately not be in the interests of *anyone* in health services – including top managers and policy-makers.

References

Alvesson, M. and Deetz, S. (2000) *Doing critical management research*, London: Sage.

Alvesson, M. and Willmott, H. (1996) *Making sense of management: A critical introduction*, London: Sage.

Axelsson, R. (1998) 'Towards an evidence-based health care management', *International Journal of Health Planning and Management*, 13, 307–317.

Briner, R. (2000) 'Evidence-based human resource management' in L. Trinder (ed) *Evidence-based practice: A critical appraisal*, Oxford: Blackwell, pp. 184–211.

Burrell, G. and Morgan, G. (1979) *Sociological paradigms and organisational analysis: Elements of the sociology of corporate life*, London: Heinemann.

Clark, T. and Salaman, G. (1998) 'Telling tales: Management gurus' narratives and the construction of managerial identity', *Journal of Management Studies*, 35(2), 137–159.

Cranfield, S. and Ward, H. (2002) Managing change in the NHS (2001) Publications. (http://www.sdo.lshtm.ac.uk/pdf/changemanagement.survey.pdf) accessed 02.07.03.

Davies, H., Nutley, S. and Smith, P. (2000) 'Introducing evidence-based policy and practice in public services' in H. Davies (ed) *What works? Evidence-based policy and practice in public services*, Bristol: The Policy Press, pp. 1–12.

Deetz, S. (2003) 'Disciplinary power, conflict suppression and human resources management' in M. Alvesson (ed) *Studying management critically*, London: Sage, pp. 23–45

Donovan, C. (2005) 'The governance of social science and everyday epistemology', *Public Administration*, 83(3), 597–615.

Dopson, S. (2006) 'Debate: Why does knowledge stick? What we can learn from the case of evidence-based health care', *Public Money and Management*, (April), 26(2), 85–86.

Fuller, S. (2000) 'Why science studies has never been critical of science: Some recent lessons on how to be a helpful nuisance and a harmless radical', *Philosophy of the Social Sciences*, 30(1), 5–32.

Green, J. (2000) 'Epistemology, evidence and experience: Evidence-based health care in the work of accident alliances', *Sociology of Health & Illness*, 22(4), 453–476.

Grey, C. (1996) 'Towards a critique of managerialism: The contribution of Simone Weil', *Journal of Management Studies*, 33(5), 591–611.

Grey, C. (2004) 'Reinventing business schools: The contribution of critical management education', *Academy of Management Learning and Education*, 3(2), 178–186.

Hewison, A. (1997) 'Evidence-based medicine: What about evidence-based management?', *Journal of Nursing Management*, 5, 195–198.

Iles, V. and Sutherland, K. (2001) *Organisational change: A review for health care managers, professionals and researchers*, London: NCCSDO.

Iles, V., Cranfield, S. and Richardson, L. (2004) *Developing change management skills: A resource for health care professionals and managers. Writing: A method of inquiry*, www.sdo.lshtm.ac.uk/changemanagement{Idevelopingskills.pdf}, accessed 01.12.04.

Jack, G. and Westwood, R. (2006) 'Postcolonialism and the politics of qualitative research in international business', *Management International Review*, 46(4), 481–501.

Kovner, A. R., Elton, J. J. and Billings, J. (2000) 'Evidence-based management', *Frontiers of Health Services Management*, 16(4), 3–24.

Lambert, H., Gordon, E. and Bogdan-Lovis E. (2006), 'Introduction: Gift Horse or Trojan Horse? Social Science Perspectives on Evidence-based Health Care', *Social Science & Medicine*, 62(11), 2613–2620.

Learmonth, M. (2003) 'Making health services management research critical: A review and a suggestion', *Sociology of Health & Illness*, 25(1), 93–119.

Learmonth, M. (2006) 'Is there such a thing as "evidence-based manage-ment"?: A commentary on Rousseau's 2005 presidential address', *Academy of Management Review*, 31(4), 1089–1091.

Linstead, S. and Grafton-Small, R. (1992) 'On reading organizational culture', *Organization Studies*, 13(3), 331–355.

Llewellyn, S. (2001) ' "Two-way windows": Clinicians as medical managers', *Organization Studies*, 22(4), 593–623.

Morse, J. M. (2006) 'The politics of evidence' in N. K. Denzin and M. Giardina (eds) *Qualitative inquiry and the conservative challenge* , Walnut Creek, CA: Left Coast Press, pp. 79–92.

Ozcan, Y. A. and Smith, P. (1998) 'Towards a science of the management of health care', *Health Care Management Science*, 1, 1–4.

Parker, M. and Dent, M. (1996) 'Managers, doctors and culture: Changing an English health district', *Administration and Society*, 28(3), 335–361.

Peters, T. J. and Waterman, R. H. (1982) *In search of excellence: Lessons from America's best-run companies*, New York: Harper Row.

Pfeffer, J. and Sutton, R. (2006) *Hard facts, dangerous half-truths and total nonsense: Profiting from evidence-based management*, Boston, MA: Harvard Business School Press.

Potter, J. (1996) *Representing reality: Discourse, rhetoric and social construction*, London: Sage.

Rousseau, D. (2006) 'Is there such a thing as "evidence-based management"?', *Academy of Management Review*, 31(2), 256–269.

Sackett, D., Rosenberg, W., Muir Gray, J. A., Haynes, B. and Richardson, S. (1996) 'Evidence-based medicine: What it is and what it isn't', *British Medical Journal*, 312, 71–72.

Scott, T., Mannion, R., Marshall, M. and Davies, H. (2003) 'Does organisational culture influence health care performance? A review of the evidence', *Journal of Health Services Research Policy*, 8(2), 105–117.

Stewart, R. (2002) *Evidence-based management: A practical guide for health professionals*, Abingdon, Oxon: Radcliffe Medical Press.

Strangleman, T. and Roberts, I. (1999) 'Looking through the window of oppor-tunity: The cultural cleansing of workplace identity', *Sociology*, 33(1), 47–67.

Tenbensel, T. (2004) 'Does more evidence lead to better policy? The implications of explicit priority-setting in New Zealand's health policy for evidence-based policy', *Policy Studies*, 25(3), 189–207.

Tranfield, D., Denyer, D. and Smart, P. (2003) 'Towards a methodology for devel-oping evidence-informed management knowledge by means of systematic review', *British Journal of Management*, 14, 207–222.

Traynor, M. (2004) 'Nursing, managerialism and evidence-based practice: The constant struggle for influence' in M. Learmonth (ed) *Unmasking Health Management: A critical text*, New York: Nova Science, pp. 117–128.

Walshe, K. and Rundall, T. (2001) 'Evidence-based management: From theory to practice in health care', *The Milbank Quarterly*, 79(3), 429–457.

Willmott, H. (1993) 'Strength is ignorance; slavery is freedom: Managing culture in modern organizations', *Journal of Management Studies*, 30(4), 515–552.

7

'Speaking Truth to Power': On the Discomforts of Researching the Contemporary Policy Process

David J. Hunter

Introduction

In his classic exploration of the art and craft of policy analysis in the context of public policies, Aaron Wildavsky observes wryly:

> speaking truth to power remains the ideal of analysts who hope they have truth, but realize they have not (and in a democracy, should not have) power. No one can do analysis without becoming aware that moral considerations are integral to the enterprise. (Wildavsky 1979)

For Wildavsky, a political scientist by background, the analytical process is dedicated to making things better, not worse. Facts and values, in his view, are inseparable in action even if the evidence-based policy tradition, and its often spurious scientism, is predicated on trying to keep facts and values separate.

Reflecting on the state of policy analysis, Wildavsky goes on to explore the morality of the analyst, asking: Are analysts 'hired guns' paid to do the bidding of their clients? Should they subvert their superiors for a higher cause? When do you resign? Who do you serve? How can moral implications be made more explicit in analysis? Sometimes, though happily not too often, questions such as these arise implicitly if not explicitly in doing research, especially if its aim is to effect change or possibly challenge change where it is perceived to be dysfunctional in respect of particular values or policy objectives. As Albert Camus said to Jean Gilbert in 1956:

> In an era of bad faith, the man who does not want to renounce separating true from false is condemned to a certain kind of exile.

The policy circumstances which most cry out for independent investigation are precisely those in which bad faith is likely to be present
in epidemic proportions. These circumstances constantly threaten
researchers with exile, albeit of a kind less harsh than Camus probably
had in mind! Reflecting on a research study examining the impact of
the introduction of general management on the NHS some 16 years ago,
a group of us wrote:

> Bad faith easily catches hold where a strong government has intro-
> duced a major new policy, backed it with substantial resources and
> invested it with high symbolic significance in terms of the currently
> dominant political ideology. (Pollitt et al. 1990:171)

These words could have been written today to describe the UK government's National Health Service modernization project in England (a
distinction should be made with the other countries making up the UK
where the health care reform agenda has taken a different direction).

This chapter is concerned with the interface between research and
policy. Whether this 'twilight zone' is regarded as research or policy
analysis does not particularly matter. The important point is that much
of the research done on policy is presumably undertaken in the hope
that it may improve the way we do things around here.

Policy-making models

In their useful review of a range of policy-making models, and the role
of research underpinning them, Bowen and Zwi (2005:602) suggest six
models:

1. the knowledge-driven model
2. the problem-solving model
3. the interactive model
4. the political model
5. the enlightenment model
6. the tactical model.

The *knowledge-driven model*, which suggests that emergent research about
a social problem will lead to direct application to policy, rarely applies
although is often held dear by some researchers and, at least at a rhetorical level, by policy-makers. More often, in the real and messy world
of policy, the *political model* applies. Its basis is that decision-makers

are not receptive to research unless it serves political gain and provides supporting evidence for a predetermined course of action. If the desire is to construct a different relationship between the worlds of research and policy, that is, speaking truth to power with some authority and prospect of influence, then it might be appropriate to aspire to the *inter-active model*. It suggests that the search for knowledge moves beyond research to include a variety of sources and influences including politics and stakeholder interests. More than any other model, it aims to reflect the complexity and messiness of the policy process.

However, the adoption of this model is probably some way off. The responsibility for this state of affairs lies with policy-makers on the one hand, who continue to place a premium on tacit and experiential know-ledge (summed up in the remark: 'he/she who knows, does'), and with researchers on the other hand, who often make little attempt to under-stand the world of policy believing that it is not their business to do so. Partly as a consequence of this hands-off stance, they often commu-nicate in an esoteric language which fails to engage policy-makers or overlook opportunities to transfer knowledge with a view to influencing policy and practice.

Researchers tend not to concern themselves with policy questions because they see them as essentially political matters beyond their competence or influence. Rather, they view their role in more reduc-tionist and instrumental terms. Their job is to win research contracts, complete the research to agreed quality standards and on time, publish the results (preferably in high-ranking peer-reviewed journals) and move on to the next research project or contract.

Depressingly, and with only slight exaggeration, what preoccupies the community of researchers above all these days is their standing in the Research Assessment Exercise (RAE) and not whether their work has been influential in shaping policy or has made a difference. It is their performance in the RAE that will determine both their career prospects and possibly the fate of their research centre or institution.

The above has tended to caricature what is often a complex rela-tionship between researcher and client but there is a sense in which Wildavsky's legitimate moral concerns about the role of the analyst remain buried in the consciousness of researchers – and not without good reason. It has been a long-standing criticism of researchers in the UK and elsewhere that the gulf between them and those being researched remains unhelpfully wide. Instead of a common discourse and continuous interaction, there is often an artificial distance between them with little or no mutual interaction to aid learning. The RAE can be held partly responsible for this dysfunctional relationship although it is not the only factor. Indeed, the RAE can become a convenient excuse not to engage in a process that many researchers find uncomfortable and often distasteful. Some researchers after all manage to achieve both – a good RAE submission and policy impact. Nonetheless, a criticism of the RAE is that it has utterly failed to appreciate and value policy-relevant or applied research. Indeed, it is a criticism rather belatedly acknowledged by the government although one it seems powerless to tackle. The widespread perception outside academia is that user-focused and interdisciplinary research is regarded as potential victims of the RAE.

Whatever the disincentives in academia to do policy research which may impact on practice there are also other important issues that need to be addressed in respect of whether governments actually want policy analysis, or for that matter analysts or researchers who are prepared to speak truth to power, especially when this can be an uncomfortable process for all concerned. As John Maynard Keynes famously observed over half a century ago:

> There is nothing a government hates more than to be well-informed, for it makes the process of arriving at decisions much more complicated and difficult.

The present UK government entered office in 1997 committed to evidence-based policy and, in contrast to Keynes' claim, to making a virtue of knowledge rather than ignorance. The mantra was and remains (at least in rhetorical terms) 'what matters is what works'. Usually unstated, the assumption underpinning this view of policy and practice is that policy-making is a rational linear process that needs to be informed by relevant and appropriate research.

Even if the model is deemed flawed, it is held up as the gold standard to which all should aspire. There is no sense or appreciation that 'wicked issues', that is, issues which are deeply intractable and are imperfectly understood and to which solutions are not clear, are inherent in the public domain (Stewart 1998). As Marmot (2004:906) has written, the relationship between science and policy is complicated:

> Scientific findings do not fall on blank minds that get made up as a result. Science engages with busy minds that have strong views about how things are and ought to be.

A good example is the government's approach to public health with its focus on individual choice and on shifting the balance of responsibility between the State and the individual in favor of the individual (Hunter 2005). There is a tension between this value position with its emphasis on individual lifestyles as an explanation for poor health status and that which emphasizes the social determinants of health and views healthy public policy as a role for government regardless of whether it is perceived as the 'nanny' state (Jochelson 2006).

In other words, we are dealing with complex systems whose operations cannot be predicted or subject to simplistic interventions (Plsek and Greenhalgh 2001). As Wildavsky notes, problem-solving may give way to problem succession (cut one off and another sprouts), hence his plea for continuous dialogue and interaction between policy-makers and analysts since in his view 'the solution is part of defining the problem'.

But such a messy, ambiguous real-world view of policy does not sit easily or comfortably with the policy-maker's desire for quick and unequivocal results that will either guide action or, more often, endorse action already embarked upon (Barnes et al. 2005). The government's public sector modernization reform agenda is imbued with precisely such a conception of research and evidence. This is especially the case in those areas of government policy that are sensitive to criticism and where the stakes are high in respect of pressure to demonstrate total success and where evidence is not only merely one factor in the mix, and rarely the overriding one, but also a preference for evidence that reinforces the direction of travel rather than challenges it. Following their evaluation of Health Action Zones (HAZs) in England, Barnes et al. make the important point that it seemed that the Department of Health was of the opinion that HAZs had to be evaluated than why or how (Barnes et al. 2005).

Under the present government, health policy and the organization of health care has been at the top of the policy and political agendas since the late 1990s. At the time, the then Prime Minister pledged personally to rescue the NHS and to modernize it – a pledge he has restated regularly ever since. Never have the political stakes in respect of achieving success been so high. It is unprecedented for a politician at that level, i.e., the country's most senior politician, to make such a claim. At the same time, there has never been such a technocratic, managerial government which, paradoxically, although speaking the language of management, has simultaneously succeeded in politicizing the management task in health policy to the point where managers are regarded as merely the agents of ministers or political apparatchiks. Setting targets and performance managing their progress may be the stuff of management but in the hands of politicians masquerading as managers you get terror by targets and a performance management regime characterized by fear, bullying and a blame-oriented culture (Blackler 2006).

Discomforts of researching the policy process

The current style of policy-making presents particular problems for researchers and policy analysts. These are enshrined in the second part of the title of this chapter – the discomforts of researching the contemporary policy process. The research community has no shortage of anecdotes testifying to the following:

- grant starvation – the research is not welcome or deemed necessary
- denial of access to conduct field work
- restrictions on publication because the findings are critical or 'off message'
- give us only the good news, not the bad
- inconvenient research findings that are ignored, buried, rubbished
- researchers attacked for their motives and/or blacklisted with associated consequences when it comes to accessing research funds.

More commonly, the complaints are far less extreme and reflect a general frustration on the part of researchers that they are not listened to, or are not as engaged in the policy process as they could be, or that events move so swiftly that by the time researchers have anything useful to say it is too late. But the difficulties cannot all be laid at the door of policy-makers. Researchers often fail to understand or appreciate the complexities and nuances of the policy process and have a rather touching, if naïve, faith in evidence driving policy if only policy-makers would listen to them and heed their advice.

Some of the discomforts in conducting policy research may be illustrated with two examples. They have been chosen to represent rather extreme manifestations of particular difficulties researchers experience but this is deliberate in order to make the point. In practice, the issues are rarely as extreme.

Example 1

The first example comes from an ethnographic study of the impact of general management in the NHS in the mid-1980s (Harrison et al. 1992). Following the Griffiths report, which was highly critical of the state of management in the NHS, the change of management style from consensus teams to a single chief executive was significant and represented a potential shift of power from medicine to management (Griffiths 1983).

Four researchers, including the author, all well-versed in elite actor research and in the specifics of NHS policy-making, were successful in obtaining funds from the ESRC under its 'management in government' program. Support was also sought from central government. The Chief Scientist's organization inside what was then the Department of Health and Social Security seemed supportive. But the NHS Management Board (which no longer exists) intervened insisting that no research into general management be funded until a set of criteria had been drawn up. Reasonable enough you might think but three years later we were still waiting for the criteria and had not had a definitive response to our application. One can be charitable and put it all down to bureaucratic inertia, albeit convenient in terms of discouraging researchers. But other factors were also probably at work. Some of us had already published critical commentaries on general management, and health department civil servants – including one pivotal senior official – were known to be so enthusiastic about general management that the prospect of research challenging their convictions was not to be seriously entertained.

In such a climate of bad faith, independent, published research was not welcomed since it risked exposing fundamental flaws which could be seized upon by disgruntled NHS groups unhappy about the management model imposed on them. The failure to secure funds meant that work had to proceed with a smaller sample of health authorities than ideally would have been desirable.

The cult of managerialism continues to dominate much policy-making and practitioner thinking. It emphasizes data-driven prescriptiveness (witness the appeal of evidence-based medicine) and devalues interpretive approaches which give voice to 'alternative realities' or paradigms. Yet, when it comes to investigating and understanding contemporary policy, natural science and experimental models of research are of limited utility. What is required, often in the teeth of fierce opposition, is qualitative and interpretive approaches. When government adviser, Derek Wanless, in his report on public health bemoaned the absence of research examining what interventions work or do not work and why, he was in effect lamenting the absence of sound qualitative studies (Wanless 2004). Ethnographic research has a particularly valuable contribution to make to policy studies and to getting beneath the skin of policy and understanding the dynamics of organizational life. For these very reasons its findings can be uncomfortable, challenging and even personal. It does not produce quick prescriptions and might even generate political embarrassment by revealing conflict and competing perspectives when public discourse demands that such power plays be airbrushed out of the picture. It therefore seems particularly threatened by tendencies evident in the 1980s, and even more evident today, toward an axiomatic and often authoritarian style of policy-making. The threat is not so much that it may not get funded, though this remains a possibility as the example shows, but that it is simply dismissed or quietly ignored if it fails to endorse the prevailing orthodoxy.

Example 2

The second example shares some of the concerns arising in the first. The issue in question – the private finance initiative (PFI) as an example of a perceived creeping privatization of the NHS that is being undertaken largely by stealth in the absence of public debate – is an even hotter issue politically than managerialism.

At the time, Professor Allyson Pollock and her research team were based at UCL (Pollock has since moved to a new chair post at the University of Edinburgh). They stood out as having tenaciously (and some would say courageously) exposed many of the flaws and shortcomings of the PFI as a way of funding capital developments in the NHS, notably hospitals. In her book, *NHS plc*, she recounts the growing opposition within government to her detailed critique of the PFI and the pernicious attempts to discredit her work (Pollock 2005).

In response to growing criticism of its marketization policies, and the PFI in particular, the government established a 'rapid rebuttal unit' in the press office of the Department of Health. Whenever a paper appeared that was critical of the PFI and of government policy, the department would issue a press release claiming that the analysis was wrong or that the researchers did not understand how care was delivered or how hospitals worked, but without entering into any serious exchange on the merits of the work. If these tactics designed to counter inconvenient research data failed to discredit the researchers, then they were simply dismissed as ideologically unsound and therefore academically suspect.

Professor Pollock recounts how she personally became a target for the government's 'bullying, threats and intimidation' (Pollock 2005). Her account shows the lengths to which the government was willing to go to shield its market-driven health policies from objective analysis, especially one which challenged the direction of policy.

Professor Pollock was invited to be a special adviser to the House of Commons Health Committee on its inquiry into the PFI. Academics are frequently asked to serve as special advisers on inquiries, so the invitation was not unusual. She recalls a conversation with the then head of the PFI unit who took her aside to ask her whether it was wise or in her career interests to brief MPs against senior NHS officials. Professor Pollock was eventually dropped from her advisory position following the Health Committee's reconstitution after the May 2001 election.

Some concluding reflections – no hiding place

These two examples illustrate the argument that speaking truth to power can be a risky, frustrating and difficult business, especially when the stakes are high politically and the truth may be uncomfortable. Both of these factors can give rise to bad faith. In such circumstances, engaging policy-makers with evidence that may challenge their cherished assumptions and desires remains problematic.

The problem is becoming more acute in the NHS (in England at any rate) as a market-style system of competition and incentives is introduced by a government determined to drive through changes regardless of their efficacy or popularity. The policy is primarily being driven by ideology rather than evidence – or where evidence is cited it is selectively presented. Despite a belated move by policy-makers to invest in research to establish whether such changes will result in better public services or not, there is skepticism that the findings will be used selectively to support the reforms. In any event, the limited investment in research appears in marked contrast to the significant sums being invested in management consultants who are working at senior levels in a number of central government departments, notably the Department of Health (Craig 2006; Greer and Jarman 2007). Indeed, some of these consultants are bidding to evaluate the reforms to which they have contributed!

Of course, simplistic notions of evidence-based policy are unhelpful. A King's Fund study examining the application of evidence to policy and practice in respect of complex social interventions like Sure Start (a government program involving early interventions to improve children's social and educational welfare) asked to what extent these programs are evidence-based, what is being done to find out if they work and whether the evaluations are helping to inform policy and practice (Coote et al. 2004). Unsurprisingly, the conclusion reached is that programmes like Sure Start are largely driven by informed guesswork, expert hunches, political and other imperatives.

Where evidence is used it is done so selectively to support preconceived assumptions. Indeed, the official evaluation of Sure Start recently published (the most expensive evaluation ever undertaken of a central government programme) is critical of the programme. Paradoxically, it has widened inequalities instead of reducing them. This may be a failure of implementation rather than of the programme itself, in which case the research findings should be helpful in refocusing the initiative. But because Sure Start is seen as a flagship policy and a tangible illustration of the Chancellor's (now Prime minister) crusade against child poverty, there is a tendency either to reject any criticism of it or simply to ignore it.

Should researchers whose work seriously challenges the prevailing orthodoxy remain neutral or passive bystanders, or become unwitting accomplices in bad faith? Or should they become vocal advocates for what their findings reveal?

As researchers we could simply take the view that our job is done once the research is done and, with any luck, in the public domain for all to see. It is then for others to use it in seeking to influence policy and practice. But this would be to reject Wildavsky's belief that policy analysts, including many researchers, have a moral duty to speak truth to power and in a way that guarantees a hearing.

For many reasons, some of which have been touched on here, the funding of critical policy research seems certain to become more difficult in future. Research findings that generate political embarrassment by revealing conflict and competing perspectives are unlikely to be accorded priority when being 'on message' and managing the media have become so central to the conduct of political life. Public policy and its delivery have become so politicized that it is virtually impossible for managers and practitioners to voice dissent and speak truth to power even if they might wish to (and do so in private). Too often those managers and practitioners are seen as part of the problem rather than its solution. It seems likely that much policy research is viewed in a similar light.

There are other factors at work, too. As has already been suggested, much policy research does not produce easy or quick answers. It may do no more than offer critical perspectives, illuminating issues and asking awkward questions. Though often valuable in themselves, none of this is welcome or terribly fashionable in these instrumental times where the natural science model remains dominant and where clear answers expressing good news are wanted rather than negative comment. We live in a modern, progressive era where any change axiomatically has to be for the better. Or so we are led to believe. An alternative reading of history is that the assumption of 'progress' is misplaced. Certain changes neither improve on the present nor represent progress. As Gray (2003) has written, 'in truth there are only humans, using the growing knowledge given them by science to pursue their conflicting ends'.

As was argued at the start of this chapter, perhaps what is needed is to move toward the interactive model of policy-making where the search for knowledge moves beyond research to include other sources such as politics and interests in order to reflect the complexity of policy-making. But to achieve this requires a closer ongoing dialogue between policy-makers and researchers that is extremely rare.

With the RAE exerting a stranglehold over universities and the type of research undertaken – a process in which many academics only too willingly collude – policy relevant and/or applied research remains unattractive and of low status. Furthermore, policy-relevant research is not generally valued despite the alleged desire for it. Finally, funding for research is becoming much tighter and tougher. The introduction of full economic costs (FEC) in 2005 is likely over time to reduce the overall amount of research funding available as well as increase dependence on government departments and the major research councils. There will also be implications for the type and range of research undertaken.

Such developments, if they come to pass, are both worrying and short-sighted. To return to where we began, with Wildavsky's reflections on the art and craft of policy analysis, we need research and analysis of the type that both challenges and seeks to understand the nature of policy and its impact – that is, strong policy research that is prepared to speak truth to power and occasionally to rock the boat. Otherwise we will continue to accumulate knowledge and stockpile research findings that simply tell us what we already know and goodness knows we have enough of these already. But if that is all we do as researchers, then we are seriously failing in our moral duty to speak truth to power. There can be no hiding place.

References

Barnes, M., Bauld, L., Benzeval, M., Judge, K., Mackenzie, M. and Sullivan, H. (2005) *Health action zones: Partnerships for health equity*, London: Routledge.

Blackler, F. (2006) 'Chief executives and the modernisation of the English National Health Service', *Leadership*, 2(1), 5–30.

Bowen, S. and Zwi, A. B. (2005) 'Pathways to "evidence-informed" policy and practice: A framework for action', *PLoS Medicine*, 2(7), 600–605.

Coote, A., Allen, J. and Woodhead, D. (2004) *Finding out what works: Building knowledge about complex, community-based initiatives*, London: King's Fund.

Craig, D. (2006) *Plundering the public sector*, London: Constable.

Gray, J. (2003) *Al Qaeda and what it means to be modern*, London: Faber and Faber.

Greer, S. L. and Jarman, H. (2007) *The department of health and the civil service: From Whitehall to department of delivery to where?*, London: The Nuffield Trust.

Griffiths, R. (1983) *NHS management inquiry report*, London: Department of Health and Social Security.

Harrison, S., Hunter, D. J., Marnoch, G. and Pollitt, C. (1992) *Just managing: Power and culture in the National Health Service* Basingstoke: Macmillan.

Hunter, D. J. (2005) 'Choosing or losing health?', *Journal of Epidemiology and Community Health*, 59(12), 1010–1012.

Jochelson, K. (2006) 'Nanny or steward? The role of government in public health', *Public Health*, 120(12), 1149–1155.

Marmot, M. (2004) 'Evidence based policy or policy based evidence?', *British Medical Journal*, 328, 906–907.

Plsek, P. and Greenhalgh, T. (2001) 'The challenge of complexity in health care', *British Medical Journal*, 323, 625–628.

Pollitt, C., Harrison, S., Hunter, D. J. and Marnoch, G. (1990) 'No hiding place: On the discomforts of researching the contemporary policy process', *Journal of Social Policy*, 19(2), 169–190.

Pollock, A. (2005) *NHS plc*, London: Verso Books.

Stewart, J. (1998) 'Advance or retreat: From the traditions of public administration to the new public management and beyond', *Public Policy and Administration*, 13(4), 12–27.

Wanless, D. (2004) *Securing good health for the whole population. Final report*, London: HM Treasury.

Wildavsky, A. (1979) *The art and craft of policy analysis*, Basingstoke: Macmillan.

8
It's Part of the Job: Healthcare Restructuring and the Health and Safety of Nursing Aides

Michael J. O'Sullivan, C. Eduardo Siqueira, Kathy Sperrazza, Ainat Koren, Karen Devereaux Melillo, Lee Ann Hoff, Edna M. White-O'Sullivan and Craig Slatin

Introduction

> You name every vulgar thing, it's been said. I've been scratched, I've been bit, I've been punched in the face, I've been slapped in the face, been kicked. I've been run over by the wheelchair. The guy like ran me over on purpose and started laughing. (Focus group participant)

> We get yelled at with four letter curse words and we get it from family members, doctors and residents. And that's part of our job. (Focus group participant)

The theme of this conference is 'speaking truth to power'. This chapter describes how restructuring of the healthcare system in America during the 1990s facilitated on-going exploitation of nursing aides in long-term care facilities. Many nursing aides suffer significant physical and psychological injuries by patients. We question why these came to be generally accepted as 'part of the job' by both nursing assistants and management. This was a truth known to those in power but a burden carried by those who had little or no power to remedy the situation.

Using data collected from case studies conducted by the PHASE in Healthcare Research Project, funded by the US National Institute for Occupational Safety and Health (NIOSH) to study health disparities among healthcare workers, we investigated the apparent paradox that long-term nursing facilities, whose purpose is to preserve and protect the health of their residents, can be one of the most dangerous and unhealthy places for nursing aides to work.

Nursing home industry

There are over 18,000 nursing homes in the United States employing 1.6 million people to care for 2.5 million residents (Health, United States 2004, 2005). Over 75% of nursing home residents are sufficiently disabled that they cannot perform three or more activities of daily living. About half the long-term care employees, or about 8 million, are nursing aides and nurses. In these facilities nursing aides, rather than nurses, provide the bulk of the direct care to residents (Act now for your tomorrow 2005). The Office of the Inspector General stated that

> Nursing homes operate in an environment of high staff turnover where it is difficult to attract, train and retain an adequate work-force. Turnover among nurse's aides, who provide most of the actual hands-on care in nursing homes, means that residents are constantly receiving care from new staff that often lack experience and know-ledge of their patients. Furthermore, research correlates staff shortages and insufficient training with substandard care. (Grob 2005)

Addressing appropriate minimum nurse staffing ratios, the Centre for Medicare and Medicaid Services called for the creation of a nursing home culture which valued and respected nursing aides and nurses, and was honored by management and the workers themselves (Fuerburg 2001).

Organizational culture of healthcare

The culture of healthcare facilities has come to be accepted as an important determinant of quality of care (Sikorska-Simmons 2006). Furthermore, a 'culture change' movement spreading across the country in long-term care aims to improve quality by changing culture with these institutions (Eaton 2000). A study of nuclear energy workers (Harvery and Erdos 2002) described organizational climate as the way individuals perceive the culture and how it affects the workers' feelings of safety. Lundstrom et al. (2002) describe safety climate as the 'shared percep-tions of workers regarding the level of safety in their work environment'. The safety climate of organizations is an outgrowth of the presence and magnitude of known hazards and the persistence or resistance to removing them by management and workers. Schein (2004) characterizes organizational culture as

A pattern of shared basic assumptions that was learned by a group as it solved its problems... [and] that has worked well enough to be considered valid and, therefore, to be taught to new members as the correct way to perceive, think and feel in relation to those problems. (p.17)

Organizational culture is learned and accepted by new members through socialization and acculturation processes. A nursing home's safety climate is derived from the organizational culture, an expression of values, norms and unspoken expectations about how to feel, speak and behave while a member of the organization. Moreover, management style is an important determinant of organizational culture (Cohen and Fink 2001) and the emergent safety climate.

Management has the responsibility for minimizing exposure to health and safety risks for patients and workers and, despite an extensive body of literature and government reports identifying and proposing various remedies for reducing the number of injuries in nursing homes, injuries persist at very high levels (Waehrer et al. 2005). One wonders how the incidents described above by the nursing aides came about, why they persist and what steps managers and workers can take to deliver quality care without exposing nursing aides to excessive verbal and physical assaults.

Nursing homes in America have had a very dubious reputation for the care provided to residents or as an attractive place to work (Eaton 2000; Vladeck 1980). For nursing aides, the work is often difficult, dirty and unrewarding (Gass 2004). Investigations in the 1990s by the General Accounting Office and the Inspector General documented serious patient problems in nursing homes including malnutrition, dehydration, pressure sores, abuse and neglect beyond expectations (Fuerburg 2001). In the face of public outcries, congressional hearings concluded that inadequate nurse staffing, including nursing aides, was a root cause of many of the patients' problems (Rantz et al. 2004). Moreover, estimates of the total cost of turnover of nurses and aides, who left because of the work, was estimated to be over $1 billion a year, or an average of $250,000 per nursing home per year, a substantial sum for most facilities.

A major restructuring of the healthcare system that occurred in the 1990s was not designed to remedy the problems of high staff turnover and the resulting poor care, but primarily to contain rising costs. Restructuring meant level government funding for nursing homes and a shift from fee-for-service reimbursement to per-diem rates by insurers, including Medicaid, which pays the lion's share of nursing home costs, and significant realignment of the nursing home workforce (Coburn 2004; Zhang and Grabowski 2004). Instead of resolving the problems, restructuring driven by cost containment appears to have compounded them.

Restructuring resulted in staff downsizing accomplished by laying off staff and closing or merging nursing homes or otherwise 'right-sizing' the facilities (Gordon 2005). Nursing departments were the prime targets of downsizing (Fagin 2001) with many nurses fired or relegated to involuntary part-time work. The result was an intensification of nursing care and a de-skilling of the nursing workforce with nursing aides performing what were formerly professional nursing duties (Greiner 1996; Preuss 1998). This placed high levels of stress and discontent on nursing aides left in the facilities to soldier on. Nursing absorbed a disproportionate burden of reductions and nurses felt angered about being devalued, underpaid and because they could not provide the care they believed their patients needed (Heitlinger 2003).

Healthcare spending cuts

Many studies have mistakenly concluded that healthcare, because of its labor intensity, is a very inefficient enterprise and calling for greater efficiency by 'cutting the fat' with reductions in force (DeMoro 2000; Fagin 2001). When cuts began, many nurses chose to resign rather than accept degraded working conditions (Ulrich et al. 2002). Nursing aides, with generally fewer skills and less economic independence than nurses, quit as well. Turnover rates among nursing aides, which had already been high, soared to new levels. According to one report, nursing staff turnover in long-term care averaged 49% for registered nurses and 71% for nursing aides by 2002 (Howard 2005).

But, nursing aide positions were ones the industry needed to fill because most of the labor in nursing homes is not nursing but personal care. Consequently, low-skilled individuals were hired to fill the vacant positions but with a new twist. The new hires were often immigrants with limited English, from different races and cultural backgrounds. The length of training was short, three weeks at most, when they were assigned to nursing floors with equally inexperienced workers with similarly poor English skills. With fewer staff and the constant merry-go-round of turnover, working conditions were very stressful, often contentious and sometimes combative. Aides rapidly burned out and left for greener pastures, only to be replaced with similar individuals (General Accounting Office 2001) and, thus, the cycle was perpetuated. Newly arrived immigrants were anxious to take the jobs, using the nursing aide positions as portals into the domestic job market. However, new cultural and racial tensions were added to the already pressurized brew within the inadequately staffed nursing home workplace.

Health and safety in nursing homes

Healthcare is generally regarded by the public as a clean and safe environment but injury statistics for nursing homes belie this commonly held view. There are myriad hazards in nursing homes including infectious agents, poisonous chemicals and daunting physical demands of lifting and moving patients. In an analysis of Bureau of Labour Statistics (BLS) data, Waehrer et al. (2005) showed that occupational injury and illness rates in healthcare exceeded those for all private industry and the rate for nursing and personal care facilities (17.3 injuries per FTE/year) was more than double (8.5 per FTE/year) that of all industries combined. These facilities had injury and illness rates higher than agriculture, coal mining and construction, industries generally regarded as the most hazardous in the country. These data are part of a growing body of evidence associating specific occupational stressors with the incidence and prevalence of occupational accidents and illnesses (Flynn and Deatrick 2003; OSHA 2003; Rantz 2003, 2004; Schnelle 2004; Zhang and Grabowski 2004).

Workplace violence in nursing homes

Nursing aides in our study reported numerous instances of physical and verbal assaults and abuse. Verbal assaults were generally committed by residents against staff, but family members and fellow staff members were perpetrators as well. Assaults included slapping, punching, kicking, spitting, biting, pinching and scratching by residents. Staff repeatedly played down patient assaults as a consequence of patients' impaired mental states and often did not hold patients responsible for their behavior, nor did they always report the assaults to management.

Staff believed patients' dissatisfaction with the quality of care was a driving force behind assaults, but also related assaults to racism and discrimination. They described abusive and difficult encounters between patients and aides with different ethnic, racial or cultural backgrounds of the mostly white, female and elderly residents. Moreover, similar differences often accounted for verbal and physical assaults and abuse occurring among nursing aides themselves.

Management was aware of the behaviors and responded to incidents of chronic hostility. Management interventions included family meetings, behavior management plans and, ultimately, transfer of assaultive patients to other facilities better equipped to care for them. While abuse guidelines were in place in each facility, our analysis found that they focused exclusively on abuse of residents by staff and neglected the phenomenon of abuse on staff by residents.

Management dismissed workplace assaults as major problems at either facility, placing it relatively low on their list of concerns. Management also expressed the belief that they adequately trained their staff to report assaults, that staff actually reported incidents and that management took appropriate action to investigate and rectify the situations. This turned out to be a misconception at best or at worst, a deliberate oversight. Each facility used the MOST (Method Oriented Safety Thinking) Training System as the in-service program for general health and safety training. MOST places primary responsibility for accidents and injuries on workers and is based on the concept that aides trained in 'safe behaviors and practices' will reduce accidents and injuries (Ljungberg and Kilborn 1989). Critics of MOST believe that it ignores the role of safety systems, such as lifting devices or adequate staffing, and focuses excessively on worker behaviors as remedies for injuries. Moreover, nursing aides reported that when management investigated accidents they often looked for what workers did wrong and labeled the aides as 'the cause' rather than critically examining the facility's safety systems. This practice puts major responsibility for injuries on the backs of workers and minimizes the role of management.

Both facilities had safety committees responsible for safety surveillance, compliance with regulations, investigating incidents of injuries and ensuring follow-up training and retraining. In general, staff believed safety training programs were helpful and increased their awareness of various risks. However, one respondent believed management used in-service training to shift the burden of negligence to injured workers rather than focusing on management practices. Also, one facility used financial incentive programs to reward staff for decreased injuries.

However, it was unclear if incentives caused staff to be more cautious or simply discouraged reporting of injuries because of peer pressure to win the rewards by not reporting them. The facility discontinued the incentive program believing the benefits did not warrant the cost. The administrator acknowledged that though not intended, the program probably discouraged reporting.

Reporting and severity

Workers said they often did not report assaults or abuse when they were not seriously injured. Injuries which were not accompanied by immediate and severe pain, did not break the skin or were not recurrent were often ignored. Many workers said they did not report injuries or assaults because they did not know the procedure or did not have the time or understanding to fill out the required paperwork. This was particularly common among workers with limited English. Additionally, their experiences convinced them that often they did not get the hoped-for management support. Consequently, assaults and abuse came to be accepted as 'part of the job'. Within the organizational cultures of the facilities, workers came to expect and accept verbal and physical assaults by patients and had been acculturated to accepting them as part of normal working conditions and, therefore, they tended to disregard them.

Management and workers' compensation

Management accepted assaults as 'part of the job' as well, as long as worker compensation costs remained relatively stable. However, compensation costs are inaccurate, only 'the tip of the iceberg', as we found injury reporting policies poorly administered and record keeping haphazard, despite the safety committees and regulations. Workers' compensation benefits appeared to be neither accurately nor fully explained in the employment orientation materials we examined.

In addition, aides often viewed filing workers' compensation claims as confusing and as placing their jobs in jeopardy because they might be fired if labeled trouble makers. In addition, aides felt that compensation cash benefits were inadequate to live on. They believed the 'blame the victim' attitude of management was duplicated by workers' compensation adjusters. It appeared that these beliefs further suppressed accurate workers' compensation reporting and accounting.

Discussion

Values are at the core of organizational culture and can be either espoused or enacted. Espoused values are those that organizations declare they prize and are often highlighted in mission statements and similar documents. Enacted values are ones organizations actually put into practice. Gaps between what are espoused and actually enacted can be assessed by observing emergent staff and management behaviors (Schein 2004). We, as organizational behavior specialists, can identify gaps between espoused and enacted values, address why gaps may have developed and posit how differences may be narrowed with improvement to individual safety as well as organizational performance. The attitude of accepting assaults as 'part of the job' by aides and management indicates a gap between espoused beliefs about worker safety versus enacted policies and procedures which put aides and others at risk for assaults and abuse. Gordon (2005) believes this attitude is simply taken-for-granted pervasive throughout healthcare. Its origins may be traced to archaic practices but its remnants persist to this day, acting as a behavioral guide for nursing aides, nurses and management.

Restructuring, competitive pressures and commodification

Before restructuring, healthcare facilities competed with each other with the latest state-of-the art technologies and services, but not on price. Many patients neither knew nor cared about the cost of their healthcare. Healthcare facilities operated under fee-for-service reimbursement where costs were shifted to insurers, then passed on to the companies offering the insurance benefit and then ultimately to consumers as increased premiums and deductibles and to taxpayers as increased taxes. Governments, corporations and eventually consumers grew concerned with the unrelenting increases in costs. Globalization and job loss swelled the ranks of the uninsured, while the simultaneous shifting of financial risk to consumers increased out-of-pocket expenses. Obviously, such open-ended reimbursement could not be sustained indefinitely. Cost containment, whether in the form of HMOs or other managed competition schemes, became the fundamental justification for restructuring. Healthcare was subjected to demands found in other industries, namely production pressures versus worker safety. Competitive pressures imposed by market-based price-competition brought about a clash where profit and organizational survival conflicted with quality care (Lamm 2003) and worker safety.

Under restructuring, management attempted to rationalize inadequate staffing. While the intensity of care increased and resources decreased with workforce cutbacks, workers were asked to sacrifice their welfare for the good of patients and the facility. However, this position was never overtly expressed. However, the oft-repeated mantra of managers to staff of 'no margin, no mission' signified either to get the work done regardless of staffing or see additional job losses and ultimately closure of the facility. However, this 'survival of the fittest' mentality was a new development representing the ascendance of market-based, corporate perspectives rather than a public interest and patient-centered approach (Geyman 2004).

America, by 2000, found itself entangled in a private, market-based health insurance system which stood in stark contrast to the socialized insurance systems of other western countries where national healthcare expenditures were much lower and health status significantly higher (Woolhandler and Himmelstein 2004). However, the real, but short-lived, savings of restructuring imposed a levy which had to be paid. Later studies conclusively demonstrated that patients and workers during restructuring paid the price of the ill-conceived cost containment schemes. Payment was extracted with excessive deaths and injuries to patients, and persistently high injury rates for workers (Institute of Medicine 1999; Needleman et al. 2001, 2002, 2006). Market-driven, price-competitive restructuring ultimately proved to be neither efficient nor effective.

Conclusion

Quality patient care and safety are extremely important in healthcare and more often than not trump employee health and safety concerns. But no matter how worthy quality patient care and safety are, if not viewed within a context of a dynamic interactive system which includes the health and safety of the workers, the consequences may be serious and unintended to both patients and staff. Addressing this dilemma, a nurse said

> often there's no other way, this is just part of the job. When faced at the time with a decision of choosing between a patient with an immediate need and a potential injury that doesn't seem too real at the time, we will most likely choose the patient if we see no other alternative. There are so many simultaneous pressures that it feels

like shoveling against the tide. The realities get the best of what you may know is the right way to do something.

Our study indicates that assaults and injuries are accepted as part of the job and often go unreported and untreated, and consequently uncorrected. Breslin et al. (2006) found a similar, accepting 'part of the job' attitude and consequences particularly among younger male workers. Injury rates are extremely high in nursing homes and there are likely many more unreported ones. It appears that healthcare restructuring, with its emphasis on cost containment, instead of improving a dire situation in many nursing homes, reinforced an already perverted self-defeating and dangerous culture.

So where do we go from here?

Unionized activism and political action have led to greater public awareness of inadequate nursing services. California became the first state mandating staffing levels for hospitals, and similar legislative efforts occurred in other states. Attention to the hazards of health-care work was raised by unions and occupational health researchers. In Massachusetts, awareness of the health and safety of patients and workers led to the Massachusetts Nurses Association negotiating contracts with more emphasis on safety systems as well as better education (Wilson et al. 2006). Nursing aides, with much less insti-tutionalized power and prestige and often limited legal rights due to their immigration status, are at greater risk for continuing exploit-ation. Union organizing historically has been a road to improve-ment for impoverished workers and the Service Employees Interna-tional Union (SEIU) has made significant gains in organizing these workers.

Rather than protecting workers so they can adequately and safely provide quality care and take pride in their work and workplace, managers have chosen to sustain cultures that foster acceptance of personal injury as part of the job. Workers predictably leave these organ-izations in search of safer and less stressful employment, while care to the chronically ill and elderly residents of nursing homes remains a national problem.

We believe that the market competition in healthcare fostered by restructuring conflicted with worker health and safety as well as the health and safety of patients. When caring for the chronically ill and elderly is done with insufficiently trained and inadequate numbers of staff, we should not be surprised to encounter cultures with high worker injury rates and poor patient care and safety. Competitive practices, combined with the inherently dangerous nature of patient care, and a vulnerable and weak labor pool constitute a potent formula for assaults on and injuries to workers. The power driving healthcare restructuring in the 1990s went in the wrong direction, a truth not acknowledged by power even today.

References

Act Now for Your Tomorrow (April, 2005) 'Commission on nursing workforce for long-term care', Washington, DC: Final Report National.

Breslin, F. C., Polzer, J., MacEachen, E., Morrongiell, B., and Shannon, H. (2006) 'Workplace injury or "part of the job?": Towards a gendered understanding of injuries and complaints among young workers', *Social Science & Medicine*, 64, 782–793.

Coburn, D. (2004) 'Beyond the income inequality hypothesis: class, neo-liberalism, and health inequalities', *Social Science & Medicine*, 58, 41–56.

Cohen, A. R. and Fink, S. L. (2001) *Effective behavior in organizations*, 7th ed., New York: McGraw-Hill/Irwin.

DeMoro, D. (2000) 'Engineering a crisis: How hospitals created a shortage of nurses', *Revolution*, 1, 16–23.

Eaton, S. E. (2000) 'Beyond "unloving care" ', *International Journal of Human Resource Management*, 11(3), 591–616.

Fagin, C. M. (2001) *When care becomes a burden: Diminishing access to adequate nursing*, New York: Milbank Memorial Fund.

Flynn, L. and Deatrick, J. A. (2003) 'Home care nurses' description of important agency attributes', *Journal of Nursing Scholarship*, 35, 385–390.

Fuerburg, M. (2001) *Appropriateness of minimum nurse staffing ratios in nursing homes*, Phase II Final Report, December, Washington, DC: Centers for Medicare and Medicaid Services.

Gass, T. (2004) *Nobody's home: Candid reflections of a nursing home aide*, Ithaca, NY: ILR Press.

General Accounting Office (2001) *Nursing workforce: Recruitment and retention of nurses and nurse is a growing problem*, Washington, DC: Senate Committee on Health, Education, Labor and Pensions.

Geyman, J. P. (2004) *The corporate transformation of health care*, New York: Springer.

Gordon, S. (2005) *Nursing against the odds: How health care cost cutting, media stereotypes, and medical hubris undermine nurses and patient care. The culture and politics of health care work*, Ithaca, NY: ILR Press.

Greiner, A. (1996) *Impacts of hospital restructuring on nursing*, Washington, DC: Economic Policy Institute.

Grob, G. (2005) *Emerging practices in nursing homes*, Washington, DC: Office of the Inspector General.

Harvery, J. and Erdos, G. (2002) 'An analysis of safety culture attitudes in a highly regulated environment', *Work and Stress*, 16(1), 18–36.

Health, United States, 2004 (2005) Washington, DC: National Center for Health Statistics.

Heitlinger, A. (2003) 'The paradoxical impact of health care restructuring in Canada on nursing as a profession', *International Journal of Health Services*, 33(1), 37–54.

Howard, E. (2005) *Act now for your tomorrow*, Washington, DC: National Commission on Nursing Workforce for Long-Term Care.

Institute of Medicine (1999) *To err is human: Building a safer health system*, Washington, DC: National Academy Press.

Lamm, R. D. (2003) *The brave new world of health care: What every American needs to know about our impending health care crisis*, Golden, CO: Fulcrum Publishing.

Ljungberg, A. and Kilborn, A. (1989) 'Occupational lifting by nurses and warehouse workers', *Ergonomics*, 32(1), 59–78.

Lundstrom, T., Pugliese, G., Bartley, J., Cox, J. and Guither, C. (2002) 'Organizational and environmental factors that affect worker health and safety and patient outcomes', *American Journal of Infection Control*, 30(2), 93–106.

Needleman, J., Buerhaus, P. I., Mattke, S., Stewart, M. and Zelevinsky, K. (2001) *Nurse staffing and patient outcomes in hospitals*, Boston, MA: US Department of Health and Human Services and Harvard School of Public Health.

Needleman, J., Peter, B., Soeren, M., Maureen, S. and Katya, Z. (2002) 'Nurse staffing levels and the quality of care in hospitals', *New England Journal of Medicine*, 346(22), 1715–1722.

Needleman, J., Buerhaus, P. I., Stewart, M., Zelevinsky, K. and Mattke, S. (2006) 'Nurse staffing in hospitals: Is there a business case for quality?', *Health Affairs*, 25(1), 204–211.

OSHA (2003) *Guidelines for preventing workplace violence for health-care and social-service workers*, Washington, DC: US Occupational Safety and Health Administration, US Department of Labor.

Preuss, G. (1998) *Sharing care – the changing nature of nursing in hospitals*, Washington, DC: Economic Policy Institute.

Rantz, M. J., Hicks, L., Grando, V., Petroski, G. F., Madsen, R. W., Mehr, D. R. and Conn, V. e. a. (2004) 'Nursing home quality, cost, staffing and staff mix', *The Gerontologist*, 44(1), 24–38.

Schein, E. H. (2004) *Organizational culture and leadership*, 3rd ed., San Francisco, CA: Jossey-Bass.

Schnelle, J. F. (2004) 'Determining the relationship between staffing and quality', *Gerontologist*, 44, 10–12.

Sikorska-Simmons, E. (2006) 'Organizational culture and work related attitudes among staff in assisted living', *Journal of Gerontological Nursing*, February, 19–27.

Ulrich, C. M., Wallen, G., Grady, C., Foley, M. E., Rosenstein, A. H., Rabetoy, C. A. P. and Miller, B. H. (2002) 'The nursing shortage and the quality of care', *New England Journal of Medicine*, 347, 1118–1119.

Vladeck, B. C. (1980) *Unloving care*, New York: Twentieth Century Fund.

Waehrer, G., Leigh, J. P. and Miller, T. R. (2005) 'Costs of occupational injury and illness within the health services sector', *International Journal of Health Services*, 35(2), 343–359.

Wilson, B., Slatin, C. and O'Sullivan, M. (2006) 'Nurses respond to healthcare restructuring', *Journal of Health and Social Policy*, 21(4), 51–72.

Woolhandler, S. and Himmelstein, D. U. (2004) 'The high costs of for-profit care', *Canadian Medical Association Journal*, 170(12), 1814–1815.

Zhang, X. and Grabowski, D. C. (2004) 'Nursing home staffing and quality under the nursing home reform act', *Gerontologist*, 44(1), 13–23.

9
Chasing Chameleons, Chimeras and Caterpillars: Evaluating an Organizational Innovation in the National Health Service

Catherine Pope, Andrée le May and John Gabbay

Introduction

Although some might argue that too little attention is paid to the evaluation of health service innovations, evaluation research has burgeoned alongside the ubiquitous healthcare reform of the UK NHS which escalated under the Conservative government of the 1980s and has continued under the Labour government since the late 1990s. In terms of funding and activity health service evaluation is something of an industry: to give just one example the NHS Service Delivery and Organization (SDO) R&D Programme has spent some £6m since 2002 funding research to evaluate models of service delivery (http:/www/sdo.lshtm.ac.uk). Evaluative research is a quest for evidence and an answer to 'what works (or doesn't) for whom in which context?' often driven by a desire to inform the change process. This chapter is about one particular evaluative research project which examined an organizational innovation introduced as part of wider NHS reforms undertaken by the New Labour government. Our focus is not on answering the 'what works' question per se, but instead we critically examine what makes evaluation research difficult. We draw on our experience of researching one innovation, but the challenges arising from the specifics of this particular project are not unique; indeed we argue that the chameleons, chimeras and caterpillars we encountered may well be persistent features of evaluative research.

Between 2003 and 2006 we studied the implementation of NHS Treatment Centres (TCs) (Bate et al. 2007). We sought to identify the organizational and social factors associated with the implementation process, outcomes and ultimately the success (or otherwise) of this new model of delivery. The study design was longitudinal; we were anxious to capture the 'dynamics and effects of time, process, discontinuity and context' (Pettigrew et al. 2001:697). We were also interested in the influence of power and politics within and across multiple organizational levels (Pettigrew et al. 2001; Poole and Van de Ven 2004) and were therefore concerned to examine the relationships between the emerging TCs and their host organizations and the Primary Care Trusts (PCTs), strategic health authorities (SHAs) and the central government environment which surrounded them. Our research team was multi-disciplinary drawing on allegiances to organizational science, sociology and anthropology, professional backgrounds in nursing and medicine and operational research expertise. Despite collectively having spent many years researching health services, we were perhaps unprepared for the slippery, elusive nature of our research subject. It is this aspect of evaluation we describe in this chapter.

The NHS treatment centre programme

TCs (initially called Diagnostic and Treatment Centres) were one of a series of government-led initiatives directed at hospital waiting lists outlined in the *NHS Plan* (Department of Health 2000). They were modelled on 'surgi-centres' found in the USA since the 1970s and on the Ambulatory Care and Diagnosis centre (ACAD) set up in London in the 1990s. In essence TCs entailed the separation of elective (i.e. planned) surgery from emergency treatment, to ensure that unpredictable emergency work did not interrupt the flow of planned admissions. The *NHS Plan* proposed developing some 20 TCs, some within the NHS and some in the private sector, but by the end of 2005 there were 80 NHS and independent sector centres (IS-TCs), undertaking an additional 250,000 operations per year. TCs were meant to go beyond redesigning spaces and patient flows to embrace a whole new philosophy of care. They represented a fundamental rethink, a 'new way of working', firmly centred on the patient. In organizational change terms TCs heralded 'second-order' transformation, not 'first-order' incremental change (Seo et al. 2004). The Modernisation Agency (MA), which had been created to oversee and guide NHS modernization, had the task of coordinating a collaborative programme to support TCs. The MA defined the core characteristics of TCs (Box 9.1)

Box 9.1 NHS Modernization Agency's 'Defining Characteristics of a TC' (2003)

'The Goal of a Treatment Centre is to deliver high quality, cost effective scheduled diagnostic and/or treatment services that optimize service efficiency and clinical outcomes and maximize patient satisfaction.

The Defining Characteristics of a Treatment Centre are that

1. it embodies throughout its life the very best and most forward thinking practice in the design and delivery of the services it provides.
2. it delivers a high volume of activity in a pre-defined range of routine treatments and/or diagnostics
3. it delivers scheduled care that is not affected by demand for, or provision of, unscheduled care either on the same site or elsewhere
4. its services are streamlined and modern, using defined patient pathways
5. its services are planned and booked, with an emphasis on patient choice and convenience together with organizational ability to deliver
6. it has a clear and trusted identity that is valued by its patients and by its other stakeholders
7. it provides a high quality, positive patient experience
8. it creates a positive environment that enhances the working lives of the people who work in it
9. it adds significantly to the capacity of the NHS to treat its patients successfully'

http://www.modern.nhs.uk/scripts/default.asp?site_id=31
(viewed 29/05/04)

The TC project

Our evaluation adopted a case study design (Eisenhardt 1989; Yin 2003), principally using organizationally focused interviews, supported by observation and documentary analysis, to build up detailed descriptions of the development and implementation of eight TCs. While much of the fieldwork was located at the micro-level, we also studied meso- and macro-levels (SHA, PCT and national agencies such as the MA and Department of Health). Cases were purposively selected to represent differences in scale, type and geographical location. One TC (I) closed early on in the fieldwork and was replaced. These cases ranged from relatively small-scale initiatives (a single ward, site A), a 'virtual' TC (I), to what were in essence 'mini-hospitals' (sites C and F) treating twice as many patients as the smallest site (site B). Some TCs were new (stage 2 of site A), others were extensions to (sites B, E, F and H) or refurbishments of facilities within the 'host' organization (sites D and G). The earliest date of opening was in 2000 (stage I of site A) with the latest (stage 2 of site A) scheduled to open in 2007–08.

We conducted some 200 interviews with key stakeholders from the TCs, the 'host' organizations and a range of external 'stakeholders' (such as service commissioners from PCTs and SHAs). Additional data were derived from non-participant observation of management meetings and national events and documentary sources including business plans, minutes, architectural drawings, photographs, web material and patient information leaflets.

Findings

Given this volume of data, the task of evaluating TCs should have been straightforward. Yet throughout the analysis we were confronted by the sense that our subject was metamorphosing, continually, during the research. Our analytical notes, instead of providing answers, were full of questions like, what is a TC? Is case 'A' really a TC? The case studies seldom resembled the TC specification in macro-level policy – whether in the original *NHS Plan* or its operationalization by the MA, or TCs as conceived in our project proposal. The research object, the 'thing' being evaluated did not appear to exist. In its place we found misrepresentation, adaptation and evolution, which we began to refer to as chimeras, chameleons and caterpillars. Such is the nature of the metamorphosis that TCs resemble any or all of these three forms during their evolution, as we show below.

Chimera: a fabulous fire spouting monster with a lion's head, a serpent's tail and a goat's body; ... an organism made up of genetically distinct tissues.

Some of our TCs had this fabulous (in the literary sense) aspect in as much as they did not exist as declared. While it would be pushing the analogy too far to suggest these were fire spouting hybrids, these cases appeared to be amalgams of other forms of service delivery, extensions to other organizational innovations or simply current practice. Early visits to the case study sites led us to wonder whether or not some would manage to become full-fledged TCs. Those involved in Stage 1 of case 'A' (stage 1) aspired to TC status but made little progress in achieving this during the study. This TC remained a collection of existing services (a short stay ward for elective patients, designed to provide more flexible space to help the Trust make better use of beds and reduce trolley waits, a day surgery unit and a pre-operative assessment unit all on same site) and lacked the coherence of a TC envisaged by the *NHS Plan* or the MA. Ambitious plans for Stage 2, a new build where beds, theatres and diagnostic services would be clustered together, did not materialize during the timeframe of our project. The local health economy reviewed its priorities, and competition from other TCs increased, making the landscape more hostile and the development of Stage 2 unlikely.

Site I was billed as one of the 'first DTCs'. It was hailed in the Trust annual report as 'one of just four of its kind... [this] new centre, which part-opened in [date] will soon offer rapid diagnosis and treatment for patients in a wide variety of specialties, including orthopedics, general surgery, ophthalmology, ear, nose and throat and gynecology'. In the subsequent annual report the TC was still a strong presence, but was described as a 'virtual' centre – albeit next to an impressive photo-graph of new building work. On closer inspection this virtual designa-tion covered a series of 'projects' with various service modernization and waiting list reduction objectives. The deputy director of operations described how 'we pinched some rebuilding that was already going on in the Trust to provide some additional theatre and ward space'. Creative use of TC funding enabled the organization to open a new ward, run additional ophthalmic and orthopaedic surgery, provide additional day case facilities and to purchase a second MRI scanner. They also opened a delayed transfer ward – to provide a 'buffer zone' for patients that were about to be discharged or transferred to free up inpatient beds. Some of these initiatives were successful: the additional MRI scanner reduced waiting to 4 weeks and the deputy director of operations felt that 'modernization', such as the use of clinical pathways, had improved patient care and diffused into other areas of service delivery.

It was difficult to see how to evaluate this virtual TC. Beyond the glossy representations, the TC did not exist. We were anxious that all our chosen sites would have these chimerical qualities. In the event, this TC was short lived; in the 18 months following its first announcement the Chief Executive who had been largely responsible for championing it left the organization as the Trust went into a severe financial crisis. There followed a dramatic reprioritization and the new ward that had been perhaps the most visible, tangible element of the TC, closed. The virtual projects were dispersed or absorbed into other activities and the TC closed in the following year. By the time of the publication of the next annual report the TC had disappeared (a search on the term 'treatment centre' in the annual report produced 0 hits).

Chameleon: a small lizard famous for changing its colour; an inconstant, changeable or readily adaptable person.

Clearly, TCs are not lizards, but some of the sites appeared to share this reptilian adaptive capability for fading into the background of the wider organizational context in order to survive. Such was their ability to camouflage and blend in that these sites lost their innovative distinctiveness and settled for incremental rather than radical change.

Perhaps the strongest example of this was site C, a former private hospital bought by a neighbouring NHS Trust. Architecturally impressive and historically interesting this site continued to retain a private sector 'feel', even when owned by the NHS, such that staff commented on just how different this site was from typical NHS facilities:

It's really quite different. When you walk through the door, you notice that because there's a huge, marble atrium...we're very much advantaged here...we're opposite a big park, beautiful grounds...you see people out in the gardens alongside the fountain...And there are quite a few people who work here who could probably go and work somewhere else but I think they enjoy it so much that they just stay within the place. I think those sort of things come across to the patients as well. And I think when you're working in a place that is as aesthetically better looking, you can tell that the patients...we get letters all the time from patients saying, this is such a wonderful place. And it's probably because it looks...it's an NHS hospital but it's very private-looking...and it's got a very private feel about it. So that sort of thing comes through, probably from both staff and patients. (IT Manager)

The matron and several other key TC staff were former employees of the private hospital and they carried with them the culture and working practices of the previous administration. Staff talked about modernization in terms of mimicking the private sector. Architecture, history and culture coalesced to make this site resemble a private hospital.

However, this TC was underused and developed a large financial deficit. New managers were brought in and the Trust sought to manage this 'failing business'. Rather than cling on to the (expensive) private sector image and practices – predicated on a careful definition of suitable patients who fitted modernized care pathways and were suitable for fast-tracking through surgery – the TC began to take on any work it could find. This included more complicated, longer stay cases and 'loss leader' activity, much of which failed to cover costs. While the impressive architecture remained, the TC no longer resembled the wonderful private hospital and became (another) problematic part of the wider, troubled Trust.

Similar issues were encountered at site G where despite early attempts to forge an individual identity (including sticking steadfastly to the DTC designation, even when the 'D' had been dropped elsewhere) a growing financial crisis led the Trust management to re-absorb the TC into the existing Trust structure. Within three years, attempts to save the TC had failed and it was officially closed.

Caterpillar: A butterfly or moth grub which transforms into a chrysalis from which emerges a butterfly or moth.

Of course we are playing with the alliterative 'c's here, but the TCs which resembled caterpillars seemed to share this creature's potential for radical transformation into something quite different. One of the most interesting case studies was site F which embodied unrealized potential – a caterpillar which failed to transform. This site was initially designed as a multi-million pound extension to a new hospital. It planned to have one of the highest activity levels of our case studies, some 7000 extra cases per annum, and its design, processes and ambition (documented in the business case) and the architects' images resembled the MA specification of what a TC should be. The TC team worked on developing care pathways, thinking about the look and feel of the place, planning to increase and modernize activity on a grand scale. However, having successfully negotiated construction of the new building, the host Trust encountered financial and contractual problems. Key purchasers pulled out leaving the TC empty beds and in the absence of replacement activity the Trust was forced to retrench. It closed wards in the main hospital and 'mothballed' (closed and sealed) most of TC in order to open a small number of beds in the new building. This TC resembled some rare luna moth, emerging from its chrysalis only to find it had just a week to live.

A more positive transformation was found in site D. This site transformed, amid political furore and media attention, from a downgraded hospital with a clutch of day care beds into a state of the art TC. This transformation was strongly supported by the local community, the Trust 'top-team', local political activists and the TC staff. They all saw the TC as an opportunity to put the site 'on the map' by transforming local healthcare through the development of a high-quality service in a newly created modern, purpose-built environment. From inception this TC was expected to revolutionize healthcare in the local community and beyond. As the project progressed this vision became a reality transforming the old hospital into a new TC that was not only:

> lovely, ... Every time I go round there there's a feel of plenty of space and not many people and yet they are pushing through much more activity these days. ... But there is this feeling; it's not intimidating; it's very accessible and the whole experience seems to be very pleasant ... It's light and airy and very modern. It's more like walking into a modern library or modern building than a hospital which is great. ... It's not typical NHS and I think that's a good thing. We need to break the mould really of what the NHS currently looks like – fuddy duddy. (PCT Chief Executive)

But also one that was seen:

> as fulfilling the new consumerist model of care espoused by the government – care when you want it in a good environment. (Surgical manager)

This TC grasped the radical transformational opportunities presented by the TC initiative, in part drawing on the TC manager's extensive experience of a similar initiative, and used the MA blueprint to change from a run down hospital into a new, 'lovely' show-case TC. This transformational process, in common with the chameleon-like ability to blend into the background described earlier, makes evaluation tricky. It is difficult to pin down and follow the object of evaluation. While site D at least provided an object of study, a 'real' TC, it was so embedded in the peculiar local politics and dependent on particular personalities that it was difficult to see what might be learned. At times we asked, even of this site, 'is this a TC or just a way of keeping the hospital open?'

The examples above focus on the micro-level but there were equally important transformations in macro (government) policy and practice. These included apparently superficial changes such as the name change from DTC to TC, and major restructuring, such as the disbanding of the MA and the TC programme team. Government shifted focus onto the private sector TCs and introduced new initiatives including 'Patient Choice' (designed to allow patients greater choice about where they were treated) and 'payment by results' (PbR), which launched a new financial mechanism based on pre-set tariffs for activity. These initiatives cut across the intentions and practical feasibility of the TC programme, often working against them. Patient Choice introduced greater uncertainty about activity flows and spread patients more widely around the healthcare system, while PbR in some sites meant a reduction in the price they were paid for activity. Meanwhile health ministers with greater and lesser interest in TCs came and went, shifting the demands and the focus on the TC programme. Once a key motif in the Prime Minister's speeches, NHS TCs sank below the government's horizon and were seldom mentioned.

Discussion

This project raised three important questions. Firstly, how did a clearly prescribed initiative give rise to such diversity of product? TCs had a clear policy objective (i.e. the reduction in waiting times), a set of key defining features related to their development (MA desiderata) and a timeline to do it in. Yet they evolved differently from vision to product (some rapidly, some more slowly, some never), they were constructed to suit local needs rather than the national blueprint; they strove to stand out from each other rather than conform. A multiplicity of truths emerged. Quite apart from the divergence between the national and local policies, there was usually a wide range of perceptions about the nature and purpose of a given TC even within each local context.

Secondly, how can policy makers reconcile the need to achieve global political imperatives with the need for local diversity and creativity – the creation of a multiplicity of truths? Several of the TCs worked creatively, diverging from the blueprint in order to achieve something that would work for them and by doing this achieve the policy objectives required of them by an NHS whose prescriptions were in turn both muted and mutated by the realities of local implementation.

Thirdly, how can researchers expose and manage such an array of truths when there is an expectation of measuring success against (moving) targets and criteria defined by policy makers but which are being imperceptibly, perhaps deceptively, transformed by front line managers and staff? In this research environment the results may themselves become part of what is being studied. A positivist evaluative model reifies: we end up trying to measure local products against a politically constructed set of patterns that have little relevance or validity in local settings. Yet capturing the richness and variability of these multiple forms puts researchers, their funders and local managers at risk from powerful forces that will resent being told that their subject is elusive and changeable.

Conclusions

At the end of this piece of evaluative research only one of the nine case study sites could be accurately described as a TC – 'the thing' we set out to evaluate. But this situation is not uncommon in such research. Chimeras, chameleons and caterpillars are unexceptional in the landscape of evaluation. Past projects which members of this research team have worked on included a project on 'stroke units' which uncovered radically different and competing views about what a stroke unit was; an evaluation of 'Promoting Action on Clinical Effectiveness' which was meant to examine discrete projects' impact on practice but which turned into a study of how and why some people struggled to change other people's minds and practices; a study of 'Advanced Access to Primary Care' wherein the intervention diffused and diluted so that it was not possible to conduct a before and after study as planned; and a commission to write a report on an outreach care service which disappeared before the research began. The transformations we encountered are not unique to the NHS or to the UK policy environment. Thus, Pressman and Wildavsky's (1973) classic study of 'How great expectations in Washington are dashed in Oakland' which looked at how different US states attempt to implement federal programmes, demonstrated the same kinds of dislocation between policy and local implementation that we encountered in our study of TCs.

Evaluative research uncovers a multiplicity of truths. The object/subject of evaluation is frustratingly mischievous and challenging as shown in this study of TCs. In the act of engaging in this research, writing project protocols and attempting to evaluate organizational change we collude in the reification of these objects/subjects. Yet we are forced to transform our research to follow the unfolding social construction of reality. Perhaps we need to speak this truth more loudly. In so doing we note that there are implications for policy makers who may need to recognize the multiple truths that follow from policy initiatives. Elsewhere we have talked about the need for 'headroom' or flexible space in policy to allow this (Pope et al. 2006). Likewise the funders of research, as well as those engaged in evaluation must also see that evaluation research needs to adapt and flex to keep up with the transformations (and multiple truths) it uncovers.

Acknowledgements

We thank our colleagues Paul Bate and Glenn Robert who were part of the team that carried out the qualitative portion of the research project described here. The research on which this chapter was based on was funded by the UK National Health Service (NHS) Service Delivery and Organization (SDO) R&D Programme.

References

Bate, P., Gabbay, J., Gallivan, S., Jit M, le May A, Pope, C., Robert, G. and Utley, M. (2007) *The development and implementation of NHS Treatment Centres as an organisational innovation*, London: NHS Service Development and Organisation, Project SDO/45/2003, http:/www.sdo.lshtm.ac.uk.

Department of Health (2000) *The NHS Plan: A plan for investment, a plan for reform*, Cm 4818-I, London: The Stationery Office.

Eisenhardt, K. M. (1989) 'Building theories from case study research', *Academy of Management Review*, 14(4), 532–550.

Pettigrew, A. M., Woodman, R. W. and Cameron, K. (2001) 'Studying organizational change and development: Challenges for future research', *Academy of Management Journal*, 44(4), 697–713.

Poole, M. S. and Van de Ven, A. (2004) *Handbook of organizational change and innovation*, Oxford: Oxford University Press.

Pope, C., Robert, G., Bate, S. P., Gabbay, J. and Le May, A. (2006) 'Lost in translation: metamorphosis of meanings and discourse in organisational innovation and change processes: A multi-level case study', *Public Administration*, 84, 59–79

Pressman, J. L. and Wildavsky, A. B. (1973) *Implementation: How great expectations in Washington are dashed in Oakland: Or, why it's amazing that federal programs work at all, this being a saga of the economic development administration as told by two sympathetic observers who seek to build morals on a foundation of ruined hopes*, Berkeley, CA: University of California Press.

Seo, M-G., Putnam, L. L. and Bartunek, J. M. (2004) 'Dualities and tensions of planned organizational change', in M. S. Poole and A. H. Van de Ven, *Handbook of organizational change and innovation*, Oxford: Oxford University Press.

Yin, R. K. (2003) *Case study research: Design and methods*, 3rd ed., Thousand Oaks, CA: Sage.

10
Engaging the Public Voice in Health Care Decision-Making

Ann Casebeer, Gail MacKean, Julia Abelson, Bretta Maloff, Richard Musto and Pierre-Gerlier Forest

> Health policy decision-makers are grappling with increasingly complex and ethically controversial decisions at a time when citizens are demanding more involvement in these decision processes.
>
> (Abelson et al. 2004)

Introduction

Health care systems around the world have a long history demonstrating inadequate and/or limited engagement of public voices in decision-making processes. In an attempt to increase the capacity for greater public involvement in policy and decision-making within Canadian health care jurisdictions, a team of Canadian researchers and decision makers embarked on a three-year (2001–04) national collaborative program of applied research. The aims of this research were to unpack the meaning of effectiveness in the context of public participation methods, to develop guiding principles for the design and implement-ation of more effective public participation methods and to rigorously assess the implementation of new public participation methods with health regions across Canada.

This research project was a comparative study of public participation analyzing experiences from five Canadian provinces: Nova Scotia; Quebec; Ontario; Saskatchewan; and Alberta. There were three project phases consisting of (1) case studies of public participation processes that had recently taken place in each of the five provinces; (2) a survey of Canadian health regions and their experiences with public participa-tion; and (3) the design, implementation and comparative evaluation of new public involvement methods using a standardized national public consultation method (national process) across all five sites and a site-specific method (local process) both within and across sites.

Using the Alberta experience as an example of the valuable perspectives that public participants are able to voice, our chapter discusses the learnings from the third phase of the research where 'real time' public participation interventions were tested and compared. We demonstrate that, through the use of good process and collaborative partnership, the public can 'speak truth' to powerful health care decision makers and be heard in discussions of health and wellness issues facing their local communities and respective health care systems.

Background

Public participation in health policy and decision-making is being widely discussed in the international health policy and management literature (Abelson 2001; Abelson et al. 2003, 2004; Church et al. 2002; Dickinson 2002; Florin and Dixon 2004; Litva et al. 2002; Morone and Kilbreth 2003; Wiseman et al. 2003). Health care policy and decision makers are increasingly recognizing that there are different levels of policy and decision-making at which public can participate; that there are different kinds of public; and, that a variety of strategies can be used to engage these public (Abelson 2001; Barnes et al. 2003; Graham and Phillips 1998; Maloff et al. 2000; Thurston et al. 2005). There remains considerable lack of clarity, however, about what effective public participation actually looks like in a health care context (Florin and Dixon 2004; Thurston et al. 2005). A decade of scholarly contributions (e.g. theoretically based evaluation frameworks and empirical studies) has enhanced our understanding about the factors that embody effective public involvement processes (Abelson et al. 2003; Beierle and Cayford 2002; Webler 1995, 2001). Much of this knowledge base has been developed in sectors other than health care and draws on the literature examining the responsiveness of governance in a range of public service areas (Vigoda 2002). The authors of a recent systematic review of public participation in environmental decisions synthesized critical findings and concluded that 'process matters' and pointed to the association between broad acceptance of the decision 'outcomes' when 'processes in which agencies are responsive, participants are motivated, the quality of deliberation is high, and participants have at least a moderate degree of control over the process' (Abelson et al. 2003).

Beginning with Arnstein's seminal work (1969), we also know that 'power matters'. Power, and the sharing of it, has been inherent in, if not central to, much of the writing on public participation for more than three decades (Arnstein 1969; Morone and Kilbreth 2003). Drawing from the literature concerning the value of good public participation process, including findings from our own research (Abelson et al. 2004), we recognize the important interplay between good public participation processes and the multiple sources of power and influence within health care decision-making.

Our study demonstrates that deliberative public consultation processes can expand the influence of public voices attempting to speak 'truths' to power within usual health care decision-making processes (Abelson et al. 2007). The Calgary site was particularly successful in demonstrating a link between good process and subsequent action. The health region's experiences in the intervention phase (phase 3) of this national research project, with a deliberative public consultation process, are described to share knowledge of what processes were used and how they made a difference.

Study methods

Criteria for informed, effective and meaningful public participation, developed from findings in phases 1 and 2, guided the development of the intervention to be tested in phase 3. These criteria were as follows:

- clear communication about the purpose of the consultation and its relationship to the larger decision-making process(es);
- identifiable links between the consultation and the decision outcome(s);
- information presented honestly, clearly and with integrity;
- procedural rules that promote power and information sharing among and between participants and decision makers; and
- processes that are viewed as legitimate by citizens and decision makers.

The intervention developed was a one-day, face-to-face deliberative consultation meeting, to be implemented in each of the five research sites across Canada. A quasi-experimental design was used in which the following key attributes of the common (national) method were controlled:

- participant sampling and recruitment (20–25 participants selected from the community);

- length, structure and external facilitation of the participatory method;
- provision of background information in advance of the meeting; and
- evaluation methods.

In each of the five research sites, the health region identified their consultation issue in consultation with the local and national research teams. In Calgary, the issue selected for this public consultation intervention was health promotion services for young children (aged 0–6 years) and their families residing in the South of Anderson Road (SOAR) communities. In this context, Calgary Health Region officials were interested in understanding the needs and priorities of members of the public living in these communities in order to enhance decision-making capacity and responsiveness.

Within the context of the national study, local sites were encouraged to conduct two public consultations, one following the nationally prescribed 'deliberative' process and another using a method that varied on one or more of the key attributes described above. In the 'deliberative' approach (the national process), participants were limited to a predetermined selection of options provided for the consultation session and, through dialogue and debate, they ranked options to arrive at the preferred option. In contrast, the regionally developed approach (the local process) was 'generative' where options were developed within the consultation meeting through dialogue and brainstorming, and while priorities were identified, reaching common ground was not required. The intent of the pre-reading material for the local process was on expanding understanding rather than narrowing the focus as in the national (deliberative) process. In Calgary, the local process focused on capturing the priority health promotion issues for families with young children in these communities. The national process focused on agreeing what strategies should be used to address the priority issues identified within the local process.[1]

Sampling and recruitment

As the focus of these public consultations was health promotion for young children and their families, the intent was to recruit citizens living in the SOAR communities[2] who had an interest in this issue. Participants for both public consultation days were recruited through 80 organizations that worked with young children in SOAR (28 agencies, 15 community associations, 14 day cares, 23 public elementary schools and 1 community health centre). Local residency status was an inclusion criterion. A random sample of 50 SOAR residents, stratified by geographic area of residence, was selected from the 88 names of residents submitted by the recruiting organizations. Twenty-five participants were invited to attend each of the two consultation meetings.

Data collection

Data were collected to evaluate both public consultation days. Results reported in this chapter link to two primary evaluation objectives for these public consultations:

1. to compare the public consultation processes, using feedback from the public participants and the local project team (including the participating decision makers, independent facilitators and researchers);
2. to assess the effects of the public consultations on health region learning and decision-making.

The evaluation consisted of participant surveys administered at three time points. Baseline and post-meeting surveys were administered at the beginning and the end of each of the two consultation meeting days, respectively. A follow-up survey was sent out three to four months following each of the consultations to assess regional health authority efforts to take action on the results of the public participation. Calgary Health Region staff and decision-maker assessments of the public consultation processes were solicited through a short email survey prior to each consultation day and through qualitative debriefing sessions.

Findings

The public participants

Of the 50 participants invited to attend the two public consultation days a total of 44 citizens participated: 26 in the local process day and 18 in the national process day. All but one participant were female; most were between the ages of 30 and 45, and parents of children 9 years of age and younger. The participants were comparatively highly educated, with the majority having some kind of post-secondary education ranging from community college diplomas to university graduate or professional degrees. Most participants had lived in a SOAR community for five years or more and were active volunteers in community organizations.

Evaluations of the public consultation processes

Public participant assessments

As part of the evaluation, the team was interested in learning about the participants' expectations of these consultation days, and whether these expectations had been met. Through the baseline survey, participants were asked what they hoped to get out of the consultation day. Many of the participants indicated that they came to get information for themselves and for others in their communities, so that they could help kids. Others wrote about making a contribution to their community through participating in this day, and a few mentioned learning about the research project. Through the post-meeting survey, participants were asked to indicate the extent to which the consultation day had met their expectations. All of the participants in both public consultation days (100%) felt that either all or some of their expectations had been met. In this survey, public participants were asked to indicate the extent that they agreed or disagreed with a series of statements about the consultation days (using a 4-point Likert scale). The majority of the participants agreed or strongly agreed with the statements outlined in Table 10.1.

The most well-received component of both days was that participants felt that the formats promoted discussion, although participants in the national process felt more strongly about the format promoting discussion than did participants in the local process consultation (94% strongly agreed with the statement vs. 75%, respectively). Although the feedback from the public participants was overwhelmingly positive, the comparatively weaker aspect of both days was the clarity of the communication around the purpose of the consultations and the amount of time available to discuss the issues in a comprehensive way.

Almost all of the participants believed that the consultation day in which they participated was an extremely useful way of bringing together citizens to discuss these types of health issues (i.e. 79% of participants in the local process consultation; 94% of the participants in the national process consultation). Some final comments made by the participants on their post-meeting survey are included below.

Table 10.1 Public participants' views on the two consultations

	Strongly agree		Agree		Disagree [a]	
	Local process [b]	National process [c]	Local process	National process	Local process	National process
The purpose of the meeting was clearly communicated	13 (54%)	9 (56%)	11 (46%)	6 (38%)		1
Participants were provided with support (e.g. info., handouts, AV material) to guide their discussions throughout the day	17 (71%)	12 (75%)	6 (25%)	3 (19%)		1
Info. was communicated clearly	19 (79%)	11 (69%)	4 (17%)	4 (25%)		1
The format of the meeting promoted discussion	18 (75%)	15 (94%)	5 (21%)	1 (6%)		
Participants had equal opportunities to participate in discussions	19 (79%)	13 (81%)	4 (17%)	3 (19%)		
Participants had enough time to discuss the issues in a comprehensive way	15 (63%)	7 (44%)	6 (25%)	6 (38%)	3[d]	1

[a] The strongly disagree columns are not included in this table as none of the participants had checked anything off here.
[b] The total number of respondents on the first consultation day (local process) was 24, out of a total possible of 26.
[c] The total number of respondents on the second consultation day (national process) was 16, out of a total possible of 18.
[d] Two of these three respondents checked halfway between agree and disagree, which would be 'neutral'.

...Was a great day. Thanks for letting the community be involved.

I would be happy to participate again. It was a great experience. The honorarium is a good way to initially interest people.

I'm grateful to live in a city, province and country that values individuals' perspectives.

In response to open-ended questions about what they liked best and least about the day, the majority of participants' positive comments were around the organization of the day itself including the excellent facilitation, the good food and the provision of honorariums. They also enjoyed the opportunity to network and to participate in good discussions with a diverse group of people. What participants liked least about both days was that there 'wasn't enough time' to discuss the issues in the depth that they would have liked, and they wanted 'more detailed information' to inform their discussions. Finally, some of the participants in the national process day did not like having to focus their discussion on pre-identified options.

Local research team and decision-makers' assessments

The pre-day email survey

The team involved in the planning for these public consultation days included five CHR decision makers, two university researchers and the two facilitators. The email survey sent out prior to each of the days was sent to the five region decision-maker members of the research team and focused on eliciting their views concerning planning time and the value of this approach to public participation. For both consultation days the majority of the respondents felt that the *planning time* involved was about the same as they had anticipated, and that the time spent was about right given the scope and context of the decision-making process. Some respondents said that the planning time was difficult to comment on because of the difficulty in separating out the time spent preparing for the consultation days from the time spent on the research component. There was recognition, by the end of the planning for the national process, that the planning required for a deliberative public consultation process is considerable. It was also felt that the planning time required for future consultations would be less, as experience was gained with the process.

With respect to issues about the value of these public consultation days, those raised were primarily concerned with accountability and the maintenance of relationships. There was also concern that the national process consultation might not be as successful as the local process consultation day, because public participants would be given pre-identified options that they might not feel any commitment to and because the amount of background reading and preparation required might 'scare away' some of the potential participants. The CHR staff team members were asked what criteria they would use to judge the success of the days. The two main criteria cited by the respondents were (1) that the participants are able to participate meaningfully (and they evaluate their participation positively) and (2) that the perspectives provided by the participants are incorporated into the region's planning and program development processes. One respondent described evidence of success as follows:

> Ensuring a feedback loop to the community; following up with those citizens who have offered to be involved in future initiatives. Demonstrating a genuine commitment to considering the information and using the relevant data in planning.

Finally, the CHR team members described what they found the least and most satisfying aspects of planning. The least satisfying aspects were the administrative details (e.g. ordering lunch, pulling together supplies, booking the facility) and the too short timeline between the local process and national process consultation days. The most satisfying aspects included: working on the local research team, which was described as 'a true collaborative effort'; the energy and commitment of everyone on the team; and increasing our understanding of public participation.

The post-day debriefing sessions

With respect to what worked well, both public consultation days were characterized by: a high level of participant engagement; a high quality of information provided by the participants; and a high concentration and energy level that was sustained throughout both days. The participants appeared to feel that they could meaningfully contribute to the discussion of issues and identification of either strategies or priorities. This success can be attributed to a number of processes, including good recruitment and invitation protocol, careful planning and formatting, clear and helpful background materials, neutral and skilled facilitators and flexible and responsive approaches to small group work.

Regarding the local process consultation, using an adapted population health model as a planning tool to support the small group work of

brainstorming strategies to address the highest priority health promotion issues worked well. The use of this tool helped to build confidence,
support the small groups' autonomy and guide the process without
being too prescriptive.

Additional factors contributing to the success of the national process
consultation included discussing the more concrete issue of the two
first, allowing participants to warm up to the process before tackling the
more complex issue, providing sufficient detail for meaningful deliberation and decisions, having the 'parking lot' there for participants
to record new ideas while staying on track with the assigned options,
allowing latitude around modifying the options and shifting the focus
from forcing consensus, to reaching common ground.

In comparing the two days, the national process was more demanding
for the facilitators, as the format required increased perceptiveness,
mental agility, flexibility, people skills and negotiation skills. During
the local process, there was a greater sense of cohesion and good feeling
throughout the day. The national process day concluded similarly, but
it was a much bumpier ride. The local process, because of its more open-
ended format, appeared to provide more scope for creative thinking
by the participants. The national process had potential for this as
well, although it demanded skilled facilitation to permit an appropriate
amount of flexibility.

On the national process day, there was real value in having the participants deliberate around a limited number of options, in some detail,
and on finding some common ground on which options they preferred.
This process forced the participants to clarify their thinking around
each of these issues and to carefully examine their own positions. The
national process also allowed the participants to delve more deeply and
move the issues further along. Both the local and the national processes
provided valuable, but different kinds, of information as components
on a continuum of participation that included both generative and
deliberative consultation methods. The national process consultation
may have had greater validity for the participants, because the issues
and options were generated through a previous consultation with other
citizens living in the same communities.

Effects of the public consultation days on health region decision-making

One way of evaluating the ultimate success of a public participation
process is by looking at the extent to which the public participants'
ideas are being shared and incorporated into pertinent planning and

decision-making. Summarized here is what has been done to date with the information collected through the public consultation days.

The two priority issues generated through the local process consultation day (nutrition and activity and valuing children) were selected as the issues to be discussed and deliberated around on the national process consultation day. Calgary Health Region personnel are actively sharing the ideas and information that came out of the two days. An overview of both the processes and outcomes, for both days, was presented to senior managers in the Calgary Health Region and to the community organizations in SOAR. The Calgary Health Region held a meeting with interested community organizations, to discuss the ideas that came out of these two public consultation days, many of which went beyond the mandate of the region, in order to forge new connections and collaborative initiatives.

Most importantly, the region is already using the ideas that came out of both the consultation days, to advance initiatives that were already in the works and to create new initiatives. Some examples are as follows:

- A child care providers' resource package has been developed and planning is underway for its distribution.
- A comprehensive community services resource binder has been completed for parents' use.
- A SOAR website is being constructed to facilitate timely communication about parent and/or child programs that may be of interest to families and those working with young children.
- A distribution list of participants at both consultations has been created to provide them with timely and consistent information on local services and programs for families with young children.
- In partnership with the city of Calgary and the local YMCA, a child development component is being added to a long-standing parenting program to increase learning opportunities for children alongside their parents.
- A community mobilization project on healthy eating and active living is underway in one of the neighbourhoods.

In addition, community organizations have collaborated to address community needs voiced by citizen participations, including: providing administration support for maintaining the website and list serves; and providing space for programming in a low-income housing unit.

The perspectives and views shared by the citizens participating in both public consultation processes are being used to make a difference. The actions undertaken by the Calgary Health Region and other community partners reflect the knowledge and decisions that public participants voiced in both the local and national processes, and, in subsequent forums, have enabled ongoing community involvement. Public participation processes have significantly shaped regional progress in supporting healthy children and families and in creating opportunities for ongoing input from the communities themselves.

Discussion and implications

The valuable perspectives that the public were able to bring to the discussion of health and wellness issues facing young children and their families, and strategies to address these issues, have already contributed value to the region's planning and decision-making concerning healthy children in healthy communities. What the project teams have learned about engaging the public in discussing important health issues such as this will advance our understanding both locally and nationally about how to work with the public more effectively. The success of the two public consultations indicate that the public is able, and willing, to participate in complex consultation processes, and that public participants are able to provide perspectives that have the potential to improve the quality and responsiveness of health services planning and delivery.

When combined with the messages from the other provincial sites within the wider national study and what is known from the wider public participation literature, there are clear and hopeful messages concerning the ability of public voices to inform health care decision-making processes. This is more likely to occur when public participation processes take place in a context that supports and promotes involving citizens in relevant policy and decision-making processes, and when high-quality public participation processes are developed and employed based on what we know about good practice. In the Calgary site, this good practice demonstrated the value of combining several efforts and processes, including

- the use of both generative and deliberative public participation processes;
- a multi-disciplinary and collaborative local project team, including regional planners and providers; independent facilitators and researchers; decision maker partners and champions; and
- willing and invested public participants.

We believe that the conditions for an effective public consultation process articulated by Cayton (2004), in his editorial responding to an earlier paper written based on Phase 1 of this national research project (Abelson et al. 2004), were exemplified in the public consultation processes we have described in this chapter. Cayton stated:

> People taking part in consultations need to be engaged as partners; their expertise acknowledged; objectives need to be explicit; information needs to be shared; and, communication before, during and after the process needs to be thought through. None of this is difficult, but in the end only if we truly intend to involve people and change what we do as a result, will ... the public have reason to take part.

Experience from the Calgary site suggests that deliberative processes that are part of a longer term, local and continuing commitment to encourage public participation in decision-making, are more likely to lead to ongoing exchanges of knowledge and preferences, truly enabling responsive changes to be implemented. Further research and practice initiatives are needed to confirm and advance this case experience.

The benefits of multi-disciplinary collaboration, creating a strong academia–practice–public partnership for advancing knowledge in this area, also merit additional investigation. Our experience of the quiet observer presence of the researchers on the consultation days seemed to strike the appropriate stance, focusing on the community participants as the experts and the researchers as learners. A collaborative approach to team process allowed the research and practice issues and goals to merge, ensuring that both sets of needs were met. Clarity of roles and processes can enhance both research and practice expectations, overlapping and eventually blurring distinctions and avoiding tensions that some applied research projects encounter. The combined financial and intellectual resources of practitioners and researchers enabled improved efforts at public consultation to be advanced, in our case, in support of improved health services contribution to healthy children and families in the involved communities. These findings are congruent with Vigoda's (2002) suggestions for a positive role for academia in furthering the nature and understanding of enhanced collaborative partnership for more empowered public participation processes and outcomes.

High-quality public participation practices facilitate open and honest discussion among the public participants, as well as between the public participants and the sponsoring health organization. These 'best practices' are about people working together and about inviting and allowing public voices to influence those health policies and decisions that will affect their lives and the lives of their fellow citizens. The case reported on here illustrated that members of the public bring a valuable contextual knowledge that is otherwise missing from health policy and decision-making processes, and that helps us move from a theoretical perspective of what could or should work to what can work in the real world. In our case these public voices spoke about and knew about their communities and their children, the priority health issues and the kinds of strategies to address these issues that would be more likely to work in their communities. All parties worked hard to create an environment that nurtured good process and allowed a space for real, honest discussion. These spaces of consultation were embedding public participation in an organizational context that formally endorses and values public participation and contribution to decision-making. We believe that this intensifies and extends the value that can emerge from one-off exercises situated within less supportive decision-making environments, as longer-term relationships between health organizations and communities increase trust and create environments where good things can happen, not just on a single day or two – but across time.

Acknowledgements

The local and national project teams would like to extend a sincere thank-you to our funders; the Canadian Health Services Research Foundation and the Alberta Heritage Foundation for Medical Research; and the decision maker partners on all sites across the country. Special recognition and gratitude is reserved for the members of the SOAR communities who came out to participate on these days, as well as to the organizations that helped with the recruitment. The enthusiastic participation of all these people resulted in extraordinarily successful public participation processes.

Notes

1. To access detailed descriptions of the consultation processes and the region's public participation framework, go to http://www.calgaryhealthregion.ca/programs/comdev/frameworks.htm.
2. SOAR – This group of communities (approximately 25) encompasses a relatively large population group (over 50,000) south of Anderson Road. It is primarily comprised of young, educated families. Although an affluent population, there are significant pockets of low-income and immigrant populations.

There are also transportation challenges due to the north – south transportation corridors that split the area plus limited public transportation due to the rapid growth of this area.

References

Abelson. J. (2001) 'Understanding the role of contextual influences on local health-care decision making: Case study results from Ontario, Canada', *Social Science & Medicine*, 53(6), 777–793.

Abelson, J. and Forest, P.-G. (February 2004) *Towards more meaningful, informed and effective public consultation: Final report to the Canadian Health Services Research Foundation* (unpublished manuscript), www.chsrf.ca.

Abelson, J., Forest. P. G., Eyles, J., Casebeer, A. and MacKean, G. (2004) 'Will it make a difference if I show up and share: A citizens' perspective on improving public involvement processes for health system decision-making?', *Journal of Health Services and Policy Research*, 9(4), 205–212.

Abelson, J., Forest, P.-G., Eyles, J., Smith, P., Martin, E. and Gauvin, F.-P. (2003) 'Deliberations about deliberation: Issues in the design and evaluation of public consultation processes', *Social Science & Medicine*, 57, 239–251.

Abelson, J., Forest, P.-G., Eyles, J., Casebeer, A., Martin, E., and Mackean, G. and the Effective Public Consultation Team (2007) 'Exploring the role of context in the implementation of a deliberative public participation experiment: Results from a Canadian comparative study', *Social Science & Medicine* (in press).

Arnstein, S. R. (1969) 'A ladder of public participation', *American Institute of Planners Journal*, 35, 216–224.

Barnes, M., Newman, J., Knops, A. and Sullivan, H. (2003) 'Constituting "the public" in public participation', *Public Administration*, 81(2), 379–399.

Beierle, T. C. and Cayford, J. (2002) *Democracy in practice: Public participation in environmental decisions*, Washington, DC: Resources for the Future.

Cayton, H. (October 2004) 'Patient and public involvement', *Journal of Health Services Research and Policy*, 9(4), 2, 193–194(2).

Church, J., Saunders, D., Wanke, M., Pong, R., Spooner, C. and Dorgan, M. (2002) 'Citizen participation in health decision-making: Past experience and future prospects', *Journal of Public Health Policy*, 23(1), 12–32.

Dickinson, H. D. (October 2002) 'How can the public be meaningfully involved in developing and maintaining an overall vision for the health system consistent with its values and principles', Commission on the Future of Health Care in Canada. Discussion paper no. 33.

Florin, D. and Dixon, J. (2004) 'Public involvement in health care', *BMJ*, 328(7432), 159–161.

Graham, K. A. and Phillips, S. D. (1998) 'Making public participation more effective: Issues for local government' in K. A. Graham, S. D. Phillips (eds) *Citizen engagement: Lessons in participation from local government*, Toronto, ON: The Institute of Public Administration in Canada, pp. 1–24.

Litva, A., Coast, J., Donovan,. J, Eyles, J., Shepherd, M., Tacchi, J., Abelson, J. and Morgan, K. (2002) 'The public is too subjective: Public involvement at different levels of decision-making', *Social Science & Medicine*, 54(12), 1825–1837.

Maloff, B., Bilan, D. and Thurston, W. E. (2000) 'Enhancing public input into decision making: Development of the Calgary Regional Health Authority Public Participation Framework', *Family and Community Health*, 23(1), 66–78.

Morone, J. A. and Kilbreth, E. H. (2003) 'Power to the people? Restoring citizen participation', *Journal of Health Politics, Policy and Law*, 28(2–3), 271–288.

Thurston, W. E., MacKean, G., Vollman, A., Casebeer, A., Weber, M., Maloff, B. and Bader, J. P. (2005) 'Public participation in regional health policy: A theoretical framework', *Health Policy* , 73, 237–252.

Vigoda, E. (2002) 'From responsiveness to collaboration: Governance, citizens, and the next generation of public administration', *Public Administration Review*, 62(5), 527–540.

Webler, T. (1995) ' "Right" discourse in citizen participation: An evaluative yardstick' in O. Renn, T. Webler and P. Wiedelmann (eds) *Fairness and competence in citizen participation: Evaluating models for environmental discourse* Boston, MA: Kluwer Academic, pp. 35–86.

Webler, T. (2001) 'What is a good public participation process? Five perspectives from the public', *Environmental Management*, 27(3), 435–450.

Wiseman, V., Mooney, G., Berry, G. and Tang, K. C. (2003) 'Involving the general public in priority setting: Experiences from Australia', *Social Science & Medicine*, 56(5), 1001–1012.

11

The Swampy Lowland: Using Hyperlinks to Navigate the Multiple Realities of Partnership

Marion Macalpine and Sheila Marsh

> In the swampy lowland, messy, confusing problems defy technical solution.... in the swamp lie the problems of greatest human concern.
>
> (Schon 1987:3)

Introduction

Our 'swampy lowland' is the complexity of 'partnership' working within health and social care in the UK public sector. Our long-term multi-layered research project 'swampy ground' uses a website to build and communicate many different layers of 'truth' within complex partnerships that aim to improve people's lives, often people with little power. We use multi-voice research to gain ethical access to the perspectives of different actors in partnerships, often in sensitive situations where much is difficult to make public. Our work spans from 2000 to 2006 and presents multiple 'truths' and ways of seeing and analyzing, through the use of web pages and hypertext (www.swampyground.org), exploring what happens on the ground in the translation of policy into practice.

We summarize the context of the first phase of research, what we did and our findings. We then review contextual changes which triggered our second phase and discuss how our ideas on 'speaking truth to power' developed through drawing on theoretical domains of policy and discourse that are key to our evolving study. Finally we consider what we have learnt from the work as a whole about where managers can act in line with their own values in the current discursive context, and in what situations they are silenced and feel they 'must not let the cat out of the bag'. What emerges is the key importance of creating shared meanings in the face of the intensity of the different realities exposed by this multi-voice research. While such shared meaning was temporary, fluid and relied on constant attention, it enabled managers to make spaces to act.

Phase one of the 'swampy ground' research: '*I ache with hate*'

At the turn of the millennium, in the context of the spirited UK government's focus on building partnerships across the 'Berlin Wall' that separates health and social care in the UK, we were working with a group of cross-sectoral, cross-professional managers[1] in a metropolitan area to explore what was happening on the ground for them in building new partnerships. These managers were involved in partnerships for particular client groups, for example providing services for adults with learning disabilities; or for professional groups and their development, for example developing private residential homes as teaching homes. With the exception of Huxham's groundbreaking work (Huxham 1996; Huxham and Vangen 1996), at this time relatively little academic literature dealt with the messy realities of building partnerships 'on the ground' in the public sector. Our aim was to contribute 'live' stories to enhance existing theoretical work on partnership and on power:

- *Partnership*: Webb (1991) on mandated partnerships, Cameron and Cranfield (1998) on action, process and learning from partnerships, Pratt et al. (2000) on whole systems, Follett on cooperation and integration (in Graham 1987)
- *Power:* Chambers on 'uppers' and 'lowers' (1997); Marsh and Macalpine (1995) on the professional/user continuum of involvement in planning and provision of services; Huxham and Vangen (2000) on constraints and opportunities for leadership within partnerships.

Our methodology comprised two stages:

1. We met managers interested in participating as a group. Each told the story of a key partnership in which they were engaged. Following this the group explored key themes from all the stories. The taped discussion was transcribed and their stories agreed by them were displayed on the website.
2. Each participant contacted their key partners, asking them if they would tell their story of the partnership; we interviewed separately

those who agreed. Their stories of the partnership were also taped, written up and agreed for display on the website, creating multi-layered accounts of six different partnerships.

We as researchers considered key themes from each 'case' and its multiple viewpoints; then we identified themes and questions across them all. The methodology was designed to provide a space for the participants to reflect on their work, deeply embedded as they were in their partnerships, and for us all to 'hear' the other voices involved in each partnership.

In our findings we were struck by the stark differences in how the same situation was viewed. We used the Tamara story[2] to express the strength of the multiple perspectives: it was not simply that there were many different perspectives on one reality, but partners constructed different realities .The impact of mandated partnerships produced deep conflict and strong emotions: 'I ache with hate' was left written on an office whiteboard following a 'partnership' meeting. Warfare metaphors predominated, such as 'entrenchment...being in a trench', 'ignoring the war', the 'seduction of conflict', having an 'ally'.[3] Other key themes concerned choices facing leaders within their partnerships, such as to engage the 'resistors' or dilute their influence by 'widening the circle' (Axelrod 2000), to compromise or stand firm on your views.

Other key issues for managers included: achieving clarity in complexity through simple rules, such as involving service users to bring order to a highly conflicted inter-sectoral battleground; maintaining momentum but taking the time to forge relationships; and being aware of others' perceptions of who has power. We also noted a familiar silence about issues of power/identity, such as ethnicity and gender and how these impacted on partnerships: silence on ethnicity is especially common in organizational settings where white people are in a majority, leaving perceptions of power imbalance due to 'race' unexamined and un-discussable (Macalpine and Marsh 2005; Marsh and Macalpine 1998).

We developed the website as a public dissemination tool: web technology, both web pages and hyperlinks across them, enabled us to express the many levels of the research. Each viewpoint within a partnership has its own page as well as hyperlinks to issues in the partnership, to themes from the whole study, and to relevant theories or frameworks which illuminate and reflect what the person is saying.

In this first phase of research, partnerships were in the early stages of implementing government policy on partnership. The participants were in new situations, setting up partnerships. They were concerned with the difficulties of carrying out this mandate and focused on internal issues, involving raw emotions. We were left with a number of intriguing questions concerning decisions within partnerships: who stands for whose interests in making those decisions; what 'being representative' means; how power/identity issues impact within partnerships and on decisions; and how to understand the extent of rage expressed.

The changing context for 'partnership' working

By 2006 we wanted to explore the impact of major changes in the external context and the now established and ubiquitous discourse of 'partnership'. All the managers we worked with were by then involved in multiple inter-organizational, inter-professional and inter-sectoral partnerships. At the same time there was a growing cynicism and awareness of the rhetoric of partnership (Tomlinson 2005). 'Partnership' was increasingly being used in government discourse to include both the independent and voluntary sectors. The term obscured two very different types of service provider: the corporate for-profit sector involved through the private finance initiative or through direct contracts and marketization (Bovaird 2006; Lister 2005; Pollock 2004); and voluntary/community organizations, increasingly recruited into contractual relationships and away from their independent civil society role. There was growing support for new social enterprises as partners with the public sector. All this was applied to health and education. Meanwhile in social care the term 'externalization' was used to express the shift whereby local government divested itself of the provider role in favor of contracting out to preferred 'partners'. A further shift was the growing statutory requirement for user involvement, and 'user-centred' services, including for children, for older people and in mental health, alongside pressures to 'balance the books', especially for the NHS.

In developing the research we wanted to take account of these changes as well as the findings and questions arising from our earlier research. We therefore researched partnerships concerning: the 'externalization' of services for adults with learning difficulties; the setting up and development of a Sure Start project for young families; the development of integrated Intermediate Care[4] provision; partnership work to improve police/mental health/social work liaison and practice.

Policy and discourse: perspectives to view 'partnership'

To illuminate our continuing questions concerning decisions within partnerships and engage with the changing context, we drew on concepts of policy and discourse.

Policy

The 'policy' discipline is an important thicket within the diverse forest of partnership literature that offers us new perspectives. Bogason (2004) helpfully sets out the range of approaches to public policy development from 'rational', top-down policy formulation based on a discourse of expertise, to the 'mutual adjustment' approach exemplified by Lindblom's evergreen 'muddling through' (1959). Our participants and their partners work in the paradoxical policy context of strong *central* diktats which nevertheless require increased *local* autonomy. Turning to policy implementation, Heclo draws attention to the 'networks of interaction' whereby policies emerge (1972:106 quoted in Bogason 2004:10). Linked to this the notion of autonomous actors in a long *chain of decision makers* is an intriguing way to explore what happens on the ground (Pressman and Wildavsky 1973, cited in Bogason 2004:10). Both ideas helpfully emphasize the multi-organizational aspect of the process and suggest important questions concerning how the new 'swampy ground' partnerships actually carry out policy and the degree of autonomy that actors in the swamp may have.

Discourse

Bogason also refers to discourse and 'deliberative policy analysis' citing Fischer and Forester:

> Policy-making is a constant discursive struggle over the criteria of social classification, the boundaries of problem categories, the intersubjective interpretation of common experiences, the conceptual framing of problems, and the definition of ideas that guide the ways that people create the shared meanings which motivate them to act.
> (1993:1–2 quoted in Bogason 2004:18).

Discourse is a key concept in exploring how policy is disseminated and (potentially) turned into action on the ground. People are embedded in their own discursive practices and the process of attempting to 'recruit' them to new discourses is not straightforward: some concepts and related practices 'take off' and others are ignored or resisted. The imperative to form partnerships has been adopted widely – reflected in proliferating partnership boards and forums in health and social care. But at the same time it remains hard to form 'shared meaning' and this has been a key question in Phase two of the research.

The connected notions of policy and discourse triggered us to explore the idea of the discursive construction not only of policy, but also of practitioners' consent to its implementation. We saw (and participated in) the speed of enthusiastic adoption initially of the very term 'partnership'. Now with the addition of 'choice'; and 'contestability', these terms often connote private sector involvement.[5] Public sector 'partnership' is now termed 'integration' with 'partnership' moving beyond working practices or protocols to the forming of new organizations to bring professions and services together (Bovaird 2006; Tomlinson 2005).

Thus these theoretical domains linked to where we ended Phase one and raised the following questions for our further work:

- How far people in the partnerships were recruited to evolving policy discourses or alternatively contested them. This relates to power exerted both top-down through directives and through hegemonic influence, i.e., partnership becoming 'common sense' and not problematized.
- How far shared meanings were created at a local level. This implicates Foucauldian notions of *power/knowledge* (Foucault 2002).

In Phase two we used the same methodology as the earlier research. Issues and themes arising from the new case studies helped us develop more understanding of these two questions.

Findings from Phase two: 'not letting the cat out of the bag'

In exploring these two issues we focus on what emerged concerning practice on the ground and the space for action by local managers involved in these partnerships. Our aim arising from the Phase one work was to explore managers' agency within the discursive context of 'partnership'.

How far people in the partnerships were recruited to evolving policy discourses or alternatively contested them

Here we discuss examples of policy/discourse issues which these cases illuminate: increasing *marketization* of how people's needs are met and increasing focus on *user involvement/empowerment*. Case material from different partners illustrates a range of responses to these mandates. It also shows how managers responded to the tensions that arose where top-down policy was ambiguous or contradictory; and to those areas where paradoxically national policy required local autonomy.

As we noted earlier, the different discursive constructions of partnership include marketization through both commercial contracts and 'externalization'. We found examples of actors adopting and internalizing aspects of this discourse as well as challenging it. In several of the cases, market-based vocabulary was used unquestioningly: 'core business', 'clean tenders', 'commercial confidentiality', although a carer felt the latter hampered democratic involvement: 'Commercial confidentiality. It's like secret stuff. But we should know.'

In the learning disability case study, the policy of externalization was strongly opposed within the minds of many people involved, but the key finding was that those who disagreed with it could not challenge it or even discuss it together, even those at a senior level. The service manager underlined the silencing process: *'We are all really good at not letting the cat out of the bag'* (i.e., their own personal opposition). The users' key concern was for continuity of both friends and staff in services they will use for a lifetime: *'Will the staff be the same? Will we still be able to see our friends?'* It became clear, however, that legal requirements intended to maintain terms and conditions when the service is transferred to another employer [6] were 'a moveable feast' and there was no guarantee that the same staff would continue to be employed at the same level. 'Externalization' was used to obscure incompatible policy priorities. Meeting user and carer needs for longer hours of support and providing holistic care were incompatible with a standstill budget. The council was not transparent about this; externalization enabled them not to confront this. The Partnership Board for Learning Disability was not involved in these decisions.

However, the commissioner challenged the process of externalization where he could. Discussions with councilors were 'sprinkled with fiery moments: [I said] "No you can't, it's going to take longer than you think"'; he did not make cuts, and did not reduce numbers of clients by changing eligibility criteria.

This case illustrates the complexity of actors' response to policy. There was an acceptance of the mandate for externalization, so strong that it entailed a silencing of critical voices; and yet still a space remained for action.

In three of the partnerships, the managers were highly committed to increasing user involvement and took enormous pains to make it happen, where they could. Users and carers were not involved in the decision to externalize the learning disability service: that decision was taken by councilors. However, what was notable was the extent and depth of capacity building for users to help select a provider, through advocates and 'starting from low base'. The commissioner 'would go anywhere' to meet with service users. This energy and commitment was also reflected in the gradual involvement and empowerment of Sure Start mothers led by the project director, including outreach by both professionals and mothers themselves. 'We stop people on the bus sometimes. We tell them about Sure Start.' Women from a wide range of ethnic and class backgrounds were involved. They attempted to engage 'dads' reflecting a strong strand of policy intent, even though in their view, 'men are such a different species'. In the police liaison case, the committee involved users as members; they tended to focus on their personal issues but 'bring a useful perspective, especially the emotional impact of what the work is about' (specialist mental health nurse adviser).

These positive models of user involvement were not evident in what people said about the development of Intermediate Care; these older users appeared to be more grateful than empowered: an older man commented, 'They decided to take me on.'

So where policy reflected managers' own values, as in user involvement, they energetically found ways to carry out this policy, which possibly legitimized them doing what they would have chosen in any case to do.

We now turn to managers' responses to the tensions where top-down policy was ambiguous or contradictory. In some cases, national policy encompassed competing/contested discourses: how far did this offer space for managers to act?

Within Sure Start, building facilities for children and families was key, yet unrealistic requirements for speed meant capital allocations were lost. Managers had then to use temporary premises and build a complex virtual organization across several sites. The local Social Services Department prioritized statutory national targets concerning children and was unable to develop with Sure Start the preventive work also envisaged in national policy (DfES 2004). The Sure Start coordinator therefore employed a part-time social worker from the voluntary sector, a limited substitute for statutory involvement.

Those in the police/mental health partnership faced tensions between discourses of public safety and the integration of people with mental health problems within the community. Health and social care professionals built an understanding with the police about achieving both care and risk management through a proportionate response to risks:

> [for the most violent cases], that meant 14 officers, an ambulance, and for me a week of my time. Once we explained all this [committee members] were surprised. So now they do a risk assessment first.... It's all really friendly now. It saves a lot of resources for all of us. (Police Sergeant)

They also prioritized taking people to hospital in an ambulance rather than a police van, which overwhelms and stigmatizes vulnerable users.

So, faced with these tensions, managers had to take up the action they could: either in making do, and leaving behind the aspirations for a building or statutory involvement, or working directly on the issues in tension as in the police liaison committee. However, tensions between competing policy aims at national level also created barriers locally that managers could not address. The chain of decision-makers was dislocated; links were missing. The council was disastrously ill-informed about what was involved in shifting from Sure Start to establishing Children's Centres within their Education Department. A two-way flow of information about this shift was essential; without this, inevitable uncertainty was made worse by the speed required from the top. Also functioning chains were broken, for example a national initiative for police induction training on mental health effectively halted valuable local training for officers set up by the committee.

In several cases, the managers were able to use an additional, paradoxical, space for action: where national policy required local autonomy in structures and decisions. Sure Start staff used this successfully in 'keeping to the essence' of promoting health and wellbeing for families in finding creative ways to work with mothers locally. For example they helped mothers engage in fitness classes that resulted in children's involvement too. The Police Liaison Committee chair found the space to bridge very different cultures operating within statutory constraints to change local action on the ground.

On the other hand, in the Intermediate Care case, faced with substantial local professional resistance to 'altruistic' integration (Webb 1991), managers took 10 years to achieve integrated Intermediate Care, which is only one small part of the seamless care patients and clients need.

The cases show an absence of strategic leadership above the level of the managers in these cases. They were told: 'just do it'. They acted autonomously by default or abdication as well as by choice.

How far did managers create shared meanings at a local level?

Phase one showed the strength of different realities within partnerships and the emotions these raised. Here we discuss how managers in Phase two worked with these realities. We first explore where they successfully created shared meaning and its impact.

Sure Start's temporary premises created a joint 'portal' where mothers, their children and a wide range of professionals knew they could meet each other face to face. This provided an outstanding example of creating shared meanings that was the opposite of narrow professionalism.

> Before...they never had the forum to share information, knowledge and good practice, to interrogate other practitioners' jobs to see where they might cross over, so that the two halves create a whole in a new virtual way....It's speeded up, it's cut out a lot of time-wasting trying to track down people. Lots of different agencies use this as a portal...either to see clients, or to see clients with another practitioner. They'll know that so and so will be here on a Tuesday, they can flag up an issue with a client....They will have a fruitful discussion about the best way forward for that child. The right form will be filled out immediately. Things are streamlined. (Sure Start Coordinator)

In addition partners in the Sure Start work, including parents, paid explicit attention to gender, ethnicity, age and class in involving people. The chair, a white woman, noted: 'I am going to a borough wide meeting with three other parents – one is Thai, one is Black British and one is Egyptian.'

Similarly the Police Liaison Committee offered a face-to-face opportunity for people from very different cultures to explore what they were trying to do and create shared processes. The importance of physically meeting each other and experiencing each others' different realities helped the difficult process of creating shared meaning (Follett cited in Maddock and Macalpine 2006):

> Community Safety Training officers from the police attended a violence and aggression training at the Trust recently and 'had their eyes opened', they reported back...that they felt 'privileged' at the level of support and powers they had as police staff, compared to mental

health staff.... the police on the training going round the wards saw what we had to deal with and our lack of resource to do it. (Specialist Mental Health Nurse Adviser)

We now turn to problems in creating shared meaning, and how this affected outcomes.

The usual divides between sectors, for example over performance requirements and forms, continued to hinder joint work. In the Intermediate Care case, these were exacerbated by restructuring in partner bodies, so that new senior managers were ignorant of previous shared work. The perennial question of different pay and conditions was addressed proactively, although there were no solutions:

> We know it is a national problem. What we've had to say was, look, we can't solve this on own.... We will move into the integrated structure with people taking their existing pay and conditions. We will work with whatever opportunity there is to make that feel better... [we] did some work together to show what the other benefits are in terms of leave, pensions etc. There are pay- offs. (Service manager, Social Services)

Here on the long-term path toward integration of health and social care, while there was agreement among professionals about the concept of 're-enablement' for older users, the term 'integration' had multiple meanings (see Box 11.1) which were not clarified.

Box 11.1 Multiple meanings of 'integration' in Intermediate Care case

Integration...

- Through behavior
- Through re-structuring
- Through co-location
- Through a new generic role
- Through integrated training
- Through good access to all other professionals
- Through combined referral procedures

People with learning disabilities have a *'lifetime in the service'*, so the construction of shared meanings between them, their carers and professionals is of key importance. Commercial confidentiality requirements of the contracting process inhibited shared meanings and a democratic process in the Learning Disability case. While there were good processes of consultation with users and carers, users and managers had marked differences between their perceptions of quality and 'flexibility'. The team manager thought, *'We felt we were providing a fantastic service'* while a user commented on getting personal development plans: *'Sometimes it is like waiting for paint to dry. You wait for ever.... "We'll let you know".'*

Dowling et al. (2004) suggest that much of the research on partnership focuses on processes rather than outcomes. What we see, however, in the construction of shared meanings is the intricate and important connectedness of process and outcomes.

Where are we now?

This multi-vocal research provides dense, textured material that illuminates the daily experience of people involved in partnership working. It enables us to hear the concerns of the different actors that are not often transparently shared, thus illuminating what we cannot access in our own partnerships. It helps managers, each immersed in their own singular and intense reality, to be exposed not only to others' perspectives but to the understanding that others construct different realities. It enables 'a shift that moves us from a single world to the idea that the world is multiply produced in diverse and contested social relations. The implication is that there is no single "world"' (Law and Urry 2004). Managers act within 'chains of decision-makers' and alongside partners with these different realities. This research has explored how far managers working in partnerships take up their agency in the current discursive environment.

Our question about whether people are recruited to policy discourses or contest them is too simplistic. We have found a great complexity of response among managers and their partners, and indeed within an individual. Where policy reflected their own values, unsurprisingly they pursued this energetically using the policy to legitimize their actions. Where partners disagreed with policy directives, there was a range of responses: from acceptance to determination to find a small space for action in line with personal values. Some policy discourses were so powerful that they silenced people at all levels and coerced their behavior if not their beliefs. Others were not able to overturn professional interests. Co-existing with all this we also saw some managers exploiting paradoxical central directives for local autonomy to work in line with their own values. Where there were contradictory policy discourses and policy tensions, managers either had to be content to 'make do' or they had to tackle the tensions directly through discussion. When the 'chains of decision-makers' were broken, there was little they could do.

Both phases of the research demonstrate that the kernel of collaborative working is indeed the intensity of different realities which are exposed as multiple truths. Proactive leadership helped partners address this by creating shared meanings through interaction, as in the Sure Start, Learning Disability and Police Liaison cases. What helped was shared experience face-to-face. What got in the way was not surfacing different meanings of concepts such as integration, leadership, quality, flexibility. Issues of power/identity too (i.e., concerning gender, ethnicity) rarely surfaced, with Sure Start as an exception. Hyperlinks between web pages enable us to experience and link the different realities constructed by partners. Managers across partnerships could also surface these different realities, expressed as they are in the different meanings attributed to key concepts. As Weick says, 'the action of saying makes it possible for people to . . . see what they think' (1995:30). Similarly Follett comments 'you cannot integrate differences until you know what they are' (in Tonn 2003:439). What emerges is the key importance of creating shared meanings in the face of the intensity of the different realities exposed by this multi-voice research. While such shared meaning was temporary, fluid and relied on constant attention, it enabled managers to make spaces to act.

We have been struck too by the contrast between the managers involved in the two phases: they moved from working to counter entrenched conflict to showing confident leadership that accepted complexity and uncertainty. The early phase managers had to focus on purpose, despite personal issues and emotions, in order to make progress. The later group moved beyond internal conflict to enabling users to take key roles. They were clearer about the degree of autonomy they had in making sense of an unclear remit.

This research shows how, alongside the constraints of 'collaborative inertia' (Huxham 2002), these managers found small spaces to enact their values, rooted in progressive change. In doing this, they were 'critical managers' (Marsh and Macalpine 1999), who worked where they could within the prevailing discourse of 'partnership'. The hyperlinks of the 'swampy ground' website allow us to glimpse some of these local processes of 'speaking truth to power'.

Notes

1. The managers were studying MA in Leading, Managing and Partnership Working at Thames Valley University. *'Managers'* we worked with were becoming *'leaders'* working in partnership, and the research tracks some of the leadership activities they were demonstrating.
2. In 'Tamara', the longest running play in San Francisco, both actors and audience move around the many rooms of the building following and building their own stories and understandings. This play vividly demonstrates for its audiences what in organisations and in partnerships is a truism: that there are many different 'realities' being experienced, many perspectives at play (Thatchenkery and Upadhyaya 1996).
3. All quotations in italics are from stories told by participants, see www.swampyground.org.
4. Intermediate Care in the UK is 're-enablement' provided for six weeks to those coming out of hospital to support them in their own home in order to prevent re-admission.
5. For example Prime Minister Blair in his press conference of 23 January 2006 talked about schools having 'external partners' as positive, without mentioning this meant the involvement of private firms in the running of schools.
6. As in the Transfer of Undertakings (Protection of Employment) Regulations 2006.

References

Axelrod, R. (2000) *Terms of engagement: changing the way we change organizations*, San Francisco: Berrett Koehler.

Bogason, P. (2004) *Networks in policy analysis – towards a new pragmatism, Roskilde*, Denmark: Centre for Democratic Network Governance. Accessed http://www.ruc.dk/upload/application/pdf/f51d6748/Working_Paper_2004_8.pdfon 16.1.2006.

Bovaird, T. (2006) 'Developing new forms of partnership with the "market" in the procurement of public services', *Public Administration*, 84(1), 81–102.

Cameron, M. and Cranfield, S. (1998) *Unlocking the potential: Effective partnership for improving health education* London: NHS Executive, North Thames. Aaccessed http://www.llweb.co.uk/documents/LSM_Cohort2/unlomain.pdf on 7.2.06.

Chambers, R. (1997) *Whose reality counts?*, London: Intermediate Technology Publications.

Department for Education and Science (2004) *Every child matters*, London: The Stationery Office.

Dowling, B., Powell, M. and Glendinning, C. (2004) 'Conceptualising successful partnerships', *Health and Social Care in the Community*, 12(4), 309–317.

Foucault, M. (2002) J. Faubian (ed.) *Power: Essential works of Foucault 1954–84*, London: Penguin Group, vol 3.

Graham, P. (1987) *Dynamic managing the Follett way*, London: Professional Publishing and BIM.

Huxham, C. (1996) *Collaborative advantage*, London: Sage.

Huxham, C. (2002) *Theorising collaboration practice: A quick tour of some accumulating theory.* Accessed http://www.gsb.strath.ac.uk/research/workingpapers/default.asp?curpage=9 on 4.2.06.

Huxham, C. and Vangen, S. (1996) 'Working together: Key themes in the management of relationship between public and non-profit organisations', *International Journal of Public Sector Management*, 9(7), 5–17.

Huxham, C. and Vangen, S. (2000) 'Leadership in the shaping and implementation of collaboration agendas: How things happen in a (not quite) joined-up world', *Academy of Management Journal*, 43(6), 1159–75.

Law, J. and Urry, J. (2004) 'Enacting the social', *Economy and Society*, 33(3), 390–410.

Lindblom, C. (1959) 'The science of muddling through', *Public Administration Review*, 19, 79–88.

Lister, J. (2005) *Health policy reform: Driving the wrong way?*, London: Middlesex University.

Macalpine, M. and Marsh, S. (2005) 'On being white: There's nothing I can say', *Management Learning*, 36(4), 429–450.

Maddock, S. and Macalpine, M. (2006) 'An inspiration for our time: Mary Parker Follett (1868–1933)', *British Journal of Leadership in Public Services*, 2(2), 44–48.

Marsh, S. and Macalpine, M. (1995) *Our own capabilities: Clinical nurse managers achieving strategic change*, London: The King's Fund, republished London: Hodder, 1999.

Marsh, S. and Macalpine, M. (1998) 'Negotiating a borderland: Nursing, gender and management', *Health Services Management Research*, 11, 221–227.

Marsh, S. and Macalpine, M, (1999) 'Can you have "critical management" as well as improve services?'. Paper presented to the International Critical Management Studies Conference, July.

Pollock, A. (2004) *NHS Plc*, London: Verso.

Pratt, J., Plamping, D. and Gordon, P. (2000) *Whole systems thinking*, Working papers series, London: Kings Fund.

Pressman, J. L. and Wildawsky, A. B. (1973) *Implementation.* Berkeley, CA: University of California Press.

Schon, D. (1987) *Educating the reflective practitioner* San Francisco, CA: Jossey Bass.

Swampy Ground web site at www.swampyground.org.

Thatchenkery, T. and Upadhyaya, P. (1996) 'Organisations as a play of multiple and dynamic discourses' in D. Boje, R. Gephart and T. Thatchenkery (eds) *Postmodern management and organisation theory*, London: Sage.

Tomlinson, F. (2005) 'Idealistic and pragmatic versions of the discourse of partnership', *Organization Studies*, 26(8), 1169–1188.

Tonn, J. (2003) *Mary Parker Follett: Creating democracy, transforming management*, Newhaven: Yale University Press.

Webb, A. (1991) 'Co-ordination: A problem in public sector management', *Policy and Politics*, 19(4), 229–241.

Weick, K. (1995) *Sense-making in organisations*, London: Sage.

12

Systems Thinking for Knowledge Integration: New Models for Policy-Research Collaboration

Allan Best, William K. Trochim, Jeannie Haggerty, Gregg Moor and Cameron D. Norman

Systems thinking is attracting great interest in public health as a conceptual orientation to solving complex challenges around health care renewal in developed countries. Our approach is based on the tenet that effective systems thinking relies on the development of a transdisciplinary knowledge base integrating traditional complex adaptive systems theory with community development, social ecology, social networks, and public health theory and practice (Best et al. 2003).

This chapter offers three case studies, showcasing concept mapping and social network analysis, knowledge integration, and multilevel analysis to compare and contrast primary health care models and resulting system performance in different contexts.

Case #1: The Initiative for the Study and Implementation of Systems (ISIS)

The US NCI ISIS project began as a means of exploring whether systems thinking could serve as a foundation for more effective public health efforts to combat tobacco use in the face of countervailing forces such as the tobacco industry. The first two years of ISIS brought together a transdisciplinary group of thought leaders in system dynamics, network analysis, knowledge management and informatics, tobacco control, management sciences, health policy, and several other fields to develop an action framework. This network of thinkers considered some core questions: How can the flow in *both* directions between research and practice be optimized? How can systems structure and function be best characterized to be useful to the public health community? In what ways can networks be better understood and optimized? In what ways do information and knowledge become the currency by which change occurs? The ISIS team concluded that systems thinking in public health cannot be encompassed by a single discipline or even a single 'systems thinking' approach (for example, system dynamics), but instead represents a transdisciplinary integration of approaches to public health which strive to understand and reconcile linear and non-linear, qualitative and quantitative, and reductionistic and holistic thinking and methods into a federation of systems thinking and modeling approaches (Trochim et al. 2007).

The ISIS team also recognized that the complexity of systems thinking might be dismissed as being too complicated. To the current public health stakeholder approaching the issue of systems thinking for the first time, the depth and breadth of systems science can be bewildering. Just consider a few of the topics associated with the general area of systems thinking: causal feedback (Sterman 2000); stocks and flows, open and closed systems (Sterman 2000); centralized, decentralized, hierarchical, and self-organizing systems (Kauffman 1995; Sterman 2000); non-linear systems and chaos (Strogatz 1994); complex adaptive systems (Gell-Mann 2003; Waldrop 1992); silo effects (Côté 2002); emergence (Holland 1998); general systems theory (Bertalanffy 1995); cybernetics (Francois 2004); computational simulation (Stacey et al. 2000); decision and game theory (von Neumann and Morgenstern 1944); system dynamics (Forrester 1997; Richardson 1996; Sterman 2001); evolution, biology, and ecology (Capra 1997, 2002) and set, graph, and network theory (Strogatz 2003; Watts 2003).

Contemporary public health itself can be quite bewildering. Indeed, public health can be viewed as a complex adaptive system (Trochim et al. 2007) of international, national, regional, and local public health governmental entities, a broad array of non-governmental organizations and foundations, advocacy and special interest groups, coalitions and partnerships, for-profit and non-profit medical systems, business and industry, and the public at large. The broad array of threats to well being, ranging from obesity and tobacco to bioterrorism and the threat of epidemics, can also be most aptly portrayed as a complex and adaptive system. Yet, despite the growing cognizance and support for 'systems thinking' in public health, implementation of effective systems approaches remains challenging (McKelvey 1999; Plsek and Greenhalgh 2001; Plsek and Wilson 2001; Stacey et al. 2000).

In order for the public health community to value systems thinking as a guiding approach, it must be presented in ways that are practical, manageable, and accessible. The ISIS collaborators hoped that by showcasing systems methods we believed to be particularly promising, we could break down some of this apprehension and encourage the applied transdisciplinary work vital to the advancement of public health.

A recent study on challenges of the implementation of systems thinking in public health (Trochim et al. 2006) used concept mapping methodology (Trochim 1989) to identify 100 challenges and eight clustered challenge areas. The authors propose that the eight clusters represent 'simple rules' to managing systems-based public health initiatives that behave like complex adaptive systems, and that leaders and managers of systems-based initiatives in public health could use the eight clusters to help guide the system to overcome the challenges of implementation.

Based on this empirical research into the challenges of systems thinking in public health, the authors recommended two related projects that build incrementally toward more refined research that answers why systems thinking can be so difficult to implement and how one might be more successful in doing so. The first project addresses the need for training and development in systems thinking, as well as clarification as to the construct of systems thinking. It proposes a mixed method, multivariate statistical methods approach to identify the major components of a comprehensive systems thinking curriculum for public health professionals. The second project would investigate and develop a new systems thinking methodology for understanding and improving leadership and management of public health systems.

Case #2: knowledge integration: from research to policy and practice

The second case example draws from an initiative of the National Cancer Institute of Canada, in collaboration with the US National Cancer Institute, to develop a common language and logic for the use of all researchers, decision makers, and practitioners in cancer control, as they work together to develop effective national strategies for evidence-based planning, decision-making, and practice. The environment for cancer research in Canada is changing in profound ways; there is a greater focus on research-based programs and services, evaluation and outcome measurement, interdisciplinary research, and collaboration. Research funding organizations, like the National Cancer Institute of Canada, consider these integral components of strategic planning. Terms such as 'evidence-based health care', 'translational research', 'knowledge transfer', 'research uptake', and 'dissemination science' are widely used in planning documents. However, there is little consensus on their definition or the processes by which they take place (Kerner et al. 2005).

Lack of clarity in the language and logic of research transfer creates significant obstacles to effective action (Lomas 1997, 2000; Mankoff et al. 2004). Interdisciplinary and interprofessional research application is complicated by the use of different terms to describe the same thing and ascribing different meanings to the same term, making it impossible to develop benchmarks to guide initiatives to put knowledge into practice, or indicators to evaluate them.

Vertical organizational structures in the cancer control system that separate research, clinical and preventive practice, service programs and policy areas also are barriers to effective collaboration (Lomas 2000). The explosion of discovery in the basic or fundamental sciences (for example, genomics and proteomics, imaging technologies for early detection) and maturation of the behavioral and social sciences has created a bottleneck of knowledge that is limited because of the failure of its translation across these vertical silos.

It has become clear that an understanding of the social and environmental determinants of health, and how they operate through both behavioral and biologic pathways, is a critical key to the prevention of cancer (Ellis et al. 2005; McKinlay and Marceau 2000; Singer and Ryff 2001; Smedley and Syme 2000). Thus, it is important to understand the research to policy and practice cycle as encompassing not only the transfer of basic science discoveries into clinical applications ('bench to bedside'), but also the transfer of knowledge into effective interventions producing measurable outcomes at the population level, with active community participation in the process ('bench to trench') (Crowley et al. 2004; Sung et al. 2003). Collaboration between research producers and research consumers in this translational approach is critical to reduce the cancer burden at the population level, the ultimate measure of benefit to all (Mankoff et al. 2004).

Unfortunately, current models for research transfer are not working well (Ellis et al. 2005; Greenhalgh et al. 2004); one reviewer concluded that it takes 17 years to turn 14 % of original research into benefit for patient care (Balas et al. 2000). The problem is that different stakeholders – research producers and end users – frequently operate in isolation rather than collaboratively throughout the knowledge production, synthesis, and integration cycle.

We need a framework that will facilitate improvements in the process of moving knowledge into action. Individual-focused efforts have not been highly successful (Greenhalgh et al. 2004; Grimshaw et al. 2001), and while organizational approaches have shown some promise, there is recognition that a systems approach is required given the complexity and breadth of the field (Greenhalgh et al. 2004). A consistent set of definitions and terms, reliable indicators to monitor successes in transitional research and knowledge transfer at a systems level, and a framework to guide thinking and activities are required.

The need for clear language and frameworks is not unique to cancer control. For example, public health in Canada faces similar challenges, as elegantly discussed in a *Canadian Journal of Public Health* (CJPH) report of work by the Canadian Institute of Health Research's (CIHR) Institute of Public and Population Health (Kiefer et al. 2005). The report was based on an environmental scan, literature review, and consultation with researchers, practitioners, and policy makers, to identify priorities and strategies for evidence-based decision-making in population and public health. The assessment by Greenhalgh et al. (2004) for the UK National Health Service provides a comprehensive literature review of diffusion in health service organizations.

The CJPH and Greenhalgh et al. papers offer definitions that provide a useful clarification of how some of the more common terms are used (Table 12.1).

Table 12.1 Terms commonly used in knowledge integration

Term	Definition
Dissemination	An active and strategically planned process whereby new or existing knowledge, interventions, or practices are spread (Kiefer et al. 2005)
Knowledge transfer	The imparting of research knowledge from producers to potential users (Kiefer et al. 2005)
Knowledge exchange	The interactive and iterative process of imparting meaningful knowledge between research users and producers, such that research users receive information that they perceive as relevant to them and in easily usable formats, and producers receive information about the research needs of users (Kiefer et al. 2005)
Knowledge uptake	The acquisition and review of research knowledge and its utilization, including incorporation into decision-making (Kiefer et al. 2005)
Implementation	Active and planned efforts to mainstream an innovation within an organization (Greenhalgh et al. 2004)

Table 12.2   Three generations of research application models

Time frame	Language	Key assumptions
Generation 1 1960-mid- 1990s *Linear models*	• Dissemination • Diffusion	• Knowledge is a product • The key process is a handoff from research producers to research users • Knowledge is generalizable across contexts
Generation 2 Mid-1990s to present *Relationship models*	• Knowledge exchange	• Knowledge comes from multiple sources: research, theory, and practice • The key process is interpersonal: networks of research producers and consumers collaborating throughout knowledge production–synthesis–integration • Knowledge is context-linked and must be adapted to local setting • Degree of use is a function of effective relationships and processes
Generation 3 *Systems models*	• Knowledge integration	• The knowledge cycle is tightly woven within priorities, culture, and context • Relationships mediate throughout the cycle and must be understood from a systems perspective and the organization and its strategic processes • Degree of use is a function of effective integration with the organization(s) and its systems

However, the underlying model for how the research to policy and practice cycle works is still limited. Thinking about the problem is evolving rapidly, as detailed in the CJPH and Greenhalgh et al. papers; however, more appropriate models are needed. Table 12.2 summarizes what may be seen as three stages in thinking about core processes underlying effective knowledge integration and use.

Systems models seek to address the limitations of linear and relationship models by acknowledging that knowledge production and mobilization involve different systems, actors, and perspectives – each with their own rhythms and dynamics, world views, priorities and processes, language, time scales, means of communication, and expectations. These worlds may not naturally connect, and the focus for the knowledge mobilization enterprise needs to be on the major drivers in the system: organizational structure, processes, and contexts; funders' timelines, expectations, and accountability; and decision-making and incentives for change.

Systems and networks research help clarify the logic of Table 12.2 and address the need for fresh thinking about organizational change necessary to support effective knowledge mobilization and integration. It is perhaps not surprising that this new science of knowledge integration and exchange is dependent upon transdisciplinary collaboration. These collaborations include a wide range of disciplines across the basic, clinical, and population health sciences, and those working in research, clinical practice, management, and policy areas. Given the uniquely close working relationships in the Canadian cancer research-application community, there is the opportunity to refine models for knowledge application that emphasize the powerful roles of organizations, systems, and networks in achieving evidence-based policies and practices. The transition from networks to organizations as the context for knowledge mobilization introduces the potential value of a new term: knowledge integration.

> *Knowledge integration* is defined as the effective incorporation of knowledge into the practices and policies of systems and organizations so that it informs decisions and affects outcomes.

Starting with this framework, the NCIC designed a process to maximize the lessons learned and the strength of the knowledge integration framework, as a foundation for implementation of its strategic plan. A final report included a review of the literature to summarize evidence for effective research to policy across three settings (basic, clinical, and population research), at three levels of behavior change (individual, organization, and systems) (National Cancer Institute of Canada report 2006). The report included inputs from a series of four workshops to refine and validate the framework, producing a practical tool to guide researchers, decision makers, and practitioners as they collaborate to implement cancer control strategy.

Case #3: primary health care redesign

The third example of systems thinking in action builds on current initiatives in Canada to renew primary health care (PHC). They are broadly similar to concerns and initiatives in other developed countries including Britain, Australia, New Zealand and the USA.

PHC is the first point of contact when people initiate care for a new problem, where common and chronic problems are resolved or managed, and serious conditions are referred to more specialized care. For Canadians – 85% of whom seek primary care every year – it is the 'heart of health care' (Campbell 2005). There is good evidence that a strong PHC system improves the level and distribution of health at lower cost than systems that rely more extensively on secondary and tertiary care (Macinko et al. 2003; Starfield and Shi 2002). In Canada, since 1998, four provincial and two national health care commissions have concurred that renewing how PHC is funded, organized, and delivered is key to addressing problems in the health system related to prompt access to comprehensive, evidence-based services. In 2000, the federal government committed new funds to accelerate change in PHC This led to a flurry of demonstration projects and new initiatives to improve access, chronic disease management, and integration of services in PHC.

However, PHC renewal in Canada is proving difficult. The flurry of demonstration projects was layered on a system that was already in transition. Each demonstration project focuses on one piece of the puzzle – for example improved care for diabetics or enhanced health help lines – but it is unclear how action on one component of the system impacts directly, or indirectly, on another part. Nor is it clear how the knowledge gained from the experiments will be integrated, especially given the lack of consistency in the terminology, measures, and benchmarks used in evaluating such initiatives.

Underlying all this is the idea that there is One Right Model of Care. Only recently are both researchers and policy makers recognizing that there is no single 'right' organizational model of care, and that outcomes depend on contextual community factors (Lamarche et al. 2005). New research in primary care is providing information on mitigating contextual factors and different processes applied to apparently similar structures. There has been a huge interest in better understanding the interactions of the different sub-systems that characterize primary care: the provider–patient encounter; interactions between providers intra and extra-muros; and the interface with the community.

How might systems thinking help? Recent work is providing tools that conceptualize actions within primary care as part of a dynamic system. For instance, Watson et al. (2004) developed a comprehensive logic model that extends from sociocultural and policy factors including population characteristics, through a full range of policy and service strategies, to broad population health outcomes. Although the model was inspired by a linear results-based logic model for accounting purposes, by making explicit all the components of the system and their potential areas of influence, the model sets the stage for understanding one component of care in the light of other factors.

Recently, Lamarche et al. (2005) used a configuration approach to identify which organizational features seem to cluster together in a variety of international and Canadian models of primary care. Using this approach led to a taxonomy of models that was rhetoric-free: a giant step forward in the field of PHC. They were able to apply the taxonomy to an analysis of effects and to show that no model is able to achieve all the desired outcomes at the same time. More recently, they have shown that performance of individual primary health care practices is associated not only with organizational structures within the practice, but also with the configuration of health care establishments in the immediate environment of clinics. These initiatives are challenging researchers to examine their areas of interest from the perspective of the whole health system or sociopolitical context.

As a better understanding emerges of key barriers to community strategies that link public health and health service strategies (Frisby et al. 2004), there is a crying need for measurement tools and research frameworks to enable researchers to examine problems from a holistic perspective. In addition to developing systems tools to conduct new research, we need ways of evaluating and synthesizing emerging evidence, both clinical and organizational, to generate systems learning that will guide change at the local, regional, and national levels. Furthermore, such learning needs to take into account differences both within and between jurisdictions, in order to provide responsive solutions to the challenges facing primary care reform at each level.

Summary and conclusions

We have illustrated the value of systems thinking by describing three recent policy-research examples from our work. In each case, we learned that a generic systems thinking approach added value, but that considerable work was needed to refine our understanding in the context of each example. We learned that systems thinking is an effective approach to foster deliberation across diverse disciplines and stakeholders. After an initial struggle with this diversity and the 'complexity of complexity' (the vast and varied literatures that inform this field), we found that common logic and language emerges from transdisciplinary dialogue. We found particularly useful the concept of 'simple rules' from complex adaptive systems – while each of our examples required a detailed working through of the key constructs and measures, the most powerful tools to promote dialogue, and hopefully positive change, were the much simpler frameworks and 'thinking tools' that emerged. It was exciting and productive to adapt well-established methodologies in ways that provided a toolkit for each context we explored. We discovered an almost overwhelming enthusiasm among decision makers for new ways of thinking, and new tools that help them address what they already knew were more complex challenges than existing strategies could encompass. Finally, the work came together around the concept of knowledge integration as a platform to focus collaboration between researchers and decision makers, empowering participants from multiple stakeholder groups to solve the pressing priorities of health system renewal.

These case studies provide some groundwork. We must continue to move forward, engaging research producers and users in collaborative projects, so that we can further refine our thinking and tools. We encourage others to seek out and create opportunities for diverse disciplines and stakeholders to work together using systems perspectives. By doing so, we will be able to demonstrate and evaluate the impact of systems thinking approaches in public health and realize its full potential as a facilitator of progressive change.

References

Balas, E. A., Weingarten, S., Garb, C. T., Blumenthal, D., Boren, S. A. and Brown, G. D. (2000) 'Improving preventive care by prompting physicians', *Archives of Internal Medicine*, 160, 301–308.

Bertalanffy, L. V. (1995) *General system theory: Foundations, development, applications*, rev. ed., New York: Braziller.

Best, A., Stokols, D., Green, L. W., Leischow, S., Holmes, B. and Buchholz, K. (2003) 'Health promotion and community partnering: Translating theory into effective strategy (an integrative framework for community partnering to translate theory into effective health promotion strategy)', *American Journal of Health Promotion*, 18(2), 168–176.

Campbell, C. (2005) 'MPs expected to press Martin for tough stand on health care', *Globe and Mail*, (Aug 20), A4, http://www.theglobeandmail.com/servlet/ArticleNews/TPStory/LAC/20050820/LIBERAL20/TPNational/?query=strategic+counsel.

Capra, F. (1997) *The web of life: A new synthesis of mind and matter*, London: Flamingo.

Capra, F. (2002) *The hidden connections: Integrating the hidden connections among the biological, cognitive, and social dimensions of life*, 1st ed., New York: Doubleday.

Côté, M. (2002) 'A matter of trust and respect', *CA Magazine*, 135(2), 60.

Crowley, W. F., Sherwood, L., Jr, Salber, P., Scheinberg, D., Slavkin, H., Tilson, H., Reece, E. A., Catanese, V., Johnson, S. B., Dobs, A., Genel, M., Korn, A., Reame, N., Bonow, R., Grebb, J. and Rimoin, D. (2004) 'Clinical research in the United States at a crossroads: Proposal for a novel public–private partnership to establish a national clinical research enterprise', *JAMA*, 291, 1120–1126.

Ellis, P., Robinson, R., Ciliska, D., Armour, T., Brouwers, M., O'Brien, M. A., Sussman, J. and Raina, P. (2005) 'A systematic review of studies evaluating diffusion and dissemination of selected cancer control interventions', *Health Psychology*, 24, 488–500.

Forrester, J. W. (1997) *Roadmaps: A guide to learning system dynamics*, Cambridge, MA: MIT Press.

Francois, C. (2004) *International encyclopedia of systems and cybernetics*, 2nd ed. Munchen: K G Saur.

Frisby, W., Thibault, L. and Kikulis, L. (2004) 'The organizational dynamics of under-managed partnerships in leisure service departments', *Leisure Studies*, 23, 109–126.

Gell-Mann, M. (2003) *The quark and the jaguar: Adventures in the simple and the complex*, London: Abacus.

Greenhalgh, T., Robert, G., Macfarlane, F., Bate, P. and Kryiakidou, O. (2004) 'Diffusion of innovations in service organizations: Systematic review and recommendations', *Milbank Quarterly*, 82, 581–629.

Grimshaw, J., Shirran, L., Thomas, R., Mowatt, G., Fraser, C., Bero, L., Grilli, R., Harvey, E., Oxman, A. and O'Brien, M. A. (2001) 'Changing provider behaviour: An overview of systematic reviews of interventions', *Medical Care*, 39(8:2), 112–145.

Holland, J. H. (1998) *Emergence: From chaos to order*, Reading, MA: Addison-Wesley.

Kauffman, S. A. (1995) *At home in the universe: The search for laws of self-organization and complexity*, New York: Oxford University Press.

Kerner, J., Rimer, B. and Emmons, K. (2005) 'Dissemination research and research dissemination: How can we close the gap?,' *Health Psychology*, 24, 443–446.

Kiefer, L., Frank, J., Di Ruggerio, E., Dobbins, M., Manuel, D., Gully, P. R. and Mowat, D. (2005) 'Fostering evidence-based decision-making in Canada: Examining the need for a Canadian population and public health evidence centre and research network', *Canadian Journal of Public Health*, 96(3), I1–I19.

Lamarche, P., Pineault, R. and Hébert, M. (2005) 'The influence of primary care organizational models on continuity, accessibility and comprehensiveness of services', Presented at the annual meetings of CAHSPR, Montreal, QC, September 2005.

Lomas, J. (1997) *Improving research dissemination and uptake in the health sector: Beyond the sound of one hand clapping*, Hamilton, ON: McMaster University Centre for Health Economics and Policy Analysis.

Lomas, J. (2000) 'Using linkage and exchange to move research into policy at a Canadian Foundation', *Health Affairs*, 19(3), 236–240.

Macinko, J., Starfield, B. and Shi, L. (2003) 'The contribution of PHC systems to health outcomes within Organisation for Economic Cooperation and Development (OECD) countries, 1970–1998', *Health Services Research*, 38(3), 831–865.

Mankoff, S. P., Brander, C., Ferrone, S. and Marincola, F. M. (2004) 'Lost in translation: Obstacles to translational medicine', *Journal of Translational Medicine*, 2, 14.

McKelvey, B. (1999) 'Complexity theory in organization science: Seizing the promise or becoming a fad?,' *Emergence*, 1(1), 5–32.

McKinlay, J. B. and Marceau, L.D. (2000) 'To boldly go ... ', *American Journal of Public Health*, 90(1), 25–33.

National Cancer Institute of Canada (NCIC) (2006) *The language and logic of research transfer: Finding common ground*, Final report to the NCIC Board from the Joint Working Group on Translational Research and Knowledge Integration of the Advisory Committee on Research and the Joint Advisory Committee for Cancer Control.

Plsek, P. E. and Greenhalgh, T. (2001) 'The challenge of complexity in health care', *BMJ*, 323, 625–628.

Plsek, P. E. and Wilson, T. (2001) 'Complexity, leadership, and management in healthcare organisations', *BMJ*, 323, 746–749.

Richardson, G. P. (1996) 'Problems for the future of system dynamics', *System Dynamics Review*, 12(2), 141–157.

Singer, B. H. and Ryff, C. D. (eds) (2001) *New horizons in health: An integrative approach*, Washington, DC: National Academy Press.

Smedley, B. D. and Syme, S. L. (eds) (2000) *Promoting health: Intervention strategies from social and behavioral research*, Washington, DC: National Academy Press.

Stacey, R. D., Griffin, D. and Shaw, P. (2000) *Complexity and management: Fad or radical challenge to systems thinking?*, New York: Routledge.

Starfield, B. and Shi, L. (2002) 'Policy relevant determinants of health: An international perspective', *Health Policy*, 60(3), 201–218.

Sterman, J. D. (2000) *Business dynamics: Systems thinking and modeling for a complex world*, New York: McGraw-Hill/Irwin.

Sterman, J. (2001) 'System dynamics modeling: Tools for learning in a complex world', *California Management Review* , 43(4), 8–25.

Strogatz, S. H. (1994) *Nonlinear dynamics and chaos: With applications to physics, biology, chemistry, and engineering*, Reading, MA: Addison-Wesley.

Strogatz, S. H. (2003) *Sync: The emerging science of spontaneous order*, 1st ed., New York: Hyperion.

Sung, N. S., Crowley, W. F., Jr, Genel, M., Salber, P., Sandy, L., Sherwood, L. M., Johnson, S. B., Catanese, V., Tilson, H., Getz, K., Larson, E. L., Scheinberg, D., Reece, E. A., Slavkin, H., Dobs, A., Grebb, J., Martinez, R. A., Korn, A. and Rimoin, D. (2003) 'Central challenges facing the national clinical research enterprise', *JAMA*, 289, 1278–1287.

Trochim, W. (1989) 'An introduction to concept mapping for planning and evaluation', *Evaluation and Program Planning*, 12(1), 1–16.

Trochim, W. M., Cabrera, D. A., Milstein, B., Gallagher, R. S. and Leischow, S. J. (2006) 'Practical challenges of systems thinking and modeling in public health', *American Journal of Public Health*, 96, 538–546.

Trochim W., Best, A., Clark, P. and Leischow, S. (eds) (2007) *Greater than the sum: Systems thinking in tobacco control*, NCI Tobacco Control Monograph, Bethesda, MD: US Department of Health and Human Services, National Institutes of Health, National Cancer Institute.

von Neumann, J. and Morgenstern, O. (1944) *Theory of games and economic behavior*, Princeton, NJ: Princeton University Press.

Waldrop, M. M. (1992) *Complexity: The emerging science at the edge of order and chaos*, New York: Simon and Schuster.

Watson, D. E., Broemeling, A.-M., Reid, R. J. and Black, C. (2004) *A results-based logic model for primary health care*, Vancouver, BC: Centre for Health Services and Policy Research, http://www.chspr.ubc.ca/research/phc/logicmodel.

Watts, D. J. (2003) *Six degrees: The science of a connected age*, 1st ed., New York: Norton.

13

Strategies of Persuasion: The Efforts of Nurse Practitioners in Institutionalizing a New Role

Trish Reay and Karen Golden-Biddle

Political entrepreneurs are people who get things done. They are critical to change implementation within organizations because they have the ability to use their contextual knowledge and convince others to modify their behavior (Buchanan and Badham 1999). But are political entrepreneurs also important in institutional change? Our study of nurse practitioners (NPs) in Alberta, Canada, led us to believe that political entrepreneurship was an important but overlooked component of institutional and organizational change. We followed the introduction of a new NP role (nurses with advanced education and experience) over a five-year time period, observing how this institutional change process was orchestrated and driven by individuals at the front lines. NPs themselves used their contextual knowledge to design and implement strategies in attempts to institutionalize the new role.

Unlike our findings, most literature on institutional change is focused on the system level. Thus, the process of institutionalizing has been characterized as a series of recognizable events at the field level – introduction of new practices through isolated experiments; gradual acceptance (or legitimation) of the new practices; and eventually, full institutionalization of the practices where they become taken-for-granted (Barley and Tolbert 1997; Green 2004; Greenwood et al. 2002). However, when viewed from an individual, front-line perspective, this same process of institutionalizing change becomes more complicated. As we have shown in prior work (Reay et al. 2006), legitimizing a new role requires the accomplishment of three active micro-processes as well as a series of small wins (Weick 1984) that individuals negotiate with those around them as part of their work activities.

Here, we take an even closer look at the experience of front-line professionals in introducing a new role. We focus on the micro-situated political processes associated with enacting a role that require many other people to change their work behavior. Not only do nurse practitioners introduce new practices and alter their own work behavior, but their addition to a health care team means that other health professionals must change their established behaviors and routines. In accomplishing this new work, nurse practitioners see their responsibility as persuading others to change the way they have been working. That is, nurse practitioners conceive of their 'change work' as convincing others to do something they would not otherwise do – a textbook definition of the use of power (Daft 2004).

Through our interviews, it became obvious that individual people were critical in advancing the NP role. But the literature on change (especially institutional change) has almost completely ignored individual actions in accomplishing desired outcomes. Only a few studies of institutional entrepreneurship have considered individual rather than organizational actors (e.g., Fligstein 1997; Maguire et al. 2004). But even these have shied away from addressing the political behavior (the use of power) of individuals in accomplishing desired outcomes. We highlight individual political processes in an attempt to improve our understanding of change processes that involve changing behavior. We suggest that purposeful attention to political entrepreneurship – individuals engaging in an oblique style of politics where changes occur 'under the radar' (Buchanan and Badham 1999; Clemens and Cook 1999; Meyerson and Scully 1995) – will enable a better understanding of how institutional change occurs. Thus, our research question is: How do individual actors try to persuade others to accommodate the introduction of a new role?

Changing institutionalized practices

Although accused of being overly focused on stability, institutional theory has more recently turned its attention to understanding change (Dacin et al. 2002; Scott 2001). In attempting to understand change, institutional theorists have begun to develop models that incorporate both agency and institutional forces (Emirbayer and Mische 1998; Hensmans 2003; Scott 2001). Bringing agency back into institutional explanations has largely been accomplished through the concept of institutional entrepreneurship, where actors (either organizations or individuals) take purposeful action designed to achieve particular changes. These actions may be in concert with, or in opposition to institutional pressures, but both agency and institutional forces are viewed as critical to the process of institutional change (DiMaggio 1988; Fligstein 1997; Seo and Creed 2002).

In spite of DiMaggio's (1988) original attention to both organizational and individual institutional entrepreneurs, only a few studies have profiled the actions of individuals (e.g., Fligstein 1997; Maguire et al. 2004; Reay et al. 2006; Zilber 2002). Although currently small in number, these studies that seek to understand the role of individuals in institutional change hold strong potential for bridging the long-standing divide between macro and micro explanations. By focusing on individuals in their everyday work settings, there is increased potential to gain important insights into the connections and interactions between individual actions and change in institutions. For example, Maguire et al. (2004) showed how two key individuals used their knowledge of established systems and structures to assist in the creation of a recognized field of HIV/Aids treatment and support. Similarly, Reay et al. (2006) showed how embedded individual actors used their knowledge of context to legitimize a new role at the organizational and system level.

Some of the literature on organizational change has focused on the role of individuals at the front line or in the middle of organizations. These studies highlight ways in which individuals can accomplish change objectives even when they do not hold positions of authority. In fact, some studies suggest that important changes in everyday work routines can only be successfully achieved by individuals who are close to (if not at) the front line (e.g., Floyd and Wooldridge 2000; Meyerson and Scully 1995). These individuals have been identified as change agents, political entrepreneurs (Buchanan and Badham 1999) or tempered radicals (Meyerson and Scully 1995). What they hold in common is an ability to understand their local context and use that knowledge to unobtrusively instigate changes that ultimately contribute to significant and sustainable larger scale change. This attention to individuals who are contextually savvy and politically active holds important promise in understanding the role of individuals in institutional change.

In addition to the need for more studies that focus on the actions of individuals in their everyday work, what is currently missing in the literature is attention to the role of individuals at different points in the institutional change process. We know that similar to the diffusion of innovation (Greenhalgh et al. 2004; Rogers 1995) institutional change proceeds over time from isolated experiments to legitimated new practices to fully institutionalized (taken-for-granted) practices that replace the old ways of working (Green 2004; Greenwood et al. 2002). But we have little knowledge about how individuals impact this change process at different points and how individual efforts unfold over time. We address this gap through our attention to nurse practitioners as they attempted to introduce their new role into a well-established health care system.

Research context and methodology

NPs in Canada

Nurse practitioners are relatively new in Canada. In the 1970s a few nurses received special training and worked in isolated northern settings. They used the title 'nurse practitioner' but it was not legislatively recognized. In 1995 new Alberta legislation allowed special nurses to provide 'extended health services' in areas that were medically under-serviced. This legislation was followed by a number of experimental projects where special nurses took on increased responsibilities. The number of special cases grew over time, but it was not until 2003 that legislation was passed creating the protected title of 'nurse practitioner'. In 2007 there are 130 registered NPs who work together with physicians and other health professionals as part of interdisciplinary health care teams in critical care units, active treatment hospital wards, long-term care facilities or primary health clinics. Only a few work in northern isolated regions.

Data collection and analysis

Our five-year study of how individual actors collectively sought to institutionalize the NP role began in September 2000, as part of a larger research program (Golden-Biddle et al. 2006) investigating health reform in Alberta. To address our question about how individual actors seek to persuade others to change their behavior, we conducted a total of 60 interviews with NPs over a four-year time period (2000–04): 33 were conducted early in our project (2000–01), 27 conducted later (2003–04). Our interviewees were both male and female, but to assist with anonymity and for ease of reading, we use female pronouns. Interviews were conducted at the work place, usually in offices integrated in the hospital or health unit. Interviews lasted an average of one hour in length and we were often 'shown around' the work unit after the interview concluded. We also collected documents and other archival materials related to the introduction of the NP role, and we observed monthly meetings of one committee that was charged with guiding the implementation of the role in one organization. Here, interview data are our primary source; archival data and meeting observations our secondary source.

We analyzed the processes NPs used to convince others to change their behaviors. In examining the longitudinal interview data and comparing patterns over time, we were surprised to see that the NPs used similar processes of convincing regardless of whether previous attempts had been successful or not and in spite of their increasing frustrations. We used qualitative data software to assist our coding efforts.

Convincing others to change behavior

We wanted to understand how individual NPs persuaded other health professionals to change their work behavior in order to accommodate the introduction of a new role. In previous research (Reay et al. 2006) we showed how NPs used a strategy based on achieving a series of small wins (Weick 1984) and kept their actions low key and 'under the radar' to prevent major disruptions in the power dynamics of their organizations. As 'political entrepreneurs' (Buchanan and Badham 1999), NPs used their knowledge of their own context to anticipate reactions of other professionals and designed their actions accordingly.

Since others had to adjust their actions to incorporate the new role, it was critical that NPs found ways to gain acceptance and fit themselves into well-established routines. We observed that they employed two strategies to convince others to modify their behavior so that NPs could function effectively. These were both conducted on a one-to-one basis. The strategies are (1) explaining the role and its advantages to others and (2) making work better for others so that there were few disadvantages and many advantages of accepting NPs as integral members of the health care team.

We were surprised to find that five years after the beginning of this change initiative, NPs continued to use these same strategies – sometimes in spite of their escalating frustration with the lack of progress. In most settings, the NP role became institutionalized and taken-for-granted, as expected in institutional change (Scott 2001). However, it was a lengthy process in each location, as NPs attempted to persuade people one by one. The NPs were persistent, and most people were eventually persuaded – however, frustrations arose in settings where acceptance was very slow.

In the next section we show how NPs used these two strategies of persuasion. Then we present excerpts from our data showing how NPs tried to manage the inherent frustrations, while still persisting with the same strategies.

Strategies to convince others

(1) Explaining the role to others
In the early stages, NPs were more than willing to explain their role to anyone and everyone. They saw themselves as pioneers, and they did not expect other health professionals to understand what an NP was, nor why they should be introduced into health care teams. The following quotes from our earliest interviews provide examples of their willingness to explain the role:

> I just sat down one-on-one with the nurses, and said, this is who I am. This is how I see the job. What do you guys need? As nurses, what do you need here? And then, I just tried to develop some rapport around that.

> Everywhere I go, when people say, 'What do you do?' I say I'm a nurse practitioner and I'm very specific about what I do – and they say, 'What's that?' And I take time to tell them, because how else are they going to learn what we do?

Over time, the message about NPs spread – but very slowly. Although new provincial legislation and professional regulations were developed to provide a framework for institutionalizing the role, many NPs still had to explain themselves to every new health professional they worked with. Even after several years, NPs told us about their continual efforts to explain the value of their role:

> I guess when you're trying to make a change in something that's been established for such a long time, you just have to keep at it. It's persistence, persistence and persistence. But then all of a sudden resistance backs off. . . . I think we're slowly getting there but I feel like I've been swimming uphill.

Sometimes I could order an antibiotic or order a CT scan, and it wouldn't be questioned. Other times, I'd order mouthwash and they [nurses] would phone the physician to get it okayed. I just keep at it. I've been here for four and a half years, and some days I think we're actually making headway.

In many settings, the role became increasingly institutionalized to the point where NPs were considered part of the 'normal' health care team. NPs told us about their successes:

It's an automatic now. You can't be called a Nurse Practitioner unless you're on the roster, and you're Master's prepared.

There is a big change here from five years ago. I remember having to defend who I was, what my education was. My orders would never get processed till they were blessed by the physician. But not anymore. Now I get huge respect.

(2) Making work better for others

The second strategy we identified was based on NP's belief that in order to be accepted, they had to prove their value to other health professionals – especially physicians. They purposefully tried to show individual physicians (in particular) how a nurse practitioner could make work better for them by reducing their hours of work or allowing them to focus on more complex cases. This strategy was particularly kept 'under the radar'. They took great care not to 'show off'. NPs took small actions everyday to continuously prove that they were knowledgeable about medical conditions, and that they could appropriately diagnose, prescribe and treat patients. They believed that these accumulated actions would lead to acceptance by physicians. Nurse practitioners told us how they tried to show their value:

The local doctor was overworked and threatening to leave. He just couldn't cope anymore. So to relieve a bit of the pressure – I was the answer.... I try to reduce his workload as much as I can.

I look after things five days a week, and the doctors only come here once a week. They used to have to phone in regularly, or get a lot of calls. But now I keep everything up to date. And they happily say, 'Oh, I don't have to phone in. This is already done.' And that makes their work life a lot easier.

Early in the introduction of the new role, nurse practitioners realized that they also needed to prove their value to the established nursing staff. Consequently, they began to use similar approaches to convince RNs that NPs could improve their work life:

> Nursing has been a bit tougher to convince than medicine. I just have to keep demonstrating the role and show what it has to offer and support nurses. The nursing staff has been able to call me anytime and know that it's a nurse on the other end that they can talk with. They're now more liable to call – knowing that I'm on the other end, versus a physician who might be a little more threatening.

> I really see this job as service to the nurses. The nurses – that's why this job is here, it's not really here for me. It's for the nurses. I try to think about what it is that they need. When you do that, it's very easy.

Long-term use of the persuasion strategies

Throughout the five years of data collection, we observed that NPs continued to act as political entrepreneurs by using these two persuasion strategies. In most cases the strategies were successful, and NPs became accepted and valuable team members. They developed new working relationships where physicians and NPs treated each other with respect and both benefited from the synergy.

However, in some settings NPs' strategy of 'making work better for others' had adverse effects. As some of our interviewees shared, their efforts seemed to result in both a never-ending need to persuade and a permanent state of assisting physicians as their 'handmaidens'. We heard from these NPs about their increasing frustrations as they consistently explained and demonstrated the value of the role, but had been unable to achieve acceptance. The following two examples show this frustration, and how it, for some NPs, led to their ultimate departure:

> *Interviewer:* So, this physician wanted you by his side all the time?
> *Interviewee:* Yes, and I was having difficulty with this physician because he did not understand the nurse practitioner role. He didn't understand that it was more than being the physician's handmaiden, and there was no moving him beyond that in spite of my best efforts.... I talked with management, and then I talked with the physician and said, 'I can't do this.' I know that what I said was taken to heart

and there were some changes made, but I ended up leaving and going to [another department]. They ultimately replaced me with an international medical student.

We all want to be doing research, we all want to be involved in administrative leadership, but the reality is that the physicians still don't even know that there was a change in legislation. They don't know that we're independent practitioners now. They don't know that we can make a decision without them. . . . How do I cope? I have to say, you know, going from full time to part-time has changed things for me. I was getting very frustrated before and I'm out of the politics now.

These NPs also shared their disenchantment with the longer term results of assisting other health professionals (especially residents or physicians) in reducing their workload. They explained that they were beginning to resent the fact that they were working extra hours to assist others, and received little recognition for their efforts. In some cases, they discovered that physicians used their additional time to engage in leisure activities – which was viewed particularly unfavorably by the NPs:

Well, I've been the one that stays late. Last week, two duty docs couldn't get in on time – well it was me that stayed late. . . . It's going to happen to me once this week, and then I'm going to say to her [the resident], no, you're staying because I need to go home today.

I think we're helping out physicians and it sometimes worries me a little bit that we do a lot of their discharge work. So, we'll do the discharge summary – which is tedious, but it frees them up so that they can go see people waiting in Emergency, or review consults with the residents or fellows. That seems like a really good use of their time, but if it's just so that they can go have coffee with their cronies while the NP is doing five or six discharge summaries, I don't think that's a good use of time.

In settings where NPs were hitting roadblocks, they told us about their frustrations, but they did not appear to have developed any concrete coping strategies. They suggested that they 'weren't going to do that anymore'. But it was not evident what actions (other than possibly leaving the unit) they would undertake.

Overall, then, we observed a picture of change where individuals at the front line took purposeful actions designed to facilitate the institutionalization of a new role. They did this by entering their workplace with new skills and new approaches to accomplishing work. In order to achieve the desired changes, they took on the challenges of convincing others to change their behavior in order to accommodate and support the new role. However, the task of persuading others to change carries inherent difficulties (Floyd and Wooldridge 2000; Meyerson and Scully 1995), and we observed that individuals were able to manage the associated frustrations if they were viewed as temporary. That is, if the persuading strategies were a short-term route to institutionalizing the new role (as we saw most frequently), NPs dealt with their frustrations through persistence and the celebration of small wins. But in the less usual cases where the persuading strategies were required over a very lengthy time period, the second strategy of making work better for others seemed to create unintended and unwanted consequences. Instead of achieving the acceptance and institutionalization of the NP role, this lengthy persuasion strategy seemed to lead to a helper or 'handmaiden' role for NPs rather than the quasi-independent professional role that was the original goal.

Conclusions

Although the overall story of institutionalizing NPs in Alberta is a success, we have also been interested in understanding situations where difficulties were encountered. We found that when faced with the challenge of introducing the new role, individual NPs adopted two strategies to facilitate acceptance. Although NPs did not expect these strategies to be immediately successful, they did regard them as a temporary strategy for achieving a future where NPs were independent members of health care teams. In most cases, this desired future was achieved. However, when these strategies did not result in acceptance of the role, NPs kept repeating the strategies, but became increasingly frustrated. Other than withdrawing from the situation, we did not hear about any other strategies being tried.

These findings are interesting in several ways. First, they highlight the political efforts of individuals in accomplishing institutional change which has so far received little attention in the literature. We were able to show how individuals at the front line took purposeful actions designed to convince others to change their behavior. Previous studies have pointed to the importance that persuasion strategies may play in institutional change (e.g., Maguire et al. 2004), but so far there has been little attention to the actual strategies and how they are employed. Our analyses suggest that similar to the political actions of change agents (Meyerson and Scully 1995), contextually savvy individuals play an important role by taking politically astute and usually 'under the radar' actions that guide the course of institutional change.

Second, and perhaps more significantly, we observe that the very nature of 'under the radar' strategies and the accompanying political dynamics at the individual level may result in unexpected consequences that are incongruent with desired outcomes. In our study, NPs believed that by showing others (physicians in particular) that NPs could make life easier for them, they would gain a foothold that would lead to the role's more general acceptance in the longer term. In many cases this did occur, but in other cases, physicians were pleased to have someone make their life easier, but that did not lead to acceptance of NPs as new health professionals. We suggest that this finding may help to understand the nuances of institutionalization process – potentially explaining a failure to institutionalize even when legitimacy is achieved. This may also help to understand how the nature of new practices or other institutions evolves or is modified throughout the course of an institutional change process.

Third, although individual efforts may be very effective in achieving legitimacy, as we found in previous research (Reay et al. 2006), different strategies at the organizational or system level may be required to move new practices from *legitimacy* to *fully institutionalized*. We observed that in some cases the move from isolated trials to a legitimated role and on to an institutionalized (taken-for-granted) role was fairly smooth. In other cases, the same individual actions of explaining the new role and improving the work situation for others appeared to reach a point where little progress was evident. At this point, the process of institutionalization might be stalled. Further research may help to identify whether better understanding of a 'stalling point' might provide insights into the overall process of institutionalizing. For example, it may be at points such as these that individuals need to be prepared to create organizational support if it is not already evident. That is, formal managerial support or organizational policies and procedures may be required at certain points of the institutionalizing process.

Finally, our study provides insights into the behavior of individuals involved in institutional change. Previous research has pointed out ways that individuals can take advantage of their institutional knowledge to move forward change agendas (Maguire et al. 2004; Reay et al. 2006). But our study adds richness to the literature by focusing on the political strategies of individuals in attempting to change the behavior of others as part of institutionalizing new practices. Consistent with concepts presented by Buchanan and Badham (1999), individual actors must find ways to make changes in work at the front line. Meyerson (2001) also identified the effectiveness of consistent individual actions that make (quiet) statements about important issues and contribute to the advancement of personally desired goals. Our findings show that quiet persistent actions by individuals can connect change in behavior with the larger scale process of institutionalizing new practices and a new role, but that organizational or system-level support may be needed for widespread institutionalization.

Although our study was conducted in Canada, our experience has implications for health care reform throughout the Western world. Overall, we suggest that health policies should do more than rearrange macro-level structures. As health policy makers search for ways to make service delivery more effective and efficient through such changes as the introduction of new roles, our research points to the importance of micro-level individual efforts in their institutionalization. Front-line actors (e.g., nurse practitioners) can accomplish significant changes through individual persuasion efforts. Although generally effective, these micro-level strategies may be limited, and political entrepreneurs may require organizational and system-level policies to support their efforts. Our research suggests that reform initiatives encouraging individual action while providing organizational support for new approaches hold promise for meaningful health system change.

Acknowledgement

The authors thank the *Canadian Health Services Research Foundation* and the *Alberta Heritage Foundation for Medical Research* for funding that supported this research.

References

Barley, S. R. and Tolbert, P. S. (1997) 'Institutionalization and structuration: Studying the links between action and institution', *Organization Studies*, 18, 93–117.

Buchanan, D. and Badham, R. (1999) *Power, politics, and organizational change*, Thousand Oaks, CA: Sage.

Clemens, E. S. and Cook, J. M. (1999) 'Politics and institutionalism: Explaining durability and change', *Annual Review of Sociology*, 25, 441–466.

Dacin, M. T., Goodstein, J. and Scott, W. R. (2002) 'Institutional theory and institutional change: Introduction to the special research forum', *Academy of Management Journal*, 45(1), 45–56.

Daft, R. (2004) *Organization theory and design*, 8th ed., Mason, OH: Thomson South-Western.

DiMaggio, P. (1988) 'Interest and agency in institutional theory' in L. G. Zucker, (ed) *Institutional patterns and organizations*, Cambridge, MA: Ballinger, pp. 3–21.

Emirbayer, M. and Mische, A. (1998) 'What is agency?', *American Journal of Sociology*, 103, 962–1023.

Fligstein, N. (1997) 'Social skill and institutional theory', *American Behavioral Scientist*, 40(4), 397–405.

Floyd, S. W. and Wooldridge, B. (2000) *Building strategy from the middle*, Thousand Oaks, CA: Sage.

Golden-Biddle, K., Hinings, C. R., Casebeer, A., Pablo, A. and Reay, T. (2006) *Organizational change in healthcare, with special reference to Alberta*, Canadian Health Services Research Foundation, http://www.chsrf.ca/final_research/ogc.

Green, S.E. (2004) 'A rhetorical theory of diffusion', *Academy of Management Review*, 29(4), 653–669.

Greenhalgh, T., Robert, G., Bate, P., Kyriakidou, O., Macfarlane, F. and Peacock, R. (2004) 'How to spread good ideas: A systematic review of the literature on diffusion, dissemination and sustainability of innovations in health service delivery and organisation', *National Co-ordination Centre for NHS Service Delivery and Organisation R&D*, 424.

Greenwood, R., Suddaby, R. and Hinings, C. R. (2002) 'The role of professional associations in the transformation of institutionalized fields', *Academy of Management Journal*, 45, 58–80.

Hensmans, M. (2003) 'Social movement organizations: A metaphor for strategic actors in institutional fields', *Organization Studies*, 24, 355–381.

Maguire, S., Hardy, C. and Lawrence, T. B. (2004) 'Institutional entrepreneurship in emerging fields: HIV/AIDS treatment advocacy in Canada', *Academy of Management Journal*, 47(5), 657–679.

Meyerson, D. E. (2001) 'Radical change the quiet way', *Harvard Business Review*, 79(9), 92–100.

Meyerson, D. E. and Scully, M. A. (1995) 'Tempered radicalism and the politics of ambivalence and change', *Organization Science*, 6, 585–600.

Reay, T., Golden-Biddle, K. and GermAnn, K. (2006) 'Legitimizing a new role: Small wins and micro-processes of change', *Academy of Management Journal*, 49(5), 977–998.

Rogers, E. (1995) *Diffusion of innovations*, 4th ed., New York: Free Press.

Scott, W. R. (2001) *Institutions and organizations*, 2nd ed., Thousand Oaks, CA: Sage.

Seo, M.-G. and Creed, W. E. D. (2002) 'Institutional contradictions, praxis, and institutional change: A dialectical perspective', *Academy of Management Review*, 27, 222–248.

Weick, K. E. (1984) 'Small wins: Redefining the scale of social problems', *American Psychologist*, 39, 40–49.

Zilber, T. B. (2002) 'Institutionalization as an interplay between actions, meanings, and actors: The case of a rape crisis center in Israel', *Academy of Management Journal*, 45, 234–251.

14

Knowledge to Action? The Implications for Policy and Practice of Research on Innovation Processes

Louise Fitzgerald, Sue Dopson, Ewan Ferlie and Louise Locock

Introduction

The focus of this chapter is to explore the policy and practice implications arising from research into the diffusion of innovations into use in health care. The empirical data upon which the discussion is founded thus focuses on the latter stages of the innovation process. Here, the practitioners in health care, many of whom are highly qualified clinical professionals, decide whether to accept evidence of an efficacious new intervention, whether drug, technology or service delivery process, and adopt it in their practice.

To inform this discussion, this chapter will first, briefly, allude to several relevant areas of prior research and literature.

Historically, there have been many studies on the diffusion of innovation, and researchers have stressed support building (Kimberly and Evanisko 1981) and so-called translational strategies (Callon et al. 1992) as critical to the diffusion of new knowledge. Van de Ven et al. (1999) identify the messy processes involved and the fluid and spasmodic participation by different individuals and groups during the process of innovation creation and adoption. The work of these authors serves to underline the complex and interactive processes apparent in the diffusion and adoption of innovations.

Building on this foundation, results from research in the health care sector (Bloch et al. 2006; Fairhurst and Huby 1998) raise critical questions about the problematic nature of Evidence-Based Health Care (EBHC) and effective processes for diffusing new practices in professionalized organizations.

Implementing EBHC might be usefully informed by prior research on the implementation of strategic change in health care, which has underlined that transformational change within such organizations is difficult to achieve (McNulty and Ferlie 2002). Effective change processes need to include the involvement of key stakeholders, particularly members of the clinical professions (Denis et al. 1996; Ferlie et al. 1996). Research has also highlighted the significant impact which organizational context can have on the effective implementation processes (Dawson 1992; Pettigrew et al. 1992). Pettigrew et al. (1992) in their analysis characterized the features of so-called 'receptive' contexts for change within health care settings in terms of their ability to progress a strategic change agenda. Localities were observed to achieve differential rates of change and this model helped explain the pattern of variation. These eight dimensions included consistency of strategy; continuity of leadership; involvement of professionals in the process and HR capacity. This has proved to be a model of change management in health care organizations which has retained considerable influence and impact. For example, it was recently used by Spitzer and Perrenoud (2006) to analyse organizational change processes in nursing education.

Shifting the focus to the application of research to policy, there has been extensive debate about EBHC, the issues in updating health care procedures and in influencing clinicians. So how has the policy domain used the research evidence? Different countries created distinctive policy frameworks, reflecting their higher level health system characteristics. In the UK, the Department of Health created an R&D strategy and directorate from the early 1990s onwards which operates within a centralized and planned system. New synthesizing institutions (such as the National Institute of Clinical Excellence) distill the knowledge base and recommend nationally whether new treatments are both clinically and cost effective. By contrast, in the USA, the Agency for Health Care Policy and Research (AHCPR), reauthorized as the Agency for Healthcare Research and Quality in 1999 seeks to influence a plurality of providers and sponsors and conducts research. The Canadian Health Services Research Foundation was created as an arm's length foundation in 1996 to support evidence-based decision-making, operating in a system with substantial inter-provincial variation.

UK policy in relation to EBHC has been typically top-down, formalized and prescriptive, in keeping with the government's overall stance towards public services management reform and the Department of Health's direct line management control over the bulk of the health care system. For example, currently the UK National Service Frameworks (NSFs) provide a nationally consistent set of evidence-based guidelines in important sectors (e.g. cancer services). The NHS Modernisation Agency, now incorporated into the NHS Institute for Improvement and Innovation (NIII) is a central body with a particular remit to help spread best practice in key areas of service improvement.

But do top-down interventions 'from above' succeed in putting evidence into practice at the clinical front line?

Methods

With limited space, this chapter will concentrate on the presentation of empirical evidence and the policy implications of these. This section will merely provide a brief overview of the research methods and access for the reader to more detailed sources.

The source of our analysis is an overview of a set of case studies in the UK NHS studying the careers of innovations, that is, their trajectories over time from invention to implementation or in some cases, non-implementation (Dopson and Fitzgerald 2005). These set of seven studies included 48 NHS case studies based on 800 semi-structured face-to-face interviews with clinical and managerial respondents, as well as nearly 600 telephone interviews, with further use of written questionnaires and documentary analysis. Table 14.1 provides more details of the studies.

This therefore represents a substantial database upon which to draw conclusions, and the details of the methods within individual studies can be found in prior publications (Dopson et al. 1999; Ferlie et al. 2000; Fitzgerald et al. 1999).

The process of synthesis and analysis across the studies was attempted as an exploratory methodological project, an attempt to innovate and was based on an iterative, but time-consuming process. The detailed approach to each stage of the synthesis can be found in Dopson and Fitzgerald (2005). Briefly, there were four main stages to the overall process:

> *Stage 1 – initial overview*: From this stage, we developed an initial overview of the findings, identifying common themes emerging from each team's separate key points. The major headings identified at this stage were: evidence, context, professionals and opinion leaders, translation, management/organization.
>
> *Stage 2 – pilot analysis of one theme by one researcher*: We selected a pilot theme for detailed analysis, the role of opinion leaders and one researcher developed a detailed analysis from all the data, which was then discussed and critiqued by the team.

Table 14.1 An overview of the research design and methods across the seven projects

	Design	No. of case studies	Face-to-face interviews	Telephone interviews	Written questionnaires	Document analysis	Dates
Study 1 Dopson and Gabbay (1995)	Single stage case studies on four clinical topics	4	58 (RHA and purchasing managers, clinicians and public health)			✓	Two years 1993–94
Study 2 Wood et al. (1998)	Stages: 1. Overview survey across whole region		71 (mainly front-line clinicians)			✓	Two years 1995–97
	2. Case studies, one per clinical topic	4	48 (mainly clinicians and clinical managers)			✓	Two years 1995–97
Study 3 Dawson et al. (1998)	Embedded case studies, two clinical topics in each of four hospitals	8	256 (clinical staff, plus 20 with trust and HA managers)		256 (same group as interviews)	✓	Two years 1995–97
Study 4 CSAG (1998)	Single stage case study design, full in seven sites, telephone and questionnaire only in six	13 (7 + 6)	250 (front-line clinicians and managers)	321	1317 GPs, 256 hospital clinicians	✓	Six months 1996–97

Table 14.1 (Continued)

	Design	No. of case studies	Face-to-face interviews	Telephone interviews	Written questionnaires	Document analysis	Dates
Study 5 Fitzgerald et al. (1999)	Stages: 1. Overview across four HAs on diffusion of innovation		38 (senior HA managers and GPs) + 35 (clinicians)			✓	Two years 1997–99
	2. Case studies on four innovations in primary care	4	40 (GPs and other primary care and physiotherapy staff)				
Study 6 Dopson et al. (1999)	Stages: 1. Initial round of interviews half-way through project.	16	7 (staff from King's Fund and DoH)	51 (project team members, managers and clinicians)		✓	Two years 1997–98
	2. Second round at end of project, using themes elicited during 1st stage			122 (project team members, senior managers and clinicians)	150 (front-line clinicians)	✓	Two years 1997–98
Study 7 Locock et al. (1999)	Single stage case studies, after project completion	6	18 (front-line clinicians)	65 (project team members, senior managers and clinicians)	238 (front-line clinicians)	✓	Six months 1998–99

All interviews were in-depth and semi-structured.

Stage 3 – analysis of one theme by all researchers: To support this stage and to work systematically, we prepared a draft coding structure of themes and sub-headings, which each team member then applied to the theme of the nature of the research evidence, working independently through all the documents.

Stage 4 – analysis of all themes by all researchers: At the next stage, each researcher individually applied the whole coding structure to all the themes and all the reports, looking for points of difference as well as convergence, and reflecting on (a) use of different terms to define similar areas and (b) use of similar terms but meaning different things.

In the following empirical section, we present some selected evidence on three of these themes and then, subsequently, we discuss the policy implications of these findings.

Empirical data

Our selection of empirical data is built around the three key themes which were ranked as of strong or very strong importance by all the researcher/synthesizers separately and were then assessed by the researcher/synthesizers in a later rating exercise as having the highest potential relevance for the renewal of policy. For example, the importance of context was assessed as of very strong importance in six studies and as of strong importance in a seventh. It was also seen as having important policy implications which we will develop here, particularly in respect of the micro-context.

Theme 1 – the importance of context: local, constructed and active

Whilst the literature on receptive contexts and the empirical data which supports it have tended to focus on the higher levels of strategic decision-making in organizations, our studies focused at both strategic and middle management levels in health care organizations and draw special attention to the importance of micro-contexts in implementing innovations.

The micro-context strongly shapes the strength of demand for evidence by health professionals and their ability to process it. This localized and group-based ability to process evidence and turn it into practice change is critical. Health professionals do not apply abstract, disembodied scientific research to the situation around them on an individualized basis. Instead, they discuss, relate evidence to the local health care context and actively interpret and (re)construct its local validity and usefulness.

At the micro-level, local clinical settings vary in their ability to translate evidence into practice change. This important empirical finding highlights the critical role of micro-context (Dopson and Fitzgerald 2005:177) whose factors include:

- the availability and engagement of local, credible and skilled clinical opinion leaders to sponsor an evidence-based innovation;
- a foundation of good prior relationships, especially between different clinical professional groups and between clinicians and managers;
- the historical development of the services which influences current structures and behaviours;
- the structural configuration of the location;
- change and project management capacity available to support behaviour change;
- the support of senior management as a key power resource;
- an underlying organizational climate that values the free flow of knowledge across boundaries.

Our empirical data highlight that the particular actors in each local context and the relationships and interdependencies of these actors are critical. It is evident that if the relationships between the members of professional groups are poor or conflicting, then limited cooperation will occur to implement evidence-based improvements. In our case studies, we found examples of widely varying sets of relationships. Without reasonable relationships and at least limited communication between professionals and managers, action at a local level does not occur. It may also be that the historical development of services and their current configuration may raise challenges to the development of evidence-based services, sometimes requiring the questioning of assumptions about the 'way we have always done things around here'. Thus in the case of glue ear in Study 3, there were widely differing referral patterns for patients presenting with these symptoms, and significantly different professional groups had established a varied array of power positions from one location to another.

Crucially, the actors in any organizational context make sense of their settings subjectively, by using previous experience, cognition and emotional judgment and cues.

Importantly then, the micro-context should not be seen just as a backcloth to action (as too often portrayed) but rather the two are tightly integrated – for example, the presence of a clinical product champion is a feature of micro-context, but is also strongly linked to purposive action. Actors draw on aspects of local context to legitimate their proposals for action: they draw context in.

Theme 2 – professional boundaries and the diffusion of evidence-based Innovation

Health care is characterized by many co-located professions, typically seeking to capture occupational turf or jurisdictions on the basis of their claims to expertise. Where innovations disturb traditional inter-professional divisions of labour, they may be blocked (Swan et al. 2002) by the losing profession. Non-professional actors such as lay management or patients played a marginal role in decision-making in the cases. Evidence-based health care was a highly professionalized arena, colonized by different, competing health care professions.

Our research data illustrate that it is not the physical, geographical or formal boundaries between health care organizations or the boundaries of a single profession which are significant, but rather the underpinning social and cognitive boundaries that membership of a profession creates (Ferlie et al. 2005). These social and cognitive boundaries are assembled through the period of initial training, which is predominantly uni-professional and through subsequent post-experience training, much of which remains uni-professional. One consequence of differing training and socialization processes is the existence of profession-linked hierarchies of evidence. The randomized control trial (RCT) is the method of choice within bio-medicine, but the question of what 'counts' as good-quality evidence was widely contested. There were differing views within the medical profession, particularly between general practitioners and acute hospital consultants, but widespread differences of view if one included the nursing, midwifery and Allied Health professionals.

These cognitive boundaries are reinforced by the power differentials between professions, which continue to exist within health care. In many instances, medical dominance is structurally reinforced when key influential roles, such as Clinical Director, Chair of Professional

Executive Committee in a PCT and Research and Development Director are held by doctors.

Theme 3 – the local enactment of evidence in practice

The fact that robust evidence is available and indeed accessible does not guarantee that it will be used. The social process of the enactment of evidence so that it turned from mere information to utilized knowledge was our third theme. Evidence is information; knowledge, on the other hand, is the acceptance of that evidence as valuable within a given context which leads to action. Critics of EBHC detect a rigid and reductionist emphasis on scientific evidence as the primary determinant of clinical practice (Hunter 1996), which undervalues medicine's more holistic and empathetic side, in which judgement, experience and skill are also important.

In many cases, the robustness of the scientific evidence was not clear to the individual clinician and was frequently not agreed between clinicians. Its quality was disputed and there were differences of view about what was or was not proven. In the case study of surgical methods of hernia repair (Study 2), there had been ongoing and unresolved disputes over many years. Many quotes illustrated the manner in which positions, often antagonistic positions, were adopted. This reinforces the theoretical view that knowledge is fragile, politicized and rhetorical and that the acquisition and sharing of knowledge involves human agency (Blackler 1995). Clinicians often sought out and believed data confirming their preferred treatment options rather than engaging in systematic search behaviour. A common complaint was of being flooded with a surfeit of information. One typical response to this was to refer to others with more specialist knowledge and to rely on discussion with one's peers (normally from the same profession), before deciding whether to adopt an innovation or not. There was reliance by clinicians on tacit knowledge and experience as well as explicit knowledge.

To understand the processes of enactment then, we have to combine the points raised in Themes 1 and 2, concerning the interactions with characteristics of the local contexts and the boundaries of professional groups. In transcending these barriers, the roles of individual opinion leaders are vitally important. The presence or absence of local opinion leaders may account for variation in progress in innovating (Locock et al. 2001). Opinion leaders act as specialist resources; influence; involve; negotiate; generate; and implement political strategies. Enactment therefore involves rational and emotional

elements, judgments and interpretations of the local context and adaptation to those circumstances.

Implications for policy and practice

This section seeks to draw out the key messages for policy makers and
practitioners from these research findings and to encourage closer scrutiny of the details of these findings.

Developing combined, flexible strategies for policy implementation

The challenge here is to establish what policies would best underpin the
development of EBHC. We perceive that there is a need for combined
strategies which will reduce the reliance on targets as a means of encouraging actions on the part of practitioners. One core focus needs to be
the development of knowledgeable and competent clinical managers to
work on local strategies of implementation. This strand of the strategy
would then need to be complemented by the role of national institutions in supporting local processes. The former NHSMA's policies, now
replaced by the NHSIII, included many national programmes, involving
a process of roll out of good practice. Ham et al. (2003) found not only
strong local variation in impact, but also issues about the sustainability of short-term gains. These issues of sustainability are reinforced
in Buchanan et al. (2007) work which demonstrates the fragility of
the change processes and their dependence on individual managers.
National intervention strategies need to be rethought and more attention paid to facilitating longer term development of local capacity, to
providing direction, research and creative ideas and to placing resources
with care.

Receptive contexts, the average context and positive outliers – developing local capacity

Theme 1 suggested that local clinical settings have distinctive profiles,
which affect their ability to process and enact evidence across professional boundaries. These distinctive profiles derive from a complex
configuration of factors. Across the cases, positive factors included not
only the robustness of the knowledge base, but also the presence of
credible opinion leaders and a foundation of good inter-professional
relations. Negative factors included disengagement by a key stakeholder

group and barriers between different professions, complicated by power struggles.

The implication for policy development is that it is not easy to transfer an evidence-based innovation from more to less positive micro-settings. A long haul is more likely than a quick fix. Our data suggest that a wholly positive configuration is rare. The crucial implication is that policy makers need to plan for and deal with the average context, with a mix of positive and negative features. So linear, national roll out from early leading edge sites is problematic. This finding reinforces McNulty and Ferlie's (2002)'s analysis of the differential impact of business process reengineering interventions in clinical settings and recent research on the limits to the diffusion of innovations in the NHS (Newell et al. 2003). Differing conditions explained the variable impact. The danger is that positive outliers may remain just that: outliers.

So the current UK policy emphasis on producing national frameworks may not be sufficient, without complementary interventions to enhance the underlying capability of the system, particularly at the micro-level. The transfer of good quality, experienced change agents from high-change to low-change sites is one possible policy response. Another would be to systematically develop multi-disciplinary education and training interventions to stimulate inter-professional dialogue and learning.

Developing bridging roles – using clinical opinion leaders more effectively

Our findings illustrated the importance of credible clinical opinion leaders in innovation diffusion. But how do general management and policy makers identify and engage with clinical opinion leaders to fulfil influencing roles (Locock et al. 2001)? Subjective understandings of what a clinical opinion leader is vary substantially. Self-described clinical opinion leaders may operate with covert objectives, using EBHC as a vehicle. Such clinical opinion leaders did not have as high impact as originally hoped for by EBHC advocates. Nor was their effect always positive: the influence of hostile or ambivalent opinion leaders as 'change blockers' is an important and neglected area.

Our data suggest that clinical opinion leaders could be developed from a range of roles and professions, nurses and Allied Health Professionals as well as doctors. Individuals whose roles naturally and by self-selection provide them with cross-boundary responsibilities, such as Nurse Advisors and PCT Pharmacy Advisors are prime candidates for development. The management system needs to identify and develop such clinical leaders, selecting them with care. They need exposure not only to education in relation to research evidence, but also to the theory and practice of change management. These opinion leaders should be encouraged to retain part time clinical roles to maintain professional peer group credibility. The development of local internal change agents, from among the general management cadre, would complement the movement of experienced change managers between sites. The development of HRM systems to reward and support these roles and careers is important.

Moving knowledge across professional boundaries

The themes from our research show that the enactment of evidence was often impeded by social and epistemological boundaries between the health care professions. Policy makers need to consider new mechanisms for sharing evidence and working practices across these boundaries between health care professions.

At local levels, multi-professional fora for identifying, debating and sharing such knowledge are either lacking or poorly integrated into clinical and organizational decision-making. A foundation of well-developed professional and inter-professional fora which generate real engagement and high attendance levels is needed. Such foundations are built up over time, but represent critical advantages. We stress the need for multi rather than uni-professional education and training, which may require policy level interventions into existing programmes which gravitate towards single professions. Busy clinicians need space for genuine learning and debate to rebalance a current bias to action which results in role overload.

The appointment of specific bridging or facilitation roles reduces the timescale for shared learning and shifts the negative perceptions between different professional groups. Our examples include the clinical role of a research midwife and the managerial role of the project leader. Management or clinical opinion leaders can play a creative role in organizational design, constructing receptive organizational settings. At the higher level of programme design, we found coherent implementation strategies, which stressed capacity development, were more commonly found in pilot projects and national development projects, than in naturally occurring innovations. The national policy level could play a valuable role here, as could the NHS intermediate tier (Strategic Health Authorities) which cover large geographical patches. It needs to be recognized that there are some countervailing forces (such as the speciality based Royal Colleges) which may typically act to retard bridging roles, in the interests of disciplinary defense.

Lomas (2005) highlights the importance of research synthesis in order to answer health care managers' and policy makers' questions and argues that social scientists have a central role in such synthesis. We offer this chapter to provide some specific pointers to action.

Acknowledgement

The authors acknowledge the support of the UK NHS R and D Programme for funding the research on which this paper is based.

References

Blackler, F. (1995) 'Knowledge, knowledge work and organizations', *Organization Studies*, 16(6), 1021–1046.

Bloch, R. M., Saeed, S. I., Rivard, J. C. and Rausch, C. (2006) 'Lessons learned in implementing evidence-based practices: Implications for psychiatric administrators', *Psychiatric Quarterly*, 77(4), 309.

Buchanan, D., Fitzgerald, L. and Ketley, D. (eds) (2007) *The spread and sustainability of organizational change: Modernizing health care*, Abingdon/New York: Routledge.

Callon, M., Laredo, P., Rabehariosoa, V., Gonadr, T. and Leray, T. (1992) 'The management and evaluation of technological programs and the dynamics of techno-economic networks: The case of the AFME', *Research Policy*, 21, 215–236.

CSAG (Clinical Standards Advisory Group) (1998) *Clinical effectiveness*, London: Clinical Standards Advisory Group.

Dawson, P. (1992) *Reshaping change: A processual perspective*, London: Routledge.

Dawson, S., Sutherland, K., Dopson, S., Miller, R. with Law, S. (1998) *The relationship between R&D and clinical practice in primary and secondary care: Cases of adult asthma and glue ear in children: Final report*, Judge Institute of Management Studies, University of Cambridge and Saïd Business School, University of Oxford.

Denis, J. L., Langley, A. and Cazale, L. (1996) 'Leadership and strategic change under ambiguity', *Organization Studies*, 17(4), 673–699.

Dopson, S. and Fitzgerald, L. (eds) (2005) *Knowledge to action?* Oxford: Oxford University Press.

Dopson, S. and Gabbay, J. (1995) *Evaluation of the national initiative getting research into practice and policy*, Oxford Region: Department of Health.

Dopson, S., Dawson, S., Miller, R. and Sutherland, K. (1999) 'Getting research into practice: The case of glue ear', *Quality in Health Care*, 8, 108–118.

Fairhurst, K. and Huby, G. (1998) 'From trial data to practical knowledge: A qualitative study of how general practitioners have accessed and used evidence about statin drugs in their management of hypercholesterolaemia', *British Medical Journal*, 317, 1130–1134.

Ferlie, E., Ashburner, L., Fitzgerald, L. and Pettigrew, A.M. (1996) *The new public management in action*, Oxford: Oxford University Press.

Ferlie, E., Fitzgerald, L. and Wood, M. (2000) 'Getting evidence into clinical practice: An organizational behavior perspective', *Journal of Health Services Research and Policy*, 5(1), 1–7.

Ferlie, E., Fitzgerald, L., Wood, M., and Hawkins, C. (2005) 'The (non) diffusion of innovations: The mediating role of professional groups', *Academy of Management Journal*, 48(1), 117–134.

Fitzgerald, L., Ferlie, E., Wood, M. and Hawkins, C. (1999) 'Evidence into practice? An exploratory analysis of the interpretation of evidence' in A. Mark and S. Dopson (eds), *Organization Behaviour in Health Care*, London :Macmillan 189–206.

Ham, C., Kipping, R. and McLeod, H. (2003) 'Redesigning work processes in health care – lessons from the NHS', *Milbank Quarterly*, 81(3), 415–439.

Hunter, D. (1996) 'Rationing and evidence based medicine', *Journal of Evaluation and Clinical Practice*, 2(1), 5–8.

Kimberly, J. R. and Evanisko, M. J. (1981) 'Organizational innovation: The influence of individual, organizational and contextual factors on hospital adoption of technological and administrative innovations', *Academy of Management Journal*, 24(4), 689–713.

Locock, L., Chambers, D., Surender, R., Dopson, S. and Gabbay, J. (1999) *Evaluation of the Welsh Clinical Effectiveness Initiative National Demonstration Projects: Final report*, Templeton College Oxford and the Wessex Institute for Health Research and Development, University of Southampton.

Locock, L., Dopson, S., Chambers, D. and Gabbay, J. (2001) 'Understanding the role of opinion leaders in improving clinical effectiveness', *Social Science and Medicine*, 53(6), 745–757.

Lomas, J. (2005) 'Using research to inform healthcare managers' and policy makers' questions: From summative to interpretive synthesis', *Health Care Policy*, 1(1), 55–71.

McNulty, T. and Ferlie, E. (2002) *Process transformation? A case of re-engineering in health care*, Oxford: Oxford University Press.

Newell, S., Edelman, H., Scarborough, H., Swan, J. and Bresnan, M. (2003) ' "Best practice" development and transfer in the NHS: The importance of process as well as product knowledge', *Health Services Management Research*, 16, 1–12.

Pettigrew, A.M., Ferlie, E. and McKee, L. (1992) *Shaping strategic change – Making change in large organisations, the case of the NHS*, London: Sage.

Spitzer, A. and Perrenoud, B. (2006) 'Reforms in nursing education across Western Europe – from agenda to practice', *Journal of Professional Nursing*, May/June, 2293, 150–161.

Swan, J. Scarborough, H. and Robertson, M. (2002) 'The construction of "communities of practice" in the management of innovation', *Management Learning*, 33(4), 477–496.

Van de Ven, A., Polley, D. E., Garud, R. and Venkataraman, S. (1999) *The innovation journey*, Oxford/New York: Oxford University Press.

15

Is the Best Defense a Good Offense? Marketing of Quality by US Nursing Homes

Jane Banaszak-Holl, Judith G. Calhoun and Larry R. Hearld

In recent decades, health care has seen the introduction of a greater number of corporate and managerial practices with the intended purpose of improving the organization and delivery of services (Scott et al. 2000). Although the spread of managerial logic has been slower among nursing homes, recent growth of large facilities and corporate-owned facilities has helped introduce administrative processes into this sector (Kitchener and Harrington 2004). Managerial practices are tools for improving efficiency and effectiveness, but they also play an important role institutionalizing authority and influencing external stakeholders (Scott et al. 2000). In this study, we examine how facility quality and structural characteristics affect both internal uses of quality information and attempts to influence external stakeholders' views of quality in the nursing home industry.

Quality of US nursing home care is frequently cited as poor with dramatic examples of overuse of restraints and pharmaceutical controls and uncontrolled pressure ulcers within resident populations (Institute of Medicine 1986; Wunderlich and Kohler 2001). Policy makers increasingly use regulation to address quality problems and have been moderately successful in reducing dramatic abuses (Walshe 2001). Regulation, though, has not been successful in producing high levels of service excellence, perhaps because quality of nursing home care can be difficult to both define and attain. Generally, service quality is defined and measured relative to the eyes of the beholder (Conlon et al. 2004), and quality of nursing home care is no exception in that it is highly subject to individuals' preferences and values (Chaiken 1992; Kane 2001; Kane and Kane 2000; Leatherman et al. 2003). Nursing homes striving to achieve quality care are caught in the middle between the differing perspectives of consumers and regulators. Regulators define quality using clinical indicators related to medical conditions; while consumers, though they may agree on the importance of health indicators, also desire attention to individual preferences and desires for specific types of services and amenities (Kane 2001).

Nursing home care affects all aspects of a resident's life and requires relatively long periods of daily interactions with care providers – these are a few of the reasons why factors other than health are important to consumers. Marketers define such a relationship as captive and intensive and argue that consumers' expectations of how services are provided and what happens during service encounters are key to successful captive relationships (Bitner 1990; Conlon et al. 2004).

Marketing and effective communication of an organizational identity and values is essential when intense service relationships are present (Scott and Lane 2000). Customer relations is a key way to build organizational identity and differentiates current marketing practices from more traditional marketing practices of advertising and public relations – ways that mass market organizational identity (Kotler and Armstrong 2006; Thomas 2005).

Recent activities support the argument that nursing homes will find it important to include quality in their public identities. Today, growing public sentiment supports the use of public scorecards so that consumers can then take more active roles in evaluating quality (Castle and Lowe 2004; Harrington et al. 2003). We expect that nursing homes would respond to the quality movement because past research has found nursing homes responsive to stakeholder demands for quality improvement initiatives and changes in service provision (Banaszak-Holl et al. 1996; Weech-Maldonado et al. 1999; Zinn et al. 1998).

In examining whether facilities market themselves as quality institutions, we test hypotheses from institutional and business strategy theories predicting which facilities will engage in marketing and we address three general questions: First, how do facilities market quality? Second, how does quality marketing fit with other uses of quality information and with general marketing practices? Finally, do market factors or internal business practices have a stronger impact on marketing practices? Quality must be the responsibility of providers as well as regulators and our findings identify the extent to which facilities use quality in marketing, a managerial activity central to organizational identity.

Theoretical approaches to quality marketing

We contrast two theoretical approaches to studying work practices in nursing homes. Institutional theory provides a basis for understanding how organizations engage stakeholders in defining standards and consumer expectations, focusing on how changes in managerial practices reflect shifts in social values and in the definition of what is 'socially acceptable' (Meyer and Rowan 1977). Attempts to influence stakeholder views focus on criteria or characteristics critical to differentiating providers' competitive advantage – those factors that sustain both an organization and an industry's unique identity. Physicians, for example, promoted professional standards and the right to professional autonomy when their professional identity was threatened by managed care (Scott et al. 2000).

Marketing is a key activity for promoting organizational identity and unique service characteristics. Rao and colleagues found that early car races in the history of the automobile industry were promoted by the automobile companies seeking to shape consumer preferences for fast cars (Rao 1994). Similarly, French restaurant chefs promoted new cooking techniques and fresher ingredients as unique components of Nouvelle Cuisine (Rao et al. 2003). In other markets, dimensions of quality have been used strategically in marketing and brand management (Ingram and Baum 1997). Within the hotel industry, the Marriott chain explicitly differentiates the quality and types of services available through its Marriott, Fairfield Inn and Renaissance Hotel brands.

We test whether high-quality facilities distinguish themselves from competitors and whether administrators who recognize customers as important will be more likely to market quality. Our hypotheses are as follows:

> H1. Administrators whose long-term care facilities are high quality are more likely to market quality of care.
>
> H2. Administrators who perceive customer marketing as important will be more likely to market quality of care.

Promotion and marketing activities are also key to developing thorough business functions and essential administrative acumen (Buss 1994). From a business strategy perspective, the integration of quality information into marketing depends on whether the facility uses marketing practices more generally and the availability of resources to develop managerial capabilities. As more individuals are involved in marketing decisions, they may be more likely to adopt modern marketing practices, including the use of quality information. Furthermore, increasing the number of individuals involved in decisions generates diversity in marketing practices, which can contribute to the use of new or different marketing techniques. Hence, we hypothesize that:

H3. The more managers included in marketing decision-making, the more likely a facility will market quality of care.

Facilities with more resources and that are larger should also be better able to implement the marketing of quality. We do not have precise measures for the availability of resources; however, both urban status and nonprofit ownership are key structural factors affecting access to resources and can be important to marketing practices. Rural facilities are known to use more generic marketing strategies (Zinn et al. 1994), which may in part be because rural facilities are more likely found in counties with lower per capita incomes (Mor et al. 2004). While nonprofits are driven less by the market environment (Harrington et al. 2001), they have much greater access to resources and that access to resources will be critical to marketing quality, as we have argued:

H4. Administrators who manage larger, urban, and nonprofit facilities are more likely to market quality of care.

Finally, we examine whether the availability of resources interacts with institutional factors to affect the use of marketing practices. We hypothesize that

H5. Effects predicted in hypotheses 1 and 2 will be stronger within larger and urban facilities.

Methods

This paper uses data from a survey mailed to administrators of all Medicare and Medicaid certified nursing homes in 18 counties commonly defined as southeast Michigan during the summer and fall, 2002. A total of 236 facilities were contacted and 101 responded; response rate was 44%. Follow-up with initial nonrespondents helped boost our response rate. Additional data were taken from Nursing Home Compare (at www.medicare.gov) that included facility ownership status, size, occupancy rates, presence of family councils and quality deficiencies reported on state inspections. The Nursing Home Compare website uses data from the On-Line Survey, Certification, and Report System (OSCAR), which provides information on facilities' structural character- istics and adherence to quality standards defined through regulations. While there are limitations to the OSCAR data, the Nursing Home Compare website is accessed by both consumers and researchers for quality information.

Our facility survey included 27 items on current practices for marketing, communications and promotion (Calhoun et al. 2006). We also identified the level and types of staff involved in marketing and administrators' perceptions of factors affecting the success of marketing and promotion. Respondents were provided the following definition of marketing practices: 'all of the planning, relationship management, communication and promotional activities and tools (including advertising, web services, newsletters, etc.) and activities utilized to inform and meet the needs of your key customers and residents – both current and prospective'. Survey items were developed from extensive review of the nursing home marketing literature and using faculty expertise in marketing, strategic planning and nursing home care. Pilot tests were conducted in three local nursing homes. For key concepts in the model, we created summative scales (Spector 1992) incorporating both providers' perceptions of what aspects of marketing are important and whether the facility engages in specific practices.

The survey items included both Likert ratings and checklists of activ- ities that were later coded as counts. Scale constructs were created from responses to multiple items, in some cases combining different types of questions, including those that may have required either a yes/no or limited response. All counts were converted to the 0–1 range by calculating the percent items reported out of maximum possible. Other variables were also standardized to the 0–1 range. Exploratory factor analysis was used to evaluate the relationships among measures. Given the lack of theory and evidence on marketing practices in long-term care (Calhoun et al. 2006), our scales are exploratory attempts to identify marketing practices.

Quality strategy measures

Our key measure on quality strategies includes both the extent to which facility staff identify and use quality information in the facility (i.e., quality feedback) and the subsequent promotion of quality (i.e., quality promotion). The full quality strategy scale was constructed by combining individual scales for quality promotion and quality feedback.

The quality promotion scale combines three survey items regarding (1) the perceived importance of quality promotion, (2) which activities are used to promote quality and (3) the types of quality indicators used in promotional materials. Respondents were asked first whether it was important to include quality in marketing initiatives on a scale ranging from 1 = 'not at all important' to 6 = 'extremely important'. Second, they were asked to indicate what types of marketing activities were used from a list that included: communications, personal or direct marketing, advertising, websites, yellow pages or none of the above. Finally, respondents were asked to indicate all types of quality indicators used in marketing and promotion, including quality of medical/clinical care, range of services/amenities, caring staff, continuum of care levels, home-like/community setting, state/federal regulatory ratings, staff credentials, awards received, faith-based environment, special program affiliations or others as specified. The latter two questions were converted to counts.

The quality feedback scale combined two constructs on the extent to which quality information was used within facilities to affect both routine activities and customer communication. The first construct came from a survey question that asked respondents to indicate the quality improvement initiatives their facility conducted from a list of five that included quality indicator reviews, resident and family satisfaction and staff satisfaction surveys, quality assurance committee reviews and total quality management initiatives. Respondents were also asked to indicate the types of customer relationship management (CRM) activities they used, choosing again from a list that included stakeholder advisory boards (for six types of stakeholders that include residents, referral sources, family, other payers, staff and volunteers), satisfaction surveys (for residents, families, referral sources and staff), solicitation of stakeholder feedback (from residents, family, referral sources or other payers), open house tours, alliances with other health care providers and use of customer demographic databases. For both feedback measures, respondents could enter other relevant examples and these are included in our counts.

Quality measures

We measured the quality of a facility's performance in two ways: first, by the number of deficiencies that a facility receives on its most recent annual inspection, a frequently used measure of clinical quality, and second, by occupancy rate or the percent of facility beds that are filled, an indirect measure of financial performance. Clinical and financial performance are fundamentally different; subsequently, both measures are included in analyses. Harrington and her colleagues have recently identified some problems with using aggregated deficiency data (Harrington and Carillo 1999; Harrington et al. 2001); nonetheless, health care scholars have found OSCAR deficiency data to be sufficiently accurate and useful in health services research (Harrington et al. 2000). Occupancy is critical to balancing costs with revenues in the facility and hence is used here to measure financial performance.

Consumer focus

Recognizing that one should market to customers reflects a certain level of self-awareness that we expect to affect quality marketing. We asked three questions about a facility's customer focus. First, we asked how many different consumer groups were targeted with marketing activities (respondents could check all that applied from a list including: the general public, seniors, family members, physicians, social workers, nurses, clergy and other). Second, we asked whether the facility segmented the market for marketing purposes and if yes, on what basis (geography, age, type of care or other).

Participation in marketing

Involvement of staff in marketing activities was measured using a scale based on two survey items: first, a count of the number of people contributing to the development of a facility's general marketing strategy (respondents could indicate involvement from the following list: local owners, board of directors, facility-level committees, nursing home administrator, marketing director, corporate leadership in the chain and other people). Second, the level of control an administrator felt he or she had when implementing marketing activities was coded on a scale from 1 = 'none at all' through 4 = 'a considerable amount' to 6 = 'total control'.

Structural capacity

We also include variables related to the structural or resource capacity of nursing home facilities. The size of a facility was measured using the total number of beds. Ownership was defined as either nonprofit or for-profit and government-owned facilities were dropped from these analyses because marketing is a less appropriate activity for these facilities. Urban status was defined as counties with populations of 50,000 or more using population information from the State of Michigan website and the 2000 US Census.

Control variables

Market competition is controlled in our model using a scale composed of two items assessing the administrator's perceptions of competition, because we expect differences in marketing approaches in highly competitive environments. First, nursing homes were asked to rate competitive intensity in the market from which they drew the greatest number of residents (on a range from 'Not at all' to 'Extremely competitive'). Second, nursing homes were asked to identify how many competitors operated in their service area.

Methods of analysis

Nursing Home Compare and independent *t*-tests were used to determine whether there was a response bias to our survey. These results have been reported previously (Calhoun et al. 2006). Survey respondents were similar to nonrespondents in size, occupancy rate and whether certified for Medicare and Medicaid. The majority of both respondents and nonrespondents were larger chain organizations and few in either group were hospital-based or government-owned. Respondents were statistically less likely to be part of a chain, more likely to be nonprofit and had fewer deficiencies than nonrespondents.

Effects of institutional and business strategy variables were tested using Ordinary Least Squares regression models predicting three scaled outcomes: (1) the overall quality strategy, which combines scales for quality promotion and quality feedback, and then separately for (2) quality promotion practices and (3) quality feedback practices. Hypothesis 5 is tested by including interaction terms with urban and large (having 100 beds or more) status. These results were largely insignificant and are only reported within the text.

Results

First we address the question of whether and how facilities promote quality and then test our hypotheses. Table 15.1 includes descriptive statistics on the relevant survey questions used to create construct scales. The results in the table indicate that nursing homes are engaged in key marketing activities and use quality in a number of ways.

While administrators were interested in using quality, the current level of actual activities may reflect limited use of marketing practices

Table 15.1   Descriptive statistics on strategy and control variables ($N = 101$)

Variable	Mean	SD	Min.	Max.
Consumer focus				
Total number of groups targeted	4.81	1.971	1	8
Segment audiences (1 = segment)	0.31	.458	0	1
Involvement in strategic decision-making				
Number involved in development	2.11	1.076	1	4
Control of marketing implementation	4.41	1.170	1	6
Quality performance				
Number of deficiencies	11.52	8.97	0	46
Occupancy rate	84.21	16.64	14.00	100.00
Controls				
Perceived market competition				
Competitive market	4.30	1.171	1	6
Number of competitors	8.18	6.29	0	33
Chain affiliation (1 = chain affiliated)	0.39	0.489	0	1
Size/number of beds	123.20	65.01	19	330
Urban status (Urban = 1)	0.72	0.45	0	1
Ownership (1 = Nonprofit)	0.42	0.495	0	1
Quality business strategy				
Quality feedback/communication				
Number QI initiatives conducted	3.75	0.999	1	6
Customer relationship management (CRM)	10.61	3.00	1	17
Quality promotion				
Importance of promoting quality	4.42	1.294	1	6
Numb. of marketing activities used	1.91	1.012	0	5
Numb. of quality indicators used	4.93	2.151	0	11

more generally (Calhoun et al. 2006). On average, facilities target a fair number of stakeholder groups (five out of eight potential groups) although less than half of all facilities segmented the audiences for their marketing strategies. On average, facilities also perceived themselves to be operating in fairly competitive markets (intensity of competition was rated 4.3 on a scale that ranges up to 6) and reported that they faced approximately eight competitors in their market.

Facilities reported, on average, using almost three out of five identified instruments for distinguishing customer needs. Usually two managers were involved in developing marketing practices, with administrators rating their level of control over marketing implementation fairly high – a 4 on a scale that ranges to 6, which would indicate solitary control over marketing practices.

We find that on average facilities engage in more than three of the six potential quality improvement initiatives listed and that they also use customer relationship marketing (CRM) techniques (as indicated by an average score of almost 11 on a scale of 17 for CRM techniques). Administrators rated the importance of promoting quality high (average ratings were roughly 4 in the range from 1 to 6), although they used quality in less than half of the potential marketing activities about which they were asked. When they did market quality, they usually focused on only a handful of potential quality indicators (a mean of 5 out of 11 possible).

There was a wide range of quality across facilities; facilities received, on average, almost 12 deficiencies on state inspections and reported an average occupancy rate of 84%. Within the sample, 39% of facilities were chain-affiliated, 72% were located in urban areas and 42% were nonprofit. The average facility size was 123 beds.

Table 15.2 reports the regression models predicting effects of independent variables on the three quality marketing scales. As results show, only two of the theoretically relevant variables have statistically

Table 15.2 OLS regression model predicting quality marketing practices $(N = 101)^*$

	Overall quality		Quality promotion		Quality feedback	
	B	SE	B	SE	B	SE
Intercept	2.39***	0.37	1.47***	0.35	0.92***	0.17
Market competition	−0.13	0.19	−0.10	0.18	−0.02	0.09
Market segmentation	−0.04	0.13	0.01	0.12	−0.05	0.06
Control over strategic DM	0.15	0.12	−0.06	0.12	0.21***	0.06
Consumer focus	0.51***	0.18	0.30*	0.17	0.21**	0.08
Number of deficiencies	−0.002	0.006	0.004	0.006	−0.01**	0.003
Occupancy	−0.77**	0.31	−0.39	0.30	−0.37***	0.14
Chain owned	0.04	0.11	−0.02	0.88	0.06	0.05
Size in beds	0.000	0.001	−0.001	0.001	0.01**	0.000
Is nonprofit	0.05	0.11	0.05	0.10	0.01	0.05
Is urban	−0.06	0.13	0.05	0.12	−0.011**	0.06
Herfindahl	−0.11	0.26	−0.01	0.25	−0.09	0.12
Adj. R2	0.07		0.03		0.37	

*Statistical significance: $^*p \leq 0.10$, $^{**}p \leq 0.05$, $^{***}p \leq 0.01$.

significant effects on overall use of quality in market and the relative amount of variance explained by the model is quite low, only 7%. The model explains much more of the variance for quality feedback practices (adjusted R-squared is 37%), while the model for quality promotion is an even worse fit than the overall model and predicts only 3% of the variance in quality promotion practices.

Looking at the model predicting overall marketing practices, only customer focus and occupancy rates predict outcomes. The greater the customer focus is, the more quality marketing is used, and the lower the occupancy rate is, the more quality strategies are used. Only the presence of a strong customer focus predicts promotional practices though.

The model predicting quality feedback practices offers the most interesting and most significant results. Occupancy rate has a negative effect on quality feedback practices such that the lower the occupancy rate, the greater the use of quality feedback techniques. On the other hand, a greater number of deficiencies decreased the likelihood that staff engaged in quality feedback practices. As in the overall model, the greater is the customer focus, the more quality feedback practices are used. And, in this model also, greater participation in marketing decisions leads to increased use of quality feedback practices.

Several of the predicted structural factors also have significant effects on the extent to which quality feedback practices are used in the facility. In this case, the larger is the facility, the more quality feedback practices are used while urban facilities are less likely to use quality feedback practices. On the other hand, chain ownership and nonprofit status do not have statistically significant effects on quality feedback practices or on the use of quality marketing more generally.

We predicted in hypothesis 5 that interaction effects between size and urban status and the institutionally relevant variables would be statistically significant. For the most part, this turned out not to be the case and these models are not reported here. However, there were two statistically significant interaction effects worth mentioning. First, the interaction between the number of deficiencies and facility size was significant in the quality feedback models. In other words, larger facilities used more quality feedback practices when deficiencies were high. Second, the interaction between occupancy rate and facility size was significant in the model predicting use of quality promotion practices, such that in larger facilities, lower occupancy rates led to greater use of promotion practices.

Discussion and conclusions

This study developed new measures to describe the use of quality information in managerial and specifically marketing practices and defined
two distinct practices of quality feedback, focusing on internal use of
quality information and quality promotion, using quality information
in communications and stakeholder relationships.

Overall, our model explains more of the variation in the use of
quality feedback than in quality promotion practices. The only significant predictors of quality promotion practices include institutional
factors of customer focus, indicating facilities that focus attention on
the demands of stakeholders. The lack of other significant results is
in line with prior research that has found nursing homes have relatively unsophisticated marketing activities (Becker and Kaldenberg 2000;
Clarke 1991) and facility administrators do not have to promote their
standing or proactive approaches to stakeholder management (Bonifazi
1997). Our descriptive statistics indicate that administrators viewed the
importance of marketing fairly high but were less likely to have practices
in place to study.

Analyses provided mixed support for the institutional predictors of
the development of quality marketing practices. Contrary to our expectations, there is a small indication that high-quality facilities, as measured by the (inverse) number of health deficiencies, are more likely to
promote their standing. However, lower occupancy rates led to more
quality feedback practices than higher occupancy rates and this effect
was even stronger in large facilities. There is also weak evidence that
among large facilities, poor performers (using number of health deficiencies) promote quality more than higher quality facilities. It would
appear then that facilities most in need of improving performance are
the ones most likely to focus on the use of quality for feedback and
promotional purposes, although less for promotional activity.

From additional analyses of large facilities, we found weak evidence
that among large facilities, facilities with a higher number of health deficiencies actually promoted quality more than higher quality facilities.
Results also provided mixed support for our business strategy hypotheses. Increasing the managers involved in marketing only increased
the use of quality feedback practices. Likewise, structural factors such
as size and urban status only affected the use of quality feedback practices. Our conclusions are limited by the cross-sectional nature of our
study. We think that the lack of structural differences in marketing
practices may result from the slow adoption of marketing tools more

generally, which would be in line with our descriptive finding that many marketing practices are not used routinely in nursing homes.

One of the greatest difficulties for nursing home administrators is finding sufficient time to address customer demands when they have competing demands from regulators. Hence, it makes sense that customer focus has some of the strongest effects on the use of quality in marketing practices. Indeed, little else predicts the use of quality promotion practices. Facilities are much more likely to be internally focused in their use of quality information.

This supports the argument that nursing homes do not have the time to support quality initiatives in a proactive way since much of the managerial time in facilities is spent in retrospective activity targeted to maintaining desired quality. Given current controversies over quality of care, the time is ripe though for nursing homes to become proactive in identifying quality factors and effective communication strategies that highlight their organizational identities and promote service relationships.

Acknowledgements

Funds for this project were provided by the Walter McNerney Fund at The University of Michigan. The thoughts expressed within are solely the responsibility of the authors.

References

Banaszak-Holl, J., Zinn, J. S. and Mor, V. (1996) 'The impact of market and organizational characteristics on nursing home service innovation: A resource dependency perspective', *Health Services Research*, 31, 97–117.

Becker, B. W. and Kaldenberg, D. O. (2000) 'Factors influencing the recommendation of nursing homes', *Marketing Health Services*, 20, 22–28.

Bitner, M.-J. (1990) 'Evaluating service encounters: The effects of physical surroundings and employee responses', *Journal of Marketing*, 54, 69–82.

Bonifazi, W. L. (1997) 'Cover me: How can you get your share of positive media coverage', *Contemporary Long Term Care*, December, 52–58.

Buss, D. (1994) 'Marketing: Nursing homes learn the rules to a whole new game', *Contemporary Long Term Care*, October, 30–40.

Castle, N. G. and Lowe, T. (2004) 'Report cards and nursing homes', *The Gerontologist*, 45, 48–67.

Calhoun, J. G., Banaszak-Holl, J. and Hearld, L. (2006) 'The utilization of marketing practices in the nursing home sector', *Journal of Healthcare Management*, 51, 185–200.

Chaiken, M. A. (1992) 'Marketing quality in nursing facilities', *Health Marketing Quarterly*, 10, 219–225.

Clarke, L. (1991) 'Issues and answers: Marketing to attract private-pay residents', *Contemporary Long-Term Care*, 28, 72.

Conlon, D. E., Van Dyne, L., Milner, M. and Ng, K. Y. (2004) 'The effects of physical and social context on evaluations of captive, intensive service relationships', *Academy of Management Journal*, 47, 433–445.

Harrington, C. and Carillo, H. (1999) 'The regulation and enforcement of federal nursing home standards, 1991–1997', *Medical Care Research and Review*, 56, 471–494.

Harrington, C., Zimmerman, D., Karon, S. L., Robinson, J. and Beutel, P. (2000) 'Nursing home staffing and its relationship to deficiencies', *Journals of Gerontology: Psychological and Social Sciences*, 55(5): S278–S287.

Harrington, C., O'Meara, J., Kitchener, M., Simon, L. P. and Schnelle, J. F. (2003) 'Designing a report card for nursing facilities: What information is needed and why', *The Gerontologist*, 43(Special Issue), 47–57.

Harrington, C. S., Woolhandler, S., Mullan, J., Carillo, H. and Himmelstein, D. U. (2001) 'Does investor ownership of nursing homes compromise the quality of care?', *American Journal of Public Health*, 91, 1452–1455.

Ingram, P. and Baum, J. A. C. (1997) 'Chain affiliation and the failure of Manhattan hotels, 1898–1980', *Administrative Science Quarterly*, 42, 68–102.

Institute of Medicine (1986) *Improving the quality of care in nursing homes*, Washington, DC: National Academy Press.

Kane, R. A. (2001) 'Long-term care and a good quality of life: Bringing them closer together', *The Gerontologist*, 41, 293–304.

Kane, R. L. and Kane, R. A. (2000) 'Assessment in long-term care'. *Annual Review of Public Health*, 3 659–686.

Kitchener, M. and Harrington, C. (2004) 'The U.S. long-term care field: A dialectic analysis of institution dynamics', *Journal of Health and Social Behavior*, 45(Extra Issue), 87–101.

Kotler, P. and Armstrong, G. (2006) *Principles of Marketing*, 11th ed.. Upper Saddle River, NJ: Pearson Education.

Leatherman, S., Berwick, D., Iles, D., Lewin, L. S., Davidoff, F., Nolan, T. and Bisognano, M. (2003) 'The business case for quality: Case studies and an analysis', *Health Affairs*, 22(2), 17–30.

Meyer, J. W. and Rowan, B. (1977) 'Institutionalized organizations: Formal structure as myth and ceremony', *American Journal of Sociology*, 83, 340–363.

Mor, V., Zinn, J. S., Angelelli, J., Teno, J. M., and Miller, S. C. (2004) 'Driven to tiers: Socioeconomic and racial disparities in the quality of nursing home care', *Milbank Quarterly*, 82(2), 227–256.

Rao, H. (1994) 'The social construction of reputation: Certification, contests, legitimation, and the survival of organizations in the American automobile industry, 1895–1912', *Strategic Management Journal*, 15(Summer Special Issue), 29–44.

Rao, H., Monin, P. and Durand, R. (2003) 'Institutional change in Toque Ville: Nouvelle cuisine as an identity movement in French gastronomy', *American Journal of Sociology*, 108, 795–843.

Scott, S. G. and Lane, V. R. (2000) 'A stakeholder approach to organizational identity', *Academy of Management Review*, 25, 43–62.

Scott, W. R., Ruef, M., Mendel, P. J. and Caronna, C. A. (2000) *Institutional change and healthcare organizations: From professional dominance to managed care*, Chicago, IL: University of Chicago Press.

Spector, P. E. (1992) *Summated rating scale construction: An introduction, Sage quantitative applications in the social sciences*, Newbury Park, CA: Sage.

Thomas, R. K. (2005) *Marketing health services*, Chicago, IL: Health Administration Press, American College of Health Care Executives.

Walshe, K. (2001) 'Regulating U.S. nursing homes: Are we learning from experience?', *Health Affairs*, 20(6), 128–144.

Weech-Maldonado, R., Zinn, J. S. and Brannon, D. (1999) 'Managerial implications of corporate board involvement and perceived market competition for quality improvement in nursing homes', *Journal of Healthcare Management*, 44, 382–396.

Wunderlich, G. S. and Kohler, P. O. (eds) (2001) *Improving the quality of long-term care*, Washington, DC: National Academy Press.

Zinn, J. S., Aaronson, W. E., and Rosko, M. D. (1994) 'Strategic groups, performance, and strategic response in the nursing home industry', *Health Services Research*, 29, 187–205.

Zinn, J. S., Weech-Maldonado, R. and Brannon, D. (1998) 'Resource dependence and institutional factors in TQM adoption: The case of nursing homes', *Health Services Research*, 33, 261–273.

16
Models of Medical Work Control: A Theory Elaboration from English General Practice

Martin Kitchener and Mark Exworthy

Introduction

In various attempts to contain healthcare costs and improve quality, many governments have explored new ways of controlling doctors' resource use and practice (Kitchener 2000). A common approach has involved adopting 'new public management' (NPM) techniques such as the use of performance indicators (PIs) (Pollitt and Bouckaert 2000). While studies have typically concentrated on issues such as doctors' autonomy (Harrison 1999), analyses of other professional work settings have used models of work control as the primary unit of analysis (Hoggett 1996; Kitchener 2000; Scott 1982). This paper extends that line of enquiry by adapting Kitchener et al. (2005) typology of American physician control models to frame a study of English general practitioners (GPs), a section of the medical profession which has experienced significant recent managerial reforms. The main aims are to theoretically elaborate (refine, extend, specify) Kitchener and colleagues' typology and advance understandings of work control in the focal field (Vaughan 1992).

This theory elaboration is presented in three main sections. The first introduces our revised typology which contains four models of medical work control (autonomous, custodial, heteronomous, and post-bureaucratic) that are compared on three dimensions: underpinning logic, governance systems, and aligned actors. The second section applies the typology to frame an exploratory analysis of work control in English general practice. We conclude by considering the implications of this analysis for future studies of work control in English general practice and other fields.

Models of medical work control

For more than 20 years, researchers have tracked relations between doctors, established organizations (e.g. the UK National Health Service [NHS]), and newer entities such as corporate hospital systems in the USA. Studies have typically concentrated on features of professional work (e.g. autonomy) or specific techniques such as peer review and quality incentives (Exworthy et al. 2003). In an alternative approach, ideal-typical models of professional work control have been used as heuristic devices to track and compare broader configurations of control systems (Hoggett 1996; Kitchener 2000; Scott 1982). Kitchener et al. (2005) combine insights from that body of research with data collected from large US hospital systems to present a typology of three bureaucratic models of physician control: custodial, conjoint, and heteronomous.

Following our review of literatures on organization theory and health services research, three alterations were made to that typology for this analysis of English GPs. First, drawing from studies of configurations of organizational structures and practices (e.g. Kitchener and Harrington 2004), we conceive of work control models as comprising three coherent dimensions: (1) logics (underpinning sets of ideas and values), (2) governance systems (organizational models, payment methods, job specificity, and performance review systems), and (3) aligned actors, individuals, and groups that support the model of control. Second, for parsimony, Scott's (1982) conjoint system of control (emphasizing a negotiated division of labour and power between doctors and managers) is incorporated within Ackroyd and colleagues' custodial model (1989). Third, reflecting developments within recent studies of commercial work control systems, a post-bureaucratic model is included. The revised typology of models of medical work control is summarized in Table 16.1.

Autonomous control

Autonomous models of work control exist to the extent that the State delegates, to an occupational group, responsibility for defining and implementing the goals of work, setting performance standards, and ensuring the maintenance of standards (Freidson 1970; Scott 1982). The justifying (professional) logic of this model is that the quality of expert labour is best assured through the twin techniques of (1) professional training, during which participants internalize certain values and norms (e.g. altruism, responsibility) and acquire a repertoire of standardized skills, and (2) subsequent reinforcement through involvement with

Table 16.1 A typology of professional work control models

	Autonomous	Custodial	Hetero-nomous	Post-bureaucratic
Logic	Professional	Collegial	Managerial	Cultural
Governance				
Organizational model	Self-employment, partnership	Professional bureaucracy	(Machine) bureaucracy	Network
Pay	Fee for service	Salary	Salary	Performance-related pay
Job specificity	Low	Medium	High	High
Performance review	Self, peers	Senior professionals	Management (internal)	Management (external)
Aligned actors	Profession	Profession	Management	Management

colleagues and professional associations which are variously motivated to maintain professional reputation.

The autonomous model of medical work control is well illustrated by the traditional 'staff group' model of US hospitals which involved physicians using them as 'workshops' (Kitchener et al. 2005). Under such governance arrangements, fee-for-service doctors dominated neighbouring occupations and operated the peer review system whereby only they were deemed eligible to assess the performance of their colleagues. The actors most closely aligned with this model of control in the UK are doctors, their representative associations, most governments until the early 1980s, and some social scientists (Freidson 2001).

Custodial control

Drawing on Mintzberg's (1979) characterization of the professional bureaucracy form of organization, Ackroyd et al. (1989:603) specify a 'custodial' model of control in which the primary concern of professional line managers is to 'preserve and perpetuate customary [professionally-determined] kinds and standards of service provision' including definitions and measurement of quality. Senior professionals are typically represented on executive boards although their preference for loosely coupled structures ensures that professional and administrative jurisdictions remain separate.

As recognized within Scott's (1982) conjoint model of control, the dual hierarchies typically produce a (bottom-up) 'professional bureaucratic' structure for expert labour and a top-down 'machine bureaucratic' structure for support staff. Within the professional bureaucracy, the importance placed on high trust and collegial relations between practitioners requires that senior professionals demonstrate to junior staff their independence from management and disinclination to intrude in daily routines and become involved within performance review. Thus, work supervision involves senior professionals 'coaching' or mentoring junior colleagues through peer review, rather than through direct management (Scott 1965). As the custodial model reflects the most typical accommodation of the autonomous logic within the bureaucratic structures employing expert labour, it draws support from the same groups as the autonomous model.

Heteronomous control

The heteronomous model of professional control described by Scott (1965) rests on Weber's (1947) classic formation of bureaucracy. It is underpinned by a logic of rational (managerial) economic conduct that supports three approaches to maintaining consistency and regulating action against agency goals such as equity: (1) functional specialization within a firmly ordered hierarchy, (2) a comprehensive, impersonal body of rules and procedures, and (3) the precise definition of powers and responsibilities invested in each organizational role (Reed 2000; Scott 1965).

The heteronomous control model is similar to those typically found in corporate professional firms. In such contexts, experts such as lawyers are typically constrained as corporate executives and stockholders set commercial goals (e.g. increased revenue, market share). Studies of NPM in British public services and elsewhere have examined attempts to introduce similar notions of 'regulated autonomy' (Pollitt and Bouckaert 2000). For example, Kitchener et al. (2000) report that, in UK social care agencies, a stated aim is to employ general managers (cf. social workers) to regulate the actions of service providers using managerial definitions of quality that emphasize efficiency.

Post-bureaucratic control

It has been argued that bureaucratic models of control (custodial and heteronomous) have imploded under pressures exerted by new technologies and indications of the relative effectiveness of decentralized alternatives (Exworthy and Halford 1999; Nohria and Berkley 1994). Beyond some disagreement over these 'post-bureaucratic' alternatives, the logic is typically portrayed as a managerial strategy for internalizing surveillance and control to the extent that workers are subjected to an organizational discipline in which the dictates of market rationality become unchallengeable (Grint 1994; Hoggett 1996).

In a leading characterization of post-bureaucratic control, Foucault's (1979) description of a panopticon system specifies continuous and remote (unobtrusive) supervisory observation and monitoring; hierarchical ranking and distribution; and cultural self-management and discipline, among others. Such features have been identified in relation to NHS managerial practices including total quality management and business process re-engineering (Townley 1994).

Changing modes of control in general practice

This section applies the typology introduced above to frame an exploratory historical analysis of work control systems in English general practice. We first draw on published accounts to characterize a 'traditional' mode of GP control that prevailed from 1948 until the mid-1990s. We then combine this information with findings from an empirical study of 15 practices in one English primary care organization (Exworthy et al. 2003) to illustrate an emergent mode of control.

The traditional mode of GP work control

In contrast to the relatively decentralized system of controlling US physicians (Kitchener et al. 2005), the NHS has traditionally relied on bureaucratic control (e.g. organizational hierarchy) to align the work of doctors with social goals such as universal coverage (Klein 2001). From the birth of the NHS in 1948, however, the systems of work control applied to hospital doctors and GPs have varied. Hospital doctors (providing secondary care) are more clearly under custodial control as salaried employees within organizational hierarchies (Kitchener 2000). While GPs were subjected to aspects of custodial control in the NHS, they traditionally operated within a more autonomous mode of control (Table 16.2).

Professional Logic

From 1948, GPs occupied an 'equivocal' position within the NHS (Peckham and Exworthy 2003). On the one hand, they were central to its operation, providing primary care and 'gate-keeping' access to the secondary (specialist) care. On the other hand, and unlike hospital doctors, GPs operated as independent contractors within organizational

Table 16.2   The traditional mode of GP control c.1948–early 1990s

	Feature	*Mode (PRIMARY, secondary)*
Logic	Professional	AUTONOMOUS, custodial
Governance		
Organizational model	Practice as main organizational unit, 1–6 GPs, c. 8000 registered population; administered by local Family Practitioner Committees (FPC)	CUSTODIAL, autonomous
Remuneration	Mainly capitated NHS salary administered through FPCs but some salary and FFS	CUSTODIAL, autonomous
Job specificity	Low	CUSTODIAL, autonomous
Performance review	GP, profession	AUTONOMOUS, custodial
Aligned actors	Profession, State	AUTONOMOUS, custodial

In the table, the assignment of control mode to each comparative dimension is justified using only illustrative features; fuller explanation is given in the text. Each dimension is assigned to its 'best fit' with an ideal typical mode in capitals, and secondary assignments recognize (less strong) similarities in regular font.

units called practices. These conditions were established from negotiations between the architects of the NHS and the medical profession at the inception of the NHS and were justified by GPs using the professional logic that characterizes the autonomous modes of control (Klein 1990; Loundon et al. 1998). Significantly, the professional logic was reinforced by and reflected in both the micro-level phenomenon of clinical autonomy and macro-level manifestations of influence such as the close corporatist relationships between the British Medical Association (BMA) and the Department of Health (Harrison and Dowsell 2002).

Custodial governance structure

Although the traditional mode of GP control was underpinned by a professional logic, many of its characteristics fit better with the custodial mode. For example, until the mid-1980s, general practice operated as a 'cottage industry' of loosely linked and relatively autonomous small businesses (practices) that typically comprised between one and six GPs serving around 1800 enrolled patients each (Lounden et al. 1998). The vast majority of practices' income was distributed through local family practitioners committees (FPCs) that exerted no managerial control over GPs (Allsop and May 1986).

GPs' income, negotiated periodically through the national contract between the professional and the NHS, was traditionally derived from a mix of remuneration methods based on crude capitation and salary with some incentives to encourage public health interventions such as immunization (Smith and York 2004). Unlike their US counterparts who jealously guard their fee-for-service payment scheme (indicative of autonomous control), GPs' contract payment was part of the price their profession paid for employment stability and other benefits of working with the NHS. Alongside these features of custodial control, peer review remained the primary means of quality and cost control, as required by professional logic. State support for (or lack of challenge to) the professional logic ensured that the traditional mode of GP control survived numerous NHS reorganizations in which many other parts of the NHS were re-structured.

Emergent mode of GP control

Managerial logic

From the mid-1980s, as UK governments' support for medical professions and their logics waned, medical cost inflation and quality variations were increasingly blamed on the limited capacity of the NHS to regulate doctors' resource-use and practice (DuGay 2000). The professional logic of existing control arrangements were challenged by economists' claims of 'producer capture' and management critiques of doctors being inert barriers to rationalized control. Emergent NPM 'solutions' to these issues drew from the managerial logic of bureaucratic control that emphasized placing doctors 'on tap' (to managers and clients) rather than 'on top' (Pollitt 1990). Table 16.3 outlines this mode of GP control that has emerged from the mid-1980s.

(Post)-bureaucratic governance

Operating an increasingly managerial logic of medical control from the mid-1980s, the traditional model of organization among the approximately 30,000 GPs was altered through several 'top-down' structural changes. These reforms included: the 1984 introduction of NHS 'general managers' (though their introduction had minimal impact on GPs until the advent of Primary Care Groups and Trusts in the late 1990s onwards); the 1990 GP contract (which included health targets, financial incentives to develop primary care teams, and the replacement of FPCs with

Table 16.3   An emergent mode of GP control c. mid-1980s-Present

	Feature	Mode (PRIMARY, secondary)
Logic	Managerial, cultural	HETERONOMOUS, POST-BUREAUCRATIC, custodial
Governance Organizational model	National network of primary care organizations (PCOs) with practice managers & c. 180,000–300,000 population; PCTs with corporate board	CUSTODIAL, autonomous, post-bureaucratic
Pay	Capitated salary & < 30% PRP	CUSTODIAL, autonomous, heteronomous, post-bureaucratic
Job specificity	Increasing	CUSTODIAL, heteronomous, post-bureaucratic
Performance review	Internal (clinical governance, practice manager); external (audit, inspection, PCTs)	CUSTODIAL, HETERONOMOUS, post-bureaucratic
Aligned actors	State, management	HETERONOMOUS, post-bureaucratic

In the table, the assignment of control mode to each comparative dimension is justified using only illustrative features; fuller explanation is given in the text. Each dimension is assigned to their 'best fits' with ideal typical mode in capitals, and secondary assignments that recognize other similarities in regular font.

new 'family heath services authorities' to more directly manage GP contracts); and the 1991 implementation of the NHS internal market which involved the devolution of commissioning budgets to 'fund holding' GPs (Smith and Walshe 2004). In one outcome of these structural changes, a heterogeneous collection of larger primary care organizations (incorporating GPs) has emerged (Bjoke et al. 2001).

Following the election of the Labour government in 1997, general practice in England was again restructured through the establishment of 303 Primary Care Trusts (PCTs, initially called Primary Care Groups) which consist of between 25 and 130 GPs serving an average population of 180,000 patients (Peckham and Exworthy 2003). In October 2006, the

303 English PCTs were reduced to 152, raising the average enrolled population to around 300,000. While GPs remain independent contractors within the PCTs, these new organizations wield considerable influence over GPs. This power is derived from PCTs being devolved 75% of NHS funding and being held accountable for GPs' functions including improving health and developing primary care. The control is being wielded through techniques including the increasing use of salaried status, cash-limited budgets, and managerial structures in which hybrid medical-managers figure prominently to oversee performance management.

Following the introduction of Personal Medical Services (PMS) pilot schemes in 1998, approximately 30% of GPs have opted to work under locally negotiated arrangements. While most are based mainly on salary, PCTs are able to commission GP services from any local provider thus increasing the potential for competition between practices and with independent providers. After acceptance by a national ballot of GPs, the 2004 national contract altered the system of GP remuneration significantly by introducing a system of quality incentives. About US $1.3 billion (around 18% of GP income) is distributed annually, determined by performance according to the Quality and Outcomes Framework (QOF), 146 indicators of clinical performance, practice organization, and patient experience (Smith and York 2004). One example of a clinical indicator is the 'percentage of patients with coronary heart disease whose notes have a record of total cholesterol in the previous 15 months' (CHD-7, GMS Contract 2004).

Exworthy et al. (2003) reported that GPs voiced many concerns about the appropriateness and validity of clinical PIs (which were an earlier version of QOF). Two principal concerns were notable. The first concerned perceived attempts to reduce GPs' autonomy, as some saw clinical PIs 'ruining my freedom' (quote from GP n. 9). This GP continued this theme: 'A bit like the Bishop in the Church of England, we [GPs] have absolute power on our patch and that is it. So it is very difficult to tell a GP...that you think they could pull their socks up' (GP no. 9). The second concerned a perceived attempt to shift the locus of control away from GPs (individually and collectively) to PCTs (and beyond). While some GPs also felt that the system was both technically flawed ('unscientific'; GP no. 17) and failed to measure process issues such as 'continuity of care' (GP no. 17), others claimed the system to be superfluous serving only to 'highlight what we already know' (GP no. 16).

In addition to clinical PIs, five additional tiers of regulatory capacity have been introduced over general practice: (1) a health technology appraisal agency, the National Institute for Clinical Excellence (NICE), which publishes recommendations on which services can be provided (though these recommendations are not always binding on PCTs), (2) the Healthcare Commission which reviews quality improvement, (3) the Modernization Agency led patient–process redesign work (disbanded in 2005), (4) doctors who are subject to mandatory re-licensing every five years (and the associated reform of their regulatory body, the General Medical Council), and (5) the National Clinical Assessment Authority which assesses doctors whose performance gives cause for concern. These tiers are linked to a 'national framework for the assessment of performance' comprising six dimensions including health improvement, fair access, and efficiency.

Quality assurance

In frustration that professionally dominated system of medical (subsequently, clinical) audit was unable to control manage medical errors and malpractice, the State has sponsored additional quality controls (Exworthy 1998). These include the use of formularies, dissemination of research findings through evidence-based medicine initiatives, clinical guidelines, and incorporation of clinical performance review into managerial systems (namely, 'clinical governance'). Crucially, following the earlier introduction of PIs to other areas of the UK public sector and to the assessment of financial and organizational aspects of health care (Power 1997), clinical PIs were introduced through initiatives including the development of National Service Frameworks that specify standards for conditions such as heart disease and diabetes, and the revised GP contract of 2004 (see above).

As an alternative to viewing these developments simply as a move towards heteronomous control, it is possible to represent them as an example of 'panoptic surveillance' whereby the knowledge that data about clinical behaviour exist and can be inspected may be sufficient to ensure that physicians behave as if they will be inspected: 'the surveillance is permanent in its effects even if it is discontinuous in its action' (Foucault 1979:201). It has been suggested that the transition from organizationally focused PIs to clinically oriented ones represents movements towards such post-bureaucratic control, aided by technology and an erosion of the notion of equality of competence within the profession and across society (Causer and Exworthy 1999).

It has also been argued that the effect on professionals is to transform their behaviour as they become the subject and object of this emergent mode, as 'calculating selves' (Miller 1992). Consciously, or otherwise, some GPs have expressed concerns that seem to mirror this view through concerns over the need to rely on computers to demonstrate competence for external scrutiny; for example:

> everyone is talking aboutbig brother watching us and looking at statistics and death rates and bash us over the head with them. (GP no. 3)

While some of the (particularly older) GPs in Exworthy and colleagues' study (2003) expressed anxiety over their technical capacity and motivation to input performance data onto computers, others reluctantly recognized an imperative to do so, for example: 'So even if we look after our patients wonderfully, if we don't have that information on the computer, we can't prove that we are' (GP no. 2)

Discussion and conclusions

The two goals of this chapter were to elaborate a typology of models of medical work control (Kitchener et al. 2005) and to provide a fresh account of changes amongst English GPs (Exworthy et al. 2003). In terms of theoretical elaboration, three main developments were made to the original typology. First, work control modes were re-specified to comprise three dimensions: underpinning logics, governance systems (including organizational models and performance review systems), and aligned actors. Second, for brevity, Scott's (1982) conjoint system of control was incorporated within a custodial model (Ackroyd et al. 1989). Third, reflecting developments within recent studies of control, a post-bureaucratic mode was specified.

In terms of empirical analysis, the chapter presents a fresh historical account of developments in the control of English general practice as it moves (uneasily) from a traditional mode towards an alternative, emergent mode. As the ideal-typical formulation of modes in the typology were never expected to capture all conditions at all times, it is unsurprising that both the traditional and emergent models combine elements associated with multiple ideal types. In the traditional mode, an autonomous logic underpinned a custodial governance system that was supported by the State and profession. While GPs conceded to certain structural constraints on their autonomy at the inception of the NHS, their success in maintaining the professional logic over rationalizing alternatives ensured that those structural constraints were restricted to features of custodial rather than heteronomous control.

The internal cohesion between the autonomous logic and custodial system of control may explain the resilience of the mode to repeated attempts at top-down structural reform including the introduction of the quasi-market. Also, it was not really until the mid-1980s that the UK State challenged the profession logic in a systematic way and presented an alternative, managerial logic for controlling professional work. Then, however, the State became increasingly frustrated that cost controls and quality improvements could not be secured through either the traditional mode of GP control or the quasi-market. Following the dominant ideology of the NPM reform agenda, a new managerial logic of control was promoted to underpin an alternative set of governance arrangements, central to which was the assessment of work performance.

While many reforms affecting GPs may be viewed as a movement towards heteronomous control, some may also be interpreted as indicators of a post-bureaucratic mode of control. It could be seen, for example, that new network form of organization among practices, the increased use of PIs, and the combination of NPM rhetoric and the dissemination EBM reviews represent attempts to manage GPs through a form of cultural control that is unobtrusive but which involves constant surveillance. The goal may be to use doctors to manage other doctors and persuade them all to think in more managerial terms through quality management initiatives and by encouraging them to 'rub shoulders' with managers, becoming inculcated with a managerial discourse (Exworthy and Halford 1999; Harrison and Pollitt 1994). An alternative view would suggest that, because little evidence has emerged of the achievement of consensual agreement beyond instrumental compliance of GPs, in its absence, formalization through NICE and Healthcare Commission has become the heteronomous solution.

Aside from discussions of whether the emergent features of GP control represent heteronomous or post-bureaucratic control, our account of change adds further weight to arguments concerning the flexibility of bureaucratic organizations such as the NHS to alter control modes (DuGay 2000). Our findings that some control of work is being transferred from individual GPs to an emergent administrative elite of GPs within PCTs underscores Freidson's (1970) professional re-stratification thesis (Sheaff et al. 2002). Though our focus has been primarily on performance review (namely, who sets standards, who monitors them, and who takes remedial action, where necessary), our account provides a cogent synthesis across logic, governance, and aligned actors.

A limitation of this analysis is that the empirical study from which we draw illustrations was not designed explicitly to provide information concerning the comparative dimensions of our typology. Thus, while the study provided useful information for this exploratory analysis, the next step in the theoretical elaboration would be a national study of GP modes of control. Given such limitations, this extent to which the analysis is transferable beyond the focal case (of one English PCT) is a question for future studies that will require inductive reasoning about why other cases might be replications and others might not (Ragin 1999). Such reasoning would need to consider the characteristics of PCTs (rural–urban, large–small), the potential implications for their modes of medical control, and the impact of independent PCOs. Research pursuing this approach may lead to the discovery of alternative modes of GP control, additional comparative dimensions to the typology, and potential explanations for differences in performance (e.g. Sheaff et al. 2004).

Although this study concentrated on English GPs, the typology is likely to be useful in other contexts because the modes of control were derived from studies of professional work in the UK and elsewhere. Applications to studies of UK hospital doctors and nurses would present opportunities to further elaborate the typology presented here, conceptually and empirically.

Acknowledgements

Some of the research cited in this chapter was drawn from a study funded by the UK Department of Health. We are grateful for their support and to the collaborators on that project.

References

Ackroyd, S., Hughes, J. and Soothill, K. (1989) 'Public sector services and their management', *Journal of Management Studies*, 26(6), 603–619.

Allsop, J. and May, A. (1986) *The emperor's new clothes: Family practitioner committees in the 1980s*, London; King Edward's Hospital Fund for London.

Bjoke, C., Gravelle, H. and Wilkin, D. (2001) 'Is bigger better for Primary Care Groups and Trusts?' *British Medical Journal*, 322, 599–602.

Causer, G. and Exworthy, M. (1999) 'Professionals as managers across the public sector' in M. Exworthy and S. Halford (eds) *Professionals and the new managerialism in the public sector,* Buckingham: Open University Press, Chapter 6, pp. 83–101.

DuGay, P. (2000) *In praise of bureaucracy,* London: Sage.

Exworthy, M. (1998) 'Clinical audit in the NHS internal market: From peer review to external monitoring', *Public Policy and Administration,* 13(2), 40–53.

Exworthy, M. and Halford, S. (eds) (1999) *Professionals and the new managerialism in the public sector,* Buckingham: Open University Press.

Exworthy, M., Wilkinson, E., McColl, A., Roderick, P., Smith, H., Moore, M. and Gabbay, J. (2003) 'The role of performance indicators in changing the autonomy of the general practice profession in the UK', *Social Science & Medicine,* 56, 1493–1504.

Foucault, M. (1979) *Discipline and punish: The birth of the prison,* Harmondsworth: Penguin.

Freidson, E. (1970) *Professional dominance: The social structure of medical care,* New York: Atherton Press.

Freidson, E. (2001) *Professionalism: The third logic,* Chicago, IL: University of Chicago Press.

Grint, K. (1994) 'Re-engineering history: Social resonances and business process re-engineering', *Organization,* 1(1), 179–201.

Harrison, S. (1999) 'Clinical autonomy and health policy: Past and futures' in M. Exworthy and S. Halford (eds) *Professionals and the new managerialism in the public sector,* Buckingham: Open University Press, Chapter 6, pp. 50–64.

Harrison, S. and Dowswell, G. (2002) 'Autonomy and bureaucratic accountability in primary care: What English general practitioners say', *Sociology of Health and Illness,* 24(2), 208–226.

Harrison, S. and Pollitt, C. (1994) *Controlling health professionals: The future of work and organization in the NHS,* Buckingham: Open University Press.

Hoggett, P. (1996) 'New models of control in the public service', *Public Administration,* 74, 9–32.

Kitchener, M. (2000) 'The bureaucratisation of professional roles: The case of clinical directors in UK Hospitals', *Organization,* 7(1), 129–154.

Kitchener M. and Harrington, C. (2004) 'U.S. long-term care: A dialectic analysis of institutional dynamics', *Journal of Health and Social Behavior,* 45, 87–101.

Kitchener, M., Kirkpatrick, I. and Whipp, R. (2000) 'Supervising professional work under new public management: Evidence from an invisible trade', *British Journal of Management,* 11(3), 213–226.

Kitchener, M., Caronna, C. and Shortell, S. (2005) ' "From the doctors" Workshop to the iron cage? Evolving models of physician control in US health systems', *Social Science & Medicine,* 60, 1311–1322.

Klein, R. (1990) 'The state and the profession: The politics of the double-bed', *British Medical Journal,* 301, 700–702.

Klein, R. (2001) *The new politics of the NHS,* 4th ed., Harlow: Pearson.

Loundon, I., Horder, J. and Webster, C. (1998) *General practice under the National Health Service 1948–1997,* Oxford: Clarendon Press.

Miller, P. (1992) 'Accounting and subjectivity: The invention of calculating selves and calculating spaces', *Annals of Scholarship,* 9(1/2), 61–86.

Mintzberg, H. (1979) *The structuring of organizations: A synthesis of the research,* Englewood Cliffs: Prentice Hall.

Nohria, N., and Berkley, J. D. (1994) 'The virtual organization: Bureaucracy, technology and the imposition of control' in C. Heckscher and A. Donnollon (eds) *The post bureaucratic organization: New perspectives on organizational change*, Newbury Park, CA: Sage.

Peckham, S. and Exworthy, M. (2003) *Primary care in the UK – policy, organization and management*, Basingstoke: Macmillan.

Pollitt, C. (1990) *Managerialism and the public services: The Anglo-American experience*, Oxford: Basil Blackwell.

Pollitt, C. and Bouckaert, G. (2000) *Public management reform: A comparative analysis*, Oxford: Oxford University Press.

Power, M. (1997) *The audit society*, Oxford: Oxford University Press.

Ragin, C. (1999) 'The distinctiveness of case-oriented research', *Health Services Research*, 34(5), 1137–1152.

Reed, M. (2000) 'From the "cage" to the "gaze"? The dynamics of organizational control in late modernity' in G. Morgan and L. Engwall (eds) *Regulation and organization: international perspectives*, London: Routledge, pp. 17–49.

Scott, W. R. (1965) 'Reaction to supervision in a heteronomous professional organization', *Administrative Science Quarterly*, 10, 65–81.

Scott, W. R. (1982) 'Managing professional work: Three models of control for health organizations', *Health Services Research*, 17(3), 213–240.

Sheaff, R., Smith, K. and Dickson, M. (2002) 'Is GP restratification beginning in England?', *Social Policy and Administration*, 36(7), 765–779.

Sheaff, R., Marshall, M., Rogers, A., Roland, M., Sibbald, B. and Pickhardt, S. (2004) 'Governmentality by network in English primary healthcare', *Social Policy and Administration*, 38(1), 89–103.

Smith, J. and Walshe, K. (2004) 'Big business: The corporatization of primary care in the UK and USA', *Public Money and Management*, April, 87–96.

Smith, P. and York, N. (2004) 'Quality incentives: The case of U.K. general practitioners', *Health Affairs*, 23(3), 112–118.

Townley, B. (1994) *Reframing human resource management: Power, ethics and the subject at work*, London: Sage.

Vaughan, D. (1992) 'Theory elaboration: The heuristics of case analysis' in C. C. Ragin and H. S. Becker, *What is a case? Exploring the foundations of social inquiry*, New York: Cambridge, Chapter 8, pp. 173–202.

Weber, M. (1947) *Theory of social and economic organization*, New York: Free Press.

Author Index

Subject Index